the
natural
baby

the
natural
baby

Janet Balaskas

Photographs by
Anthea Sieveking

CREATIVE
PUBLISHING
international

Published in North America in 2002 by
Creative Publishing international

Creative Publishing international
5900 Green Oak Drive
Minnetonka, MN 55343
1-800-328-3895

Project editor Cathy Meeus
Art editor Hugh Schermuly
Designer Nick Buzzard
Production Lyn Kirby
Direction Joss Pearson, Patrick Nugent

First published in the United Kingdom in 2001 by
Gaia Books Ltd, 66 Charlotte Street, London W1T 4QE
and 20 High Street, Stroud, Gloucestershire GL5 1AZ

Printed and bound in Singapore by Imago Publishing Ltd

10 9 8 7 6 5 4 3 2 1

DEDICATION

*To my extending family –
Nina and Agung, .Kira and
Mario who will soon be
parents of a new baby and
also to Kim, Ias and Theo –
when they start their
families in the future. Also
to the new generation of
grandparents – Keith, Mina,
Barry and Sindhu. My love
and appreciation to all
of you.*

While every attempt has been made to ensure that the information given in this book is
accurate and safe, it is not intended as a substitute for medical advice. The author and
publisher can accept no responsibility for any injury or damage that may occur as a
consequence of following the advice in this book.

Note: For simplicity in the text babies have been referred to as either "he" or "she" in
alternate chapters. Captions refer to the actual sex of the baby in the photograph
wherever possible.

Contents

FOREWORD   8

PREFACE   9

1 PREPARING FOR PARENTHOOD   10

Life before birth   12
The last weeks of pregnancy   14
Approaching birth   18
Meeting your baby   20

2 WELCOMING YOUR BABY   22

First hour after birth   24
Your newborn baby   28
The babymoon   30

3 FEEDING YOUR BABY   36

Why breastfeeding is best   38
Preparing to breastfeed   42
Learning together   44
The first few days   50
Baby-led feeding   52
Solving problems   54
Bottle-feeding   58
Weaning   62

4 CARING FOR YOUR BABY   68

Approaches to care   70
Holding and carrying   72
Comforting your baby   74
Elimination   78
Keeping your baby clean   83
First clothes   86
Baby massage   88

5 DEVELOPMENT AND PLAY 92

Discovering the wider world 94
Sensory awakening 98
Social baby 101
Sitting baby 104
Crawling baby 107
Walking, talking baby 110
Swimming 114

6 NIGHTTIME BABY 116

How babies sleep 118
A baby-centred approach 120
Nighttime environment 126
Settling your baby for sleep 128

7 FAMILY LIFE 132

Well mother 134
You and your partner 139
Sibling relationships 143
Support with parenting 145

8 NATURAL HEALTHCARE FOR YOUR BABY 148

Health choices 150
Complementary therapies 154
Caring for a sick baby 157
Newborn health 159
Allergies 163
Respiratory problems 164
Ear and eye problems 166
Nutrition and digestion 168
Mouth and teeth 173
Skin problems 175
Childhood infectious illnesses 179
Accidents and first aid 181

Resources 184
Index 188
Acknowledgments 191

Foreword

Natural Baby *provides a wealth of information to help new parents bring out the best in their baby, and themselves. It's so important that parents and infants get off to the right start, and this is why I particularly enjoyed reading the chapter about the early weeks with a new baby. Throughout this book, parents will learn bonding tips, which are tools that help parents study their infant and become experts in their own baby. Since parents will spend more time feeding their infants than any one interaction during the first year, the section on the benefits of breastfeeding is particularly valuable. This informative part of the book helps parents give their baby the best nutritional start – and in situations when family circumstances may be less than ideal.*

You'll also spend a lot of time comforting your baby, which is why you'll find the section on "baby wearing" particularly helpful. Carried babies cry less and they learn a lot in the arms of busy caregivers. You'll also learn a lot about a group of infants I dub "high-need babies:" bright, curious – though draining – babies who require a high degree of investment from their caregivers, yet give back a lot of joy in return.

Because of the wealth of fun and practical information throughout this book, I believe Natural Baby *will be a valuable addition to every parent's home library.*

William P. Sears, M.D.

Preface

The first year of your baby's life is crucially important. This is when he or she will be building the capacity for loving other people as well as laying the foundations for a lifetime of health and resilience. We now know that even the youngest babies are in fact thinking, feeling individuals. They have an astonishing capacity to learn and an incredible zest for life. The ordinary tasks and joys of caring for your baby are all that is needed to maximize his or her potential. The natural interactions between mother and baby come as a ready-made recipe for success. Even more so when the father is actively involved in parenting and is fully supportive.

In this book I refer frequently to the concept of "attachment parenting". This is simply a way of describing how you can care for your baby in a way that encourages the close bonds that are natural to our species. It is a philosophy of natural family living that will give your baby the essential nurturing he or she needs and make your life as new parents easier.

I want to inspire you to make the most of this unrepeatable opportunity to give your all to your baby. The precious time that you have with your baby will continue to foster the closeness between you and all the benefits this can bring. Your full acceptance of your baby's natural dependency on you in the beginning means that you will have done everything in your power to build a sound basis for your child's development. This is the most valuable investment you can make in your child's future. It is also a privilege and a wonderful opportunity for you to share the richness, intensity, and wonder of your baby's first months of life. Enjoy!

Janet Balaskas

Janet Balaskas

Preparing for parenthood

Let me invite you on a journey to the beginning of your baby's life when the original egg was fertilized. During nine months of dramatic development in the womb, this tiny embryo became a foetus and then a fully formed baby ready to be born. Take a little time to imagine what it is like for your baby to be contained in a perfect environment, nourished and protected by your body 24 hours a day. This is his first home, where he feels safe and secure. He can hear your voice and your heart beating, and feels the constant rhythm of your breathing and your movements. After the birth and in the months to come, he will regain this feeling of security every time you hold him close. Understanding this is the key to successful parenting.

In the first year after birth, babies grow and develop incredibly fast, enabling them to adapt to the challenges of survival in the world outside the womb. However, independence is achieved more slowly than for any other mammal. Some naturalists have suggested that baby humans should be considered to have an 18-month gestation, nine months of which takes place in the womb and nine months outside. The extra nurturing in the first year results in a highly developed brain and an amazing capacity for learning.

Life before birth

A MOTHER HAS A UNIQUE instinctual bond with her baby in the womb. Although the father has a less tangible link at this time, many fathers also feel an intimate sense of connection with the baby during pregnancy, which strengthens after the birth. Your baby's presence becomes most evident near to full term. It is fascinating to watch those heaving bumps and lumps move across your belly in the last few weeks. The quiet times when the baby is sleeping and the more wakeful, active times become much more noticeable as your awareness of your baby grows.

SENSES AND FEELINGS IN THE WOMB

Research reveals that even in the womb, babies are fully sentient and aware of the sounds and other stimuli around them. From as early as eight weeks, when the developing nerve endings reach the skin surface, your baby begins to register sensations through the skin. As the warm amniotic fluid and the silky membranes that line the womb softly brush against his body, he gains his first sense of his own boundaries. In late pregnancy, when your baby is closer to the surface, you naturally comfort him hundreds of times a day, as you touch or stroke your belly.

Hearing is one of the earliest senses to develop and your baby hears a whole symphony of sounds in the womb. He hears your voice and your heartbeat, the internal sounds of your digestion and every cough, sneeze, laugh, shout, cry, or song. This

By talking to your baby as you gently massage your partner's belly, you can communicate through sound as well as touch.

combination of constant and unexpected sounds and movements make him ready for the sounds and noises he will hear after birth. From at least 28 weeks, babies in the womb also hear sounds from the immediate environment, such as the voice of their father or siblings, music, and household sounds. No wonder newborn babies generally like to be near the hustle and bustle of everyday life.

Knowing that your baby hears your voice in the womb may encourage you to hum or sing for your baby sometimes. Songs and lullabies are natural messages of love and comfort that mothers have sent to their unborn babies for thousands of years. You can also introduce your baby to music you think he will like before the birth. Studies have shown that often repeated sounds or music heard in pregnancy are recognized by young babies, who may associate them later as comfort sounds.

Emotional development also begins in the womb and many people have recalled memories in therapy as adults that they believe originated before birth. In a simple way we all remember the feeling of being protected in the womb, when we relax in a warm bath or cuddle up under the covers in a cosy bed. It is now widely accepted that babies in the womb are influenced by their mother's moods and feelings. Emotions are affected by hormonal activity and, conversely mood changes can stimulate the production of different hormones. In pregnancy you produce higher levels of endorphins, hormones that give you a sense of wellbeing. These also cross the placenta and impart similar feelings to your baby. In the same way, high levels of stress hormones, such as adrenaline, which we produce when we are anxious, frightened, or angry, may also reach the baby. However, while it is best to try to avoid highly stressful situations in pregnancy, every mother experiences a mixture of feelings. You don't need to be concerned that everyday ups and downs will harm your baby: they are a normal part of your baby's preparation for living.

PRACTISING FOR LIFE

Most of the vital functions that your baby will need after birth are practised in the womb. Through movement and vigorous kicking, the growing muscles and limbs are exercised, while the baby's lungs practise the movements needed for breathing. In the final weeks of pregnancy the lungs mature in readiness for breathing. The reflexes needed for sucking, swallowing, and urinating are already beginning to function. The baby plays with the umbilical cord and learns to grasp – a vital skill for other primates, who need to cling to their mother's fur after the birth. The eyelids begin to open and close in late pregnancy, and perhaps the baby is aware of subtle light changes when your belly is exposed to direct sunlight, although he will not feel the full impact of sight until after he is born. Babies are also aware of the presence of the placenta and like to face or turn toward it. Perhaps they are comforted by the pulsating rhythms of the blood flow. This is the beginning of the "rooting reflex" that helps babies to find the breast.

The last weeks of pregnancy

F OR A MOTHER-TO-BE, late pregnancy is a time to be especially kind to yourself, so that you approach the birth of your baby in a peaceful state of mind. You need to help your body to prepare for labour by slowing down, resting and sleeping a lot more. Eat healthy, nourishing food and avoid stress, toxins, alcohol, drugs, or stimulants. Regular, non-strenuous aerobic exercise such as walking or swimming is beneficial. Gentle pregnancy yoga is especially effective for maintaining your health and wellbeing, while developing confidence in your body. As well as the physical benefits it provides an opportunity to focus inwardly on the presence of your baby and to prepare for coping with the intensity of labour. Whether or not you practise yoga, try to allow yourself regular periods of quiet contemplation to induce a positive state of mind and a sense of relaxation. Ideally, spend time close to nature, by walking in the park or countryside, or taking time to look at the moon and stars or to enjoy the warmth of the sun in your garden.

A CHANGE OF FOCUS

It may be a huge relief to give up work in late pregnancy and to have more time to yourself. If you have had an interesting career, you may be concerned about the loss of stimulation and independence that you anticipate. Remember that the work you put into your baby's first year is a long-term investment that will benefit your child for a lifetime. Many women take this opportunity to find a way to "reinvent" themselves and discover a new occupation or lifestyle that works well alongside being a mother.

Pregnancy is also a wonderful time for emotional healing. Hormonal fluctuations allow your emotions to surface more easily, giving you the opportunity to explore them.

Relaxing with your baby in late pregnancy will help you be in harmony with the energy that is gathering inside you for the birth.

As the end of pregnancy approaches, the close relationship between the father and older child or children helps to prepare them for the arrival of a new baby.

Sadness or old hurts and wounds may come to the fore. You are going through a major life change and this is to be expected. It is wise to be open to any possibility of resolving conflicts with your loved ones and creating peace and harmony around you, before your baby is born.

BECOMING A FATHER

While your partner carries the baby, your support for the mothering process and your involvement with your baby is very important to them both from the start. A new baby brings great joy as well as big changes into your life. The most obvious of these may be the added challenge of having to provide for your family in the near future as well as possibly in the long term. The more subtle changes may mean being sensitive to your partner's fluctuating emotions and being prepared to do more nurturing than you may have done before. This is all great practice for after the birth, when she will need to devote most of her time initially to caring for the baby and you will need to "mother" her. The loving attention you give to her has a very powerful and positive effect on both her and your baby.

Being there when your baby is born, especially in the first few hours after the birth, when your baby will be most alert and responsive, is likely to be one of the most amazing experiences of your life. If you are concerned about your role during the birth, attending a course of preparation classes with your partner may be very helpful. This will help you to understand what is likely to happen during labour and birth, how you can help your partner, and give you vital information for making important decisions together. Such classes will also provide an opportunity for you to meet other expectant fathers with whom you can share your feelings, concerns, and experiences.

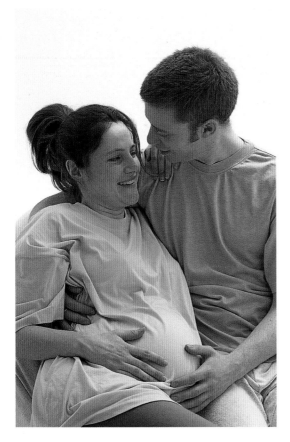

Your relationship as a couple will provide security for your baby and support for each other through the challenges of parenthood.

LOVING RELATIONSHIPS

Your baby will thrive best when your relationship with your partner is going well. This will ensure a happy and peaceful atmosphere in your home. It is not easy for any couple to sustain intimacy and good communication. This is especially true during the first year, when your baby will need so much of your time and attention. Even though it seems unspontaneous, it will help if you schedule time to be together regularly – during pregnancy and also after your baby is born. At least once a week, give yourselves an uninterrupted space to talk and listen and to share your feelings (see also Chapter 7).

If you are parenting your baby alone, you will have a special need for supportive relationships with your family and friends. This can work out very well, especially if you plan in advance and start building a committed support network. If possible, choose one consistent person to be the main "alternative parent", with whom you can share any worries and talk intimately and honestly about how things are going for you and your baby.

PREPARING YOUR HOME

It is both exciting and pleasurable to prepare for your new baby's arrival and is a natural part of the nesting instinct which many women feel in pregnancy. It also may be practical to do this now, as later on you will be fully occupied with caring for your new baby.

A NON-SMOKING HOME

Smoking is a common cause of indoor pollution and ill health and should be banned from any home where children are growing up. Babies who are subject to passive smoking are at increased risk from a range of serious disorders, including cot (crib) death (see page 161) and respiratory complaints.

Most parents are concerned to welcome their baby into a healthy home that is free from harmful pollutants. Babies are more vulnerable than adults to toxins in the environment. Because they are smaller and breathe more rapidly than adults, they tend to absorb pollutants more easily and at higher concentrations. In preparing your home for your baby, you should be aware that fumes from fresh paint, new carpets or bedding, and from chemical cleaning agents can blend into an invisible "chemical smog". As pollutants tend to be heavier than air, they collect at lower levels, just where babies and small children tend to breathe. Wherever possible, choose non-toxic, low odour paints and furnishings made from natural untreated materials. Try to complete the work well ahead of time to give any fumes time to disperse.

It may be also a good idea to give your home a spring clean, but avoid starting a big or physically strenuous project too close to your due date. Bear in mind that the latest research tells us that some normal household dirt is good for babies. It strengthens their immune system and prevents allergies, so you don't need to be too fanatical about cleaning, and there is no need for strong chemical or "antibacterial" cleaning products. There are toxic chemicals in many such cleaning products that may be more harmful than the ordinary household dirt they are intended to remove. There are several brands of natural household cleaning products available and this is a perfect opportunity to make the change. Look for the Eco labels when making your selection. Many basic household supplies, such as soap, baking soda, and vinegar, can be used instead of conventional products.

The recommended temperature for a home with a young baby is 17–21°C (63–70°F). Thermostatically controlled central heating is ideal, otherwise convector heaters fitted with a thermostat can be used and you may need a thermometer in rooms where you spend time with your baby. When bathing or massaging your baby you may wish to use a portable room heater to raise the temperature of the room. Be sure to read the section on safety in the home (page 183) for advice on making your home safe for when your baby becomes mobile.

SHOPPING FOR YOUR BABY

Before your baby is born, it is best to buy only the essential items you will need for the first few weeks. Although baby shops are packed with products for every eventuality, the most important thing very young babies need is plenty of close contact with their parents. Before making expensive purchases, take your time, talk to other parents, if possible, and consider carefully. You may want to find sources of second-hand equipment and this can be an excellent way to economize, but make sure that anything you inherit or buy is in good working order and has not been broken and repaired. Read Chapter 3, Feeding your baby, and Chapter 4, Caring for your baby, for suggestions on the basic equipment, clothing, nappy (diaper) options, and other items that are likely to be most useful.

NATURAL NURSERY

For the first 6 to 12 months of your baby's life, and possibly longer, your baby is safest sleeping at night in your bedroom (see page 121). During this time the nursery, if you have one, will probably be used mainly for storage and play. Therefore it is not essential to prepare a bedroom for your baby before the birth unless this is something you will enjoy doing. Here are some recommendations for a healthy, natural environment for a young child.

✿ Choose non-toxic materials and finishes.

✿ Washable wooden floors, cork tiles, or linoleum are preferable to fitted carpets. Select washable rugs and position them over a non-slip mat.

✿ Limit the number of electrical appliances and make sure all electrical sockets have covers or are out of reach. A "demand switch" can be installed to cut off electricity at night.

✿ Fit thermostats to radiators or convection heaters. Install radiator covers or guards.

✿ Make sure there are safety bars over any accessible windows.

✿ Minimize dust by having roller blinds or washable curtains or drapes, and light fittings that don't collect dust easily.

✿ All furniture should meet the national safety standards. Unpainted naturally treated wood is preferable to plastic or metal. Be sure that there are no sharp edges or corners.

✿ When decorating have fun and use your imagination to create a stimulating space for your child.

Approaching birth

AS YOU GET CLOSER TO THE BIRTH, your focus turns inward. Your body is preparing hormonally and you may feel calm and increasingly ready to welcome your baby. Many women enjoy the full bloom of the final weeks of pregnancy. They feel especially well and relish these last few weeks of time to themselves or with their other children. This can also be a frustrating time, especially if pregnancy goes on longer than expected. As the baby's head settles into the pelvic brim, there may be discomfort, or a feeling of heaviness in the lower abdomen. Sleep is likely to be interrupted by frequent trips to the bathroom, and sudden waves of energy that can make you wakeful at night. This is good preparation for the nighttime feeds that lie ahead. For mothers who are unwell or unsupported, the end of pregnancy can be a time to ask for additional help from your friends and family.

As well as looking forward to meeting your baby soon, its also natural to have some anxiety about what life is going to be like after the birth. You may find yourself wondering how you are going to cope with a real baby, who is not neatly packaged in the womb. Or you may be nervous about bringing your baby home from hospital for the first time and being on your own with him. These concerns can be all the more acute if you are expecting twins.

FINDING A SUPPORT NETWORK

A good way to overcome these worries is to make an effort to spend time with some new mothers and their babies while you are still pregnant. The reality of being a mother usually comes as a surprise. Talking with new mothers will help you to have realistic expectations. Mothering is a learned skill as well as an instinctive one. Ideally we would learn about looking after babies from the example of other women as we are growing up ourselves. However, in our culture this rarely happens. If you haven't had much contact with babies, look for opportunities in your neighbourhood to meet a few and if possible arrange to spend half a day with a new mother. You might explore your neighbourhood for local postnatal events organized by national or local support organizations (see page 186). You could attend once or twice while you are pregnant and then join soon after your baby is born. It will help you enormously to see breastfeeding mothers and babies and to hear what other women experience.

Even if you adore being with your baby, you are going to need some time for yourself and some purely adult stimulation, so some planning for this now is a good idea. You will want to know where to go with your baby after the birth, too, and this may be the best time to research what's available in your area.

Sitting quietly and focusing your awareness on the flow of your breathing, especially the out breaths, will help to prepare you for labour. Sense the downward pull of gravity through your lower body and imagine how this force will help your baby to descend through the pelvis during birth.

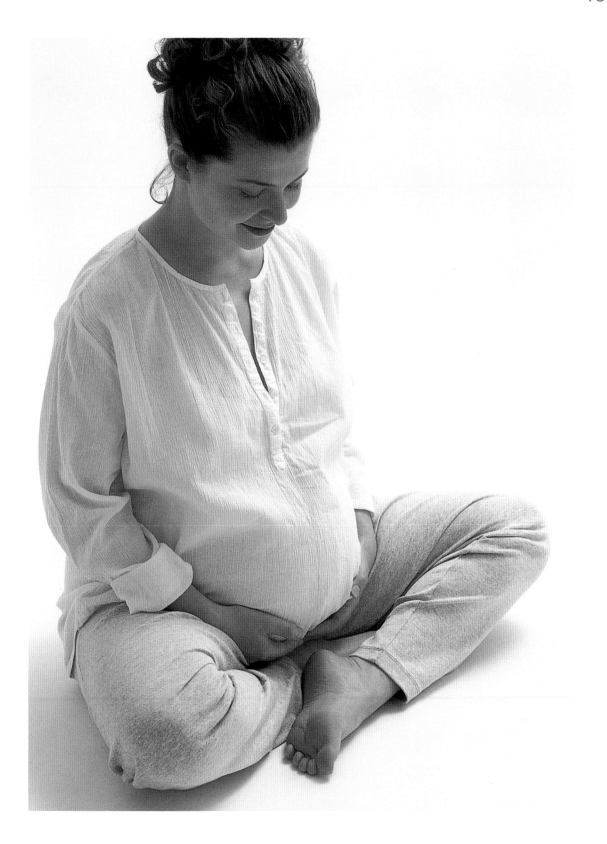

Meeting your baby

A CALM AND PRIVATE ENVIRONMENT in which you can labour undisturbed provides the best conditions for a spontaneous birth. When labour and birth happen naturally, whether on land or in water, your first meeting with your baby is immediate. There is an uninterrupted physiological continuity between the birth itself and the important events that happen in the first hour of life. While this provides an ideal start for you and your baby, it is possible to gain many of these benefits when birth is medically assisted by welcoming your baby in a similar way that will encourage the natural attachment between you and your baby.

LOVE HORMONES

Dr Michel Odent, the eminent French obstetrician and natural birth pioneer, emphasizes the vital role of hormones, both during labour and birth and in the first hour. He calls them the "love hormones", identical to the hormones which our bodies produce during love-making. The most important birth hormone is called oxytocin, produced by the hypothalamus gland deep within the mother's brain. Oxytocin is the hormone that is responsible for uterine contractions during and after labour and also promotes the intense love and attachment between mother and baby that occur immediately after the birth. This is nature's guarantee that the baby will be nurtured and will survive.

Throughout labour, the increasing level of oxytocin in your blood reaches the baby via the placenta, up until the baby is born. Both mother and baby also produce hormones called endorphins, which reach very high levels by the end of labour. They are natural painkillers produced in response to painful contractions and they too promote dependency and attachment between mother and baby. These exceptionally high levels of oxytocin and endorphins shared by mother and baby occur only at the time of birth. Nature's plan is to ensure that you and your baby fall in love and develop a strong attachment from the very beginning.

CLOSE CONTACT

A gentle and loving welcome in a warm, darkened room is the best way to greet your baby and to promote attachment. There is greater understanding today about how we can encourage normal birth physiology by increasing privacy and creating a environment that is conducive to these processes, and also by using the help of gravity and water. Many midwives specialize in helping mothers to give birth without unnecessary interventions. However, the medical model of birth still prevails strongly in our culture. Birth physiology and bonding are commonly misunderstood. How birth will happen is also unpredictable. Not every woman wants or is

able to give birth naturally and sometimes there are complications and medical assistance is needed. However, maternal behaviour is only partly hormone-led; it can also be culturally learned, for example, in the case of an adoptive mother. Bonding also takes place throughout pregnancy. Whatever happens during birth, close contact with your newborn, as soon as possible after birth, will enhance your maternal feelings.

Here at last is this little person who has become so familiar inside you for the last nine months. The first moments when you look into his eyes, stroke his body, and feel the silky softness of his skin, are unforgettable.

GREETING YOUR BABY

Some babies are calm at birth while others may cry for a while. Safe in your arms, your baby is comforted by your touch and your warm body. The birth is not over until the placenta has emerged. The baby's first sucking or closeness to the breast, stimulates the strong contractions that expel the placenta. While this is happening you will be gazing into your baby's eyes for the first time. Amazingly, your baby may seem to recognize you and he may even seem to smile up at you. As we shall see in the next chapter, the first interactions between you and your baby are very special. In the intimacy of the first hours after birth, everything functions in perfect harmony, designed by nature to protect your baby and to help him to adapt to his new world.

Welcoming your baby

Seeing, touching, and holding your baby, marvelling at her little body – this is what the first moments of motherhood are all about. In the magic intimacy of the first hour, as you welcome your new baby, an amazing interaction unfolds between you.

In the first hour after the birth, the high levels of "love hormones" that built up during labour make you and your baby especially responsive to each other. Nature ensures that you are both alert, wide eyed, and ready to meet each other. In fact, your baby will be in what is called a "quiet alert" state for several hours. As you gaze into each other's eyes for the first time, the process of recognition and falling in love begins. While most mothers feel an immediate rush of emotion for their baby, it is also normal for these feelings to arise gradually, so don't worry if you feel strangely detached at first; the intensity of labour and birth can sometimes be overwhelming. Equally, there is no need to be concerned if the close contact with your baby is not possible in the first hour, for example, for medical reasons. Instead take the first opportunity to create some private time with your baby in a warm room, undress her and hold her "skin-to-skin" and you will soon make up for lost time.

First hour after birth

FOLLOWING THE BIRTH, a mother's natural instinct is to hold her baby close to her body, directly against her naked skin. This keeps the baby warm and protects her from the cooler temperature outside the womb. It will take several weeks before your baby's own temperature regulation system begins to mature. During this time the best way to keep your baby warm is through contact with your body. Studies have shown that body contact is a more effective way of preventing heat loss in newborn babies than wrapping them and placing them in a heated crib. If the outside temperature is cool, a warmed blanket can be placed loosely over you both instead.

Body contact increases the secretion of the hormone prolactin, which stimulates milk production. It also promotes maternal attachment and the instinct to breast-feed. This natural stimulation of loving feelings is just as important for mothers who plan to bottle-feed, helping them to achieve a unique sense of connection with their baby from the start.

Your baby will love to be held close to your heartbeat, nestled into the warmth of your body and will soon learn to recognize your smell.

There is another important advantage to the baby being held exclusively in the mother's arms immediately after birth. In the womb the baby is in a sterile environment. At birth the baby enters the world of microorganisms and those that she encounters first will be dominant in her body. If these are the bacteria and other microorganisms that naturally surround the mother's body, the baby will have the immediate protection of a shared immunity to the most likely sources of infection.

MOTHER-BABY BONDING

Most researchers agree that the first hour or so after birth is a critical time. Dr Michel Odent stresses that until the placenta is expelled, the priorities are not to disturb the first contact between mother and baby and to keep the temperature of the room very warm, even overheated. This encourages the release of high levels of oxytocin (see page 20) needed to expel the placenta safely and to promote love and attachment. He believes that the unique human capacity for love has its origins in the high level of hormones that builds up in both mother and baby throughout labour and reaches a peak in the first hour after birth.

Sometimes, however, circumstances surrounding birth are less than ideal, and it is important to know that healthy attachment can also be established gradually. In her book *A Natural History of Parenting*, the biologist Susan Allport shares her view that bonding is a process that begins at birth and continues throughout the first weeks, being fully established with the first social smiles of the baby at around two to three months. She explains how rapid attachment, which is so crucial for survival in other mammals whose young are born more mature, is not so critical for humans. The bonding period is extended over several weeks of careful nurture in humans. This view can be reassuring, if love for your baby develops slowly or when ideal contact immediately after the birth is not possible. Through close contact, even adoptive parents bond successfully with their children.

A GENTLE TRANSITION TO BREATHING

In a natural birth, the umbilical cord is left intact so that the baby has two sources of oxygen until breathing is fully established. This takes 10–15 minutes. The final boost of blood that the baby gets from the cord during this time is rich in minerals. The placental circulation ceases gradually until the cord stops pulsating and compresses spontaneously. Injection of a drug called Syntometrine® to reduce uterine bleeding is commonly advised as the baby is being born. This necessitates immediate clamping of the cord and may disturb bonding. While this is needed after a medically induced birth or if there are complications, it is unnecessary after a natural birth with normal blood loss. You will need to let the midwife know in advance, if you would prefer the natural approach.

FIRST BREASTFEEDING

Newborn babies have all the instincts they need to find the breast. They have an acute sense of smell and taste and can recognize the smell of their own mother's milk, which tastes similar to the amniotic fluid. When placed on your belly or held in your arms, a powerful "rooting reflex" compels your baby to find the breast. When she feels a touch on her face she will turn her head toward it, open her mouth, and search for the nipple. She will instinctively latch on, suck, and swallow, although it sometimes takes a bit of practice to get the knack of breastfeeding right between a new mother and baby. The powerful sensations of the first sucks may surprise you at first and take a little while to get used to. You can read more about breastfeeding on pages 37–57.

Don't worry if your baby takes time to show an interest in the breast. There is no rush, it is not necessary for her to feed immediately. Sooner or later she will get hungry and want to feed. You can try to entice her by squeezing out a few drops of milk onto her lips, but don't be concerned if she seems more interested in just being close to the breast at first; she will feed when she is hungry.

THE PHYSIOLOGICAL RESPONSE

The first sucking, or simply the baby's closeness to the breast, stimulates the secretion of oxytocin in the mother, resulting in the strong cramping "after pains". These are contractions of the womb that expel the placenta, stop bleeding, and help the womb shrink back into its normal size and position. At the same time, oxytocin stimulates the muscular walls of the milk-producing glands to contract and squeeze

Holding your young baby skin-to-skin at times, especially while feeding, is a wonderful way to increase the production of the "mothering hormone" prolactin and to enhance your loving relationship with your baby.

the first milk, known as colostrum (see page 50), down the milk ducts toward the nipples. As the baby latches on and begins to feed, this in turn stimulates more contractions of the womb. The high level of oxytocin also results in tender emotional feelings while feeding and this will happen every time you breastfeed from now on. Studies show that mothers whose babies have touched their nipples and areolae within the first half hour of birth show increased nurturing behaviour. Mothers who intend to bottle-feed can also benefit from this natural boost to bonding. The breast has now taken over from the placenta as your baby's source of nourishment and for the coming weeks your baby will be feeding for long periods and at frequent intervals throughout the day and at night.

NEW FATHER

During the first half hour or so after the birth, there will be an amazing energy in the room and you will be witnessing one of the most wonderful and moving sights of your life as your partner holds your baby in her arms for the first time. Don't be surprised if you find yourself overwhelmed by emotion. The attachment between fathers and their newborn babies is profound, yet it unfolds differently from that between mother and baby. Immediate and undisturbed contact between mother and baby is a biological imperative to ensure the survival of the baby and the safety of the mother until the placenta is delivered. Your first contribution to your new family can be to help protect the deep privacy needed for this vital time.

The father's direct contact with the baby starts after birth. Once the placenta is delivered is the ideal time for you to hold your baby close and begin to get to know him.

SHARING THE WELCOME WITH BROTHERS AND SISTERS

If you have another child or children, you can introduce them to the new baby soon after the placenta has emerged or later on when you and your partner have had some time alone with the new arrival. It is a good idea to plan the timing of the first visit of your older child or children carefully to coincide with a moment when their mother is not holding the baby and can give them a cuddle first. Then give them an opportunity to hold and welcome their new sibling while she is still wakeful. In some families the children are present much earlier and sometimes even during the birth. If this is your plan then make sure that your children know what to expect and are prepared for the fact that you may change your mind if there are unexpected complications.

Your newborn baby

NEWBORN BABIES ARE EXQUISITELY SENSITIVE and receptive to everything that happens around them. Your baby can feel cool, dry air on her skin surface, which contrasts with the warm, wet amniotic fluid that surrounded her in the womb; she experiences gravity and a sense of body weight for the first time; seeing light, colour, forms, and faces in place of darkness; and hearing new and unusual sounds. The transition to full hearing and vision is gradual. This protects your baby from being overwhelmed by the stimulation of her new environment and is designed to intensify her focus on her main protector, her mother.

In the hours and days following the birth, you and your baby are supremely responsive to each other through smell and touch.

NEWBORN APPEARANCE

Proportionately, your baby's head will seem much larger than her body and her belly is rounded. Newborn babies often look a little purple or grey in colour in the very first moments after birth, although this is not so obvious in dark-skinned babies. In the next few minutes, as they start to breath and their circulation improves, they "pink up", as the midwives say. In the early days they often look quite red in colour, although their hands and feet are often pale as the circulation takes longer to reach the lower body and the extremities.

Your baby's face may look a little puffy at first, especially around the eyes, and the nose may be a little flat, or an ear may be folded, but these will regain their normal shape very quickly. Your baby's head may appear to be an unusual pointed or uneven shape. This is caused by the overlapping of the plates of the skull during birth, nature's way of moulding the baby's head to make it fit more easily through the pelvic opening at birth. This does not hurt or harm the baby and the normal shape will begin to return within hours. The skull bones will harden and fuse within the first two years. In the meantime you will notice a soft spot on the top of the baby's head called the anterior fontanelle. This is the gap where the skull plates do not yet meet. It is covered and protected by the very tough scalp and is not as delicate as it seems, so don't be afraid to touch it gently. If you ever notice that the fontanelle looks unusually indented, taut, or swollen, have your doctor check your baby as this may be a sign that your baby is unwell.

The body surface may be covered with a creamy, waxy substance called vernix. This protects the skin in the watery environment of the womb, and also helps the baby to cope with the change of temperature outside. In a few hours the vernix, which is also full of nutrients, will be absorbed through the baby's skin, so there is no need to wipe or wash it off unless there is a lot in the folds or creases. There may be some blood on your baby's body from the birth canal, and likewise there is no need to remove this immediately following the birth.

You may also notice that your baby's body is covered by a downy fuzz of delicate hair. This is called lanugo and will disappear over the next few weeks. Babies vary in the amount and colour of the hair on their heads. Blond babies often look a bit bald at first and dark babies can be born with an impressive shock of hair. This first hair may fall out in the early weeks and when it regrows may be replaced by hair of a different colour.

BIRTHMARKS

Common birthmarks are little red marks on the skin, especially on the forehead, eyelids, and at the nape of the neck. They are from enlarged blood vessels near the skin surface and will fade in 6–18 months. Mongolian blue spots are very common on dark-skinned or African and Asian babies. They look like bruises, usually on the lower back, and also disappear naturally. A raised red mark that looks like a strawberry can appear after a couple of days and should gradually fade and disappear by the time your baby is three years old. If you notice any unusual marks on your baby, discuss them with your midwife or doctor for reassurance.

NEWBORN REFLEXES

Babies are born with many instinctive reflexes designed to protect them until they learn to make conscious movements. Some newborn reflexes last only a day or two, while others last for around three months. The most basic involves the ability to maintain breathing. This remains involuntary throughout life.

A blinking reflex protects the eyes from strong light, sound, or touch.

✿ Sucking, swallowing, and rooting reflexes ensure that the baby can feed (see page 25).

✿ A strong grasp reflex enables your baby to grip anything pressed into the palm of her hand so strongly that her whole body weight can be lifted by the hands. This reflex allows primates to cling to their mother's fur from birth onward.

The splayed toes curl when you touch the sole.

✿ When exposed, held out in space, or in response to a loud noise, a newborn throws out her arms and legs with fingers outstretched as if to find something to hold onto. This is called the startle or Moro reflex. Babies do not like this sensation, so it is always best to lift and carry your baby securely in close contact with your body.

✿ A "stepping" reflex, prompts your baby to lift her feet when held upright with her feet touching a firm surface. This has nothing to do with learning to stand and walk later on.

✿ When held horizontally in water, newborn babies make reflexive swimming motions with their arms and legs.

✿ The "dive reflex" automatically closes the baby's air passages when born into water at body temperature, so that the baby doesn't inhale the water. Breathing is stimulated when the baby's face comes into contact with the air as she is lifted out of the water. The dive reflex lasts for about three months and during this period babies are naturally adapted to being in water.

See also Chapter 5, Development and play.

The babymoon

THESE EARLY DAYS WITH YOUR BABY are to be cherished. Making most of them will help to ease the transition into life after birth. Your new baby has just arrived into a whole new world which is unfamiliar and stimulating. You in turn are learning how to take care of her and how to respond to her signals.

In many traditions, the days following birth are considered special and important and it is customary for the new parents to spend this time in seclusion with their baby before welcoming visitors. You will be recovering from the birth and getting to know yourselves as mother and father of a new baby. If you are an expanding family, the adjustment for your other child or children is also important and they need extra care, involvement, and consideration. You will need plenty of time to

When you hold your baby in your arms a flood of maternal feelings can seem to come from nowhere as you begin to realize that this tiny person belongs to you. Bonding takes place every day through smell, touch, and eye contact. You need time and privacy to relax and enjoy your baby.

rest and relax together and simply delight in each other's company, keeping your surroundings calm, intimate, and quiet. Before the birth you could explain to friends and family that you will be on "babymoon" for the first week, keeping visitors to a minimum.

RECOVERY AFTER THE BIRTH

Many women feel wonderful within hours of the birth and recover quickly. If you had a long or difficult labour or a caesarean section, you may feel weak and need to recover your strength and energy slowly. But in any event you will need to take it easy and get plenty of rest in the coming weeks. During this time your womb is returning to its pre-pregnancy size and the after pains that occur as it contracts while breastfeeding may be more uncomfortable at first than you expected. Full recovery takes four to six weeks, even if you are feeling good.

According to Tibetan custom, the family spends several days alone immediately following birth. Families usually welcome these traditional days of quiet and use this time to get used to the demands of a new infant and to enact rituals and prayers for the newborn. During this time families rarely go out and visitors know that they must wait...before they welcome the new baby into the community.

Anne Hubbell Maiden and Edie Farwell
The Tibetan Art of Parenting: From Before Conception Through Early Childhood, Wisdom Publications 1997

MOTHERING THE MOTHER

In the days after giving birth the high hormone levels of pregnancy plummet. While many women continue to be on a "high", it is also normal to feel emotional and weepy at times, especially on the day when your milk comes in (see page 51).

Learning to breastfeed your baby takes time and plenty of attention. Things may go smoothly from the outset. If there are initial difficulties, as is the case with some women, this can be both physically uncomfortable and upsetting. Usually problems are solved within the first two weeks, although they can go on longer. It will help to talk to your midwife or a breastfeeding counsellor or to an understanding friend or family member if you feel low. While "baby blues" are common and transitory, true postnatal depression occurs in only 10 to 20 per cent of women. If low spirits persist, seek professional help without delay (see also page 137).

The "babymoon" is a special time to be alone together with your baby, getting to know this new member of your family.

Learning to care for your new baby is a full time occupation which begins immediately your baby is born. Most new mothers feel overwhelmed at first and devastated by continuously interrupted sleep at night. Continual tiredness can be the most challenging part of early parenting. You may feel as if you have permanent jet lag for a while. While some new babies do

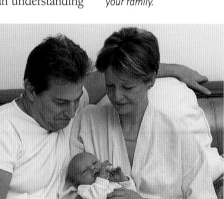

sleep for a longer stretch at night, they are far from typical. If you have other children you will be juggling your energy to respond to their needs and to help them to adjust to the new relationships within the family as well. So it is essential that someone looks after you in these early days.

You need to be brought at least three nourishing meals a day, with snacks and drinks around the clock. It makes a world of difference if someone is there to nurture you most of the time. It will probably surprise you how difficult it can be to organize yourself, get dressed, or wash your hair, or feed yourself properly when you are alone with a newborn baby. You will feel much better if someone can come and hold the baby for a while, so you can have a luxurious soak in the bath, sit down properly for an unhurried meal, or go for a short walk outdoors. You need these treats to come back refreshed for your baby.

FAMILY SUPPORT

Creating a peaceful haven for the new mother is a priority for at least the first four weeks. This role can be fulfilled by the father, other close relatives, friends, or pro-

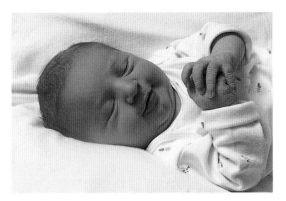

A newborn's facial expressions are fascinating to watch, especially the little windy smiles that pass across her face as she sleeps.

fessionals. Doulas are a new group of health professionals trained to give new mothers practical support after having a baby (see page 32). It is also important to acknowledge that this can also be a vulnerable time for fathers, even when they are thrilled to have a new baby. The early relationship between mother and child is very intense and the mother will be very engrossed in the baby. She will have very little energy left over for anyone else at first. It is normal for the father to feel a little left out or neglected. He may also feel overwhelmed if he is the main domestic supporter all the time and is also being woken frequently at night, especially if he needs to work as well. It is wise to plan the early weeks carefully and to ensure that you get reliable help with housework, shopping, and cooking. In this way you can truly enjoy the first few weeks following your baby's arrival.

CARING FOR YOUR BABY

A newborn baby needs to be loved, held, kept warm, nurtured, and fed throughout the day and the night. She is adapting to a very different environment from the womb, experiencing lots of new sensations and learning how to breath, digest, and eliminate waste by herself. Coming home from the hospital can be blissfully relaxing, but it can also be a little scary having sole responsibility for your baby, especially if she is your first. You may be feeling vulnerable, and caring for your baby without the support of the hospital midwives may seem daunting. It is natural for any new parent to feel this way. Learn to trust your instincts and get advice

from healthcare professionals, such as your midwife or doctor, and others you trust when you need it, and your confidence will grow. Very soon you will become the best expert on your baby.

FEEDING AND SLEEPING

In the first couple of weeks, your baby will probably sleep or feed most of the time, with short periods when she is awake and alert. Providing that you follow your baby's sleep pattern as much as possible, this will give you time to rest and recover from the birth, before your baby becomes more wakeful and demanding. In the womb your baby was fed continuously day and night through the umbilical cord, so its not surprising that most newborns need to feed frequently. After the birth, when feeding alternates with sleep, your baby experiences hunger pangs for the first time. These are uncomfortable and she learns to cry urgently when she is hungry and then feels comforted and soothed when she has been fed. This repeated satisfaction of hunger teaches your baby to trust that the world is a good place and that she is loved and cared for.

KEEPING CLOSE

Being held or in close body contact, is where your baby feels safest. In this, she is just like all the other baby mammals, who snuggle up to their mother's body, feed-

As you respond to your baby, soothing him when he is restless, feeding him when he is hungry, and comforting him when he is upset, he soon learns to trust you and to feel safe in his new surroundings.

ing more or less continually, in the early days after birth. The key to the art of mothering in the early days and weeks is to stay in close physical contact with your baby most of the time, day and night. The more you devote your attention to getting to know her, responding to her rhythms, interpreting her signals, and satisfying her needs, the more relaxed she is likely to be. A baby's needs are primal. You cannot spoil a newborn by responding immediately to her cries. They are designed to get your immediate attention to fulfil her physical needs. You will learn, with a bit of practice, if she wants to be picked up, held, or fed. If you are not sure why she is crying, try feeding her first, even if she has fed recently. She will let you know if that's not what she wants. In time you will even learn to anticipate her needs before she cries. Hold and carry her a lot and keep her in bed with you at night. This is natural behaviour for new mothers and is the way to have a contented baby.

Let your baby lie asleep on your chest for a little while after feeding, while you are awake and resting. This is very relaxing for you and makes your baby feel safe and secure.

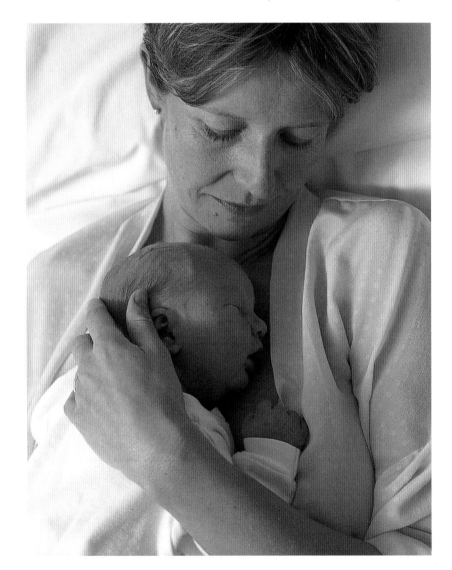

UNSETTLED BABIES

While some babies adapt remarkably easily to life outside the womb and can be contented most of the time, some babies take much longer to settle. If your baby is wakeful, cries a lot, or if you having trouble getting the knack of breastfeeding, the early days can be difficult. Some newborns are inexplicably fretful, seeming to want to feed incessantly with very short breaks between feeds and repeated bouts of inconsolable crying. The American paediatrician Dr William Sears calls them "high-need" babies. In his book *The Fussy Baby* he stresses the benefits of holding, body contact, unrestricted breastfeeding, and co-sleeping to help an unsettled baby. Although there is no cause for serious concern, a high-need baby can be wearing on new parents. Seek help from a healthcare professional or other trusted adviser, if you need it (see Why babies cry, page 75).

EARLY DAYS PRACTICAL CARE

The cord stump

The umbilical cord clamp is removed after a couple of days and the cord stump will naturally dry, shrivel, and fall off within a week. revealing the baby's "belly button" or navel. The baby does not feel this. There may be a few drops of blood around the navel, but if there is any more than this, you should consult your doctor or midwife. During this time, clean the navel twice daily with a solution of homeopathic calendula mother tincture, avoiding powders and creams. Put 10 drops into a little previously boiled warm water and apply with clean cotton wool. A drop or two of the tincture can be applied neat, directly to the base of the stump at each nappy change.

Skin

During the first few days after birth, the outer layer of your baby's skin may become dry and flaky and peel off. The skin underneath is very soft and smooth. It is best to avoid using moisturizers on a newborn's delicate skin, except for pure oils such as olive or grapeseed. Little pimples with white heads, called milk spots, may also come up on the skin as the baby acclimatizes to her new environment. There may also be small white spots over the bridge of the nose called milia. They are little blockages in the sweat and sebaceous glands, which should clear naturally in a few days.

Breathing, snuffling, and snoring

Newborn babies breathe very shallowly and much faster than an adult because their lungs are small. Their breathing can be barely visible when they are sleeping. Some babies snore and snuffle when they are asleep and all babies yawn frequently when they are awake. Sometimes their breathing can be quite noisy as the air tries to get through the narrow air passages. Unless your baby is having difficulty feeding, this is generally not a problem and will change as the nasal passages grow in the coming weeks. A good natural tip to clear the baby's nose before feeding, is to squirt a little breast milk directly up each nostril, by squeezing behind the nipple. Alternatively, your doctor may prescribe saline drops. Speak to your doctor immediately for reassurance if you are at all concerned about your baby's breathing or if your baby's chest is being sharply drawn in with each breath.

See also Chapter 4, Caring for your baby.

Feeding your baby

Breastfeeding is the natural way to feed your baby. Nutritionally, breast milk is the perfect food throughout the first year. It provides everything your growing baby needs and also provides protection from infection and disease. From your point of view it can be immensely satisfying to be able to feed your baby from your own body. The World Health Organization recommends that a baby should be exclusively breastfed for the first six months. Even after the introduction of other foods, breastfeeding can remain the mainstay of your baby's diet, until he is a year old or more.

There are sometimes good reasons why breastfeeding may not be an option. In these circumstances, bottle-feeding is a wise and valid choice. In some instances mothers use a combination of breast milk and formula feeds. They are not mutually exclusive. The following section on breastfeeding is still worth reading, as you will be able to incorporate many of the breastfeeding principles and benefits into the way that you bottle-feed your baby. In this chapter you will also find guidance about when and how to introduce solid food to your baby alongside his milk feeds.

Feeding your baby is a time to rest and relax. These hours of intimacy, peace, and pleasure are a vital part of your relationship with your baby, which fulfil his need to be nurtured and your need to love and take care of him.

Why breastfeeding is best

BREAST MILK IS THE MOST NUTRITIOUS FOOD for your newborn baby. It promotes optimum mental and physical development, provides emotional security, and strengthens the immune system. Its special qualities cannot be replicated. It is sterile, portable, just the right temperature, and is available at all times.

SCIENCE SUPPORTS NATURE

Scientists are discovering more and more about how breast milk protects babies. Compared with formula-fed babies, studies show that breastfed babies tend to have fewer and less severe gastrointestinal, respiratory, or ear infections. They are also less likely to suffer sudden infant death syndrome (SIDS or cot death) or serious illnesses. Breast milk also protects babies from viruses and bacteria that are prevalent in the environment, because the mother quickly develops the relevant antibodies (particles in the blood that are produced to fight specific infections)

WHAT BREAST MILK CONTAINS

Human breast milk is specific for our species. It contains all the essential nutrients that your baby needs. The composition of breast milk changes at different stages of development, from the newborn colostrum to the transitional milk, and then the mature milk when the baby is about two weeks old. The milk contents vary during a single feed and also at different times of the day. In addition to the immune factors, these are some of the important nutrients mature breast milk contains:

✿ The protein in breast milk is made up of 60 per cent whey protein and 40 per cent casein, the result is a soft curd that is easy to digest. Cow's milk is only 20 per cent whey protein and 80 per cent casein and takes longer to digest. It also needs to be diluted to be digestible, and the baby therefore needs to consume a greater volume of cow's milk formula than breast milk. The protein in cow's milk can cause an allergic reaction in some babies whereas human milk protein is virtually nonallergenic to babies. This is especially important for babies where there is a family history of allergy or sensitivity.

✿ There is an enzyme in breast milk called lipase, which keeps the fat globules small and easy to digest. Fat is the most efficient source of energy for babies, so easy digestibility helps optimize growth.

✿ Lactose, the sugar that is found in breast milk, is important for the development of the baby's brain and central nervous system. It also assists absorption of calcium and promotes overall growth. There is a much higher level of lactose in human milk than in cow's milk.

✿ Breast milk has all the water that babies need. Even desert nomads do not need to give their breastfed babies additional water.

✿ All the vitamins, minerals, and trace elements that babies need are in breast milk. Vitamin D and iron levels are low, but the iron is absorbed more easily than the iron in fortified formulas and there is generally no need to give supplements to your baby. But if you are vitamin D deficient yourself or if you have low iron stores or are anaemic you may wish to consider giving your baby the supplements recommended by your doctor. Going outside with your baby will expose him to sunlight, a natural source of vitamin D. High potassium and low sodium levels in breast milk are thought to protect against high blood pressure in later life.

✿ Hormones and enzymes in breast milk promote the healthy development of the baby's intestinal tract. Breast milk ensures that protective microorganisms dominate in the digestive tract.

and passes this resistance to the baby in the milk. This protects the baby even when the mother herself has a cold or 'flu. It has also been demonstrated that when a baby has an infection, the mother produces the appropriate antibodies, which are then passed back to the baby in the breast milk and so assist the baby's recovery. Breastfeeding does not mean that your baby will never get ill. His immune system will, however, be supported by this natural protection to hasten his recovery. Feeding from the breast is harder work for the baby than feeding from a bottle and this helps with development of the jaw and optimal positioning of the teeth.

A SELF-REGULATING FOOD

The composition of breast milk changes as your baby grows to suit his developing nutritional needs. The concentrated first milk, or colostrum, has a very high level of substances that boost the immune system, which is especially important to the baby in the first days of life outside the womb. As the milk supply increases, the levels of fat, lactose, and total calories increase to promote growth. A baby's brain needs very specific

BREASTFEEDING AND BRAIN DEVELOPMENT

A baby's brain more than doubles its weight in the first year of life. Certain essential fatty acids (EFAs) in breast milk provide about 60 per cent of the calories needed for this rapid brain growth. Studies have shown that breastfed babies tend to have higher IQs than formula-fed babies due to these nutrients. Some brands of baby formula now contain EFAs. Breastfeeding mothers should eat foods high in EFAs, such as oily fish, seeds, and cold-pressed olive oil

HOW BREASTFEEDING BENEFITS YOU

✿ During breastfeeding your body produces oxytocin, the hormone that reduces bleeding after birth and encourages the uterus to return to its pre-pregnancy size and position.

✿ Mothers who breastfeed tend to return more rapidly to their pre-pregnancy weight.

✿ Producing food from your own body is satisfying and empowering. You get to share hours of tenderness and bliss with your baby.

✿ Once any initial discomfort has been overcome, breastfeeding is a pleasurable, relaxing, and nurturing experience for you too. When you relax with it, breastfeeding gives you energy, rather than draining you as is commonly feared.

✿ Breastfeeding helps to prevent breast disease, reduces the risk of ovarian cancer, and improves the re-mineralization of bone after pregnancy thus reducing the risk of osteoporosis in later life.

✿ The hormone prolactin, which promotes breast-milk production, usually suppresses ovulation. While this cannot be relied upon as an effective method of contraception, the consequent lack of menstrual periods allows your iron stores to build up again. Prolactin is also has a relaxing effect, helping you to cope better with the stresses of being a new mother.

Breastfeeding promotes tender feelings for your baby.

BREAST AND NIPPLE SIZE

Whatever their size, breasts are designed to produce enough milk. Small breasts have just as many milk-producing glands as larger breasts, which simply have more fatty tissue. Flat or inverted nipples are not usually an insurmountable obstacle to breastfeeding, as the baby's sucking generally draws the nipples out. A breastfeeding counsellor can help if you are concerned or if the problem does not correct itself.

different types of fats as it grows, and the types of fat in breast milk change accordingly. When your baby moves on to a mixed diet, the milk composition adapts and changes again. In the older baby feeding mainly for comfort, the level of immune factors increase to maintain protection from disease, even though the child is consuming less breast milk.

Breast milk is so complex and variable that scientists are continually discovering new evidence about the way it naturally self-regulates. When you are fully breastfeeding you don't need to worry about your baby's nutrition. Each breastfeed is a like a complete four-course meal – the more watery milk stored in the reservoirs behind the areolae quenches the baby's thirst initially. This is followed by the more sugary milk, and then comes the protein and highly nutritious fat from the richer hind milk, followed by a watery drink at the

HOW BREAST MILK IS MADE

The hormone prolactin is produced abundantly by the pituitary gland during pregnancy, during which time it promotes enlargement of the milk-producing glands. High levels of oestrogen in pregnancy suppress milk-production, but after the birth when oestrogen levels fall, the presence of prolactin activates the milk-producing cells. The production of prolactin is maintained by regular suckling of the baby.

The let-down reflex

When you hold your baby close and he latches on, the sucking action stimulates nerve endings in the nipples, sending messages to the pituitary gland in your brain that triggers the release of prolactin and oxytocin (see page 20). Oxytocin makes the tiny muscles around the milk-producing cells contract and squeeze the milk down the milk ducts. The milk then ejects through the tiny openings in the nipples. This interaction between mother and baby is called the "let-down reflex" and occurs every time your baby needs to feed. Sometimes just thinking about feeding or hearing your baby can trigger the let down. The let-down occurs in both breasts at once. Some women experience tingling sensations as the let-down starts and its force in the early weeks may surprise you; the milk can spray out of your breasts at a quite distance.

Pituitary gland

The baby's sucking stimulates nerve endings in the mother's nipple, which transmits signals to the pituitary gland in the brain

Prolactin secreted by the anterior pituitary gland stimulates milk production

Oxytocin, produced in the posterior lobe, causes the muscles lining the milk-producing cells to contract and eject the milk

end. This is why it is important to completely finish the feed on each breast, so that your baby gets all of the essential nutrition of the hind milk. Breast milk composition also varies throughout the day and is richest when you have been resting – usually in the morning.

TOXINS IN BREAST MILK

A report was published recently by the WWF (World Wildlife Fund) highlighting the level of pollutant chemicals found in human milk. These days everyone is exposed to environmental pollution from conception onward. These chemicals come from the air we breathe, the food we eat, and even from our own mother's body in pregnancy and during breastfeeding. Such chemicals are stored in our body fat. Fatty tissue in the mother's body is broken down for the production of breast milk. During this process, chemicals that may have been stored in the mother's body fat for years may be deposited in her breast milk and passed on to the baby. In addition, traces of chemicals in the environment or diet – for example, from cigarette smoke, emissions from household products, paints and carpets, pesticides, alcohol, and medications – can end up in breast milk.

However, this does not mean that you should not breastfeed your baby. Breastfeeding is still considered by most obstetricians and paediatricians to be the best way to feed babies. The tremendous advantages of breastfeeding are considered, in most cases, by experts to outweigh any risks. It is also true that there are many hidden pollutants in formula milks, albeit different ones from those commonly found in breast milk.

The advantages of breastfeeding far outweigh the disadvantages. The issue of environmental pollutants is not simply one for breast milk but potentially affects all foods including cow's milk from which many infant formulas are derived.

Louise Silverton, Deputy General Secretary, Royal College of Midwives, *Practising Midwife*, August 1999

REDUCING BREAST-MILK CONTAMINATION

You can minimize the release of contaminants into your breast milk in the following ways:

✿ Do not to try to lose weight while breastfeeding and be sure to take in enough calories to prevent excessive breakdown of fat in which many potential contaminants are stored. There is no reason to be overly concerned if you lose a pound or two – just avoid dieting and eat normally.

✿ Don't exercise strenuously when you are breastfeeding. Moderate exercise combined with normal food intake is fine – for example, yoga, pilates, swimming, or walking. Deep breathing during exercise is a good way to clear toxins.

✿ Eat plenty of fresh and raw fruit and vegetables, which contain natural antioxidants that help to remove toxins from your body. Choose organic foods, which are naturally free from chemical pesticides and other additives.

✿ If possible, avoid exposing yourself to environmental pollutants, chemical contaminants, chemicals in cosmetics, hair dyes, and perfumes, and unnecessary medications, etc.

Preparing to breastfeed

BREASTFEEDING IS PARTLY INSTINCTIVE and partly a learned skill. It is reassuring to know that confidence comes with practice. Through a natural process of trial and error, most mothers and babies learn from each other and the majority are happily breastfeeding within a fortnight.

While the benefits of breastfeeding are widely recognized today, we are still a long way away from a breastfeeding culture. Many of us were not breastfed ourselves, and may never have had the chance to see a baby at the breast close up, unless we have a friend or relative who is breastfeeding. The disruption of birth and early body contact with interventions, and a lack of privacy or appropriate guidance, can sometimes make the start of breastfeeding more challenging than it needs to be. But with a little preparation and the right support, almost all breastfeeding difficulties can be overcome.

A wonderful exchange of giving and taking, mutual appreciation, and valuing, takes place during breast-feeding. At times your baby will take a break to look up at you and enjoy a few moments of intimate communication before turning back to the breast to continue feeding or to fall asleep.

FEELINGS ABOUT BREASTFEEDING

Feelings of love, contentment, fulfilment and satis-faction are an integral part of breastfeeding. While you comfort and nourish your baby, hormones that pro-mote attachment are stimulated (see page 24). Eye contact reinforces this exchange of love, while close body contact and gentle touch give your baby securi-ty. One of the great rewards of breastfeeding is to see how much your baby enjoys it. Breastfeeding means that your body is actively present for your baby. This makes it easier for you to understand your baby and to respond to his cues. When your baby is upset, unwell, or out of sorts, sucking for comfort will calm and reassure him, often lulling him to sleep.

Women have all kinds of feelings about their breasts and for some it can be difficult to perceive the breasts as functional organs or the body as an ongoing source of nourishment and comfort. If you have very sensi-tive breasts you may feel anxious about the addition-al handling and contact with your baby. While these concerns are very real, they are usually overcome as the connection with your baby deepens.

You or your partner may have concerns about how breastfeeding might change your breasts. The breasts actually change most in pregnancy and breastfeeding has little additional impact on their size and shape in the long term. The rich blood supply to the breast during the breastfeeding period does make the veins stand out more, but this effect is temporary.

Some women have anxieties about breastfeeding if their mother or a close relative had problems. It is important to know that most difficulties are caused by poor advice or lack of the right kind of encouragement; heredity is rarely a factor. If any concerns about breastfeeding persist, it may be very helpful to talk to a breastfeeding counsellor or therapist.

> *A man whose attitude is relaxed enough to permit women to breastfeed in comfort respects the power of women, understands the nature of babies, and encourages the natural inclination of mothers and babies to be close to one another. Our society needs more men to be like this.*
>
> Ina May Gaskin, *Babies, Breastfeeding, and Bonding,* Bergin and Garvey 1987

FATHERS AND BREASTFEEDING

The father's encouragement of breastfeeding is crucial and it will help you to provide the support that your partner needs if you understand more about the process. In the early weeks the baby's priority is to grow and to be comforted and the involvement between mother and baby is intense. As he grows, he will appreciate your presence more, but in the meantime your understanding of the mother's role is hugely important. Telling your partner how beautiful and loved she is will boost her morale and self-confidence. Having someone to provide comforting drinks, company, and affection while she feeds the baby is invaluable. Breastfeeding your newborn baby is your partner's job, but there are many important aspects of care you can undertake, for example, winding, bathing, and soothing.

The father's attitude is a key part of successful breastfeeding. Your understanding and support for two of the most important people in your life, ensures the future health and wellbeing of your family.

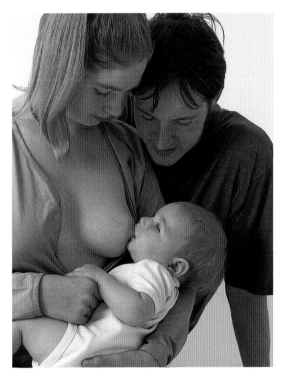

It is also good to be aware that there are issues associated with breastfeeding that many men need to deal with. Some men may feel uncomfortable with breastfeeding in public. It can also be very difficult to learn to see the breasts as functional as well as erotic. It also has to be said that jealousy of the baby getting so much pleasure and time at the breast may be an issue for even the most loving of fathers. These quite normal deeper feelings about breastfeeding need to be talked about and shared with your partner. In some cases, counselling may be helpful.

Learning together

Y OU MAY FIND THAT YOU CAN breastfeed easily and spontaneously, and the detailed guidance below may seem quite unnecessary. However, if the breast-feeding relationship takes time to establish, be patient and give yourself and your baby plenty of time. Very soon you will become experts.

Being alone with your baby without outside distractions while you feed in the early days may help you to relax and thereby encourage the milk to flow. While feeding you will need to use a breast pad or towel to absorb any leakage from the other breast. At night keep a supply of hand towels beside the bed. Compressing the non-feeding breast firmly toward the chest wall with your free arm is a trick you can use to control leakage once your baby is a month old. Before then it may cause a blocked duct. Leakage is usually abundant in the early weeks and then reduces as the milk supply becomes more closely regulated to your baby's needs.

CARE OF THE BREASTS

There is no need to wash the breasts before or after feeding. Breast milk has antibacterial properties and a daily bath or shower is all that's needed to keep your breasts clean. Over-frequent washing removes the natural lubricants and may increase the likelihood of sore nipples. After feeding allow your breasts to thoroughly dry in the air. Then express a drop or two of breast milk and spread that onto the nipples with your fingers and allow to dry. In the early days you can apply a plant-based, homeopathic or lanolin-based nipple cream. These are available at health-food stores, some pharmacies, and by mail order. There is no need to wash these off before feeding later on.

See also Common breast problems, page 135.

At the start of each feed, the release of oxytocin (see page 40) also stimulates uterine contractions. In the early days this may be uncomfortable. You can ease discomfort by taking a deep releasing breath out, and relax your body just as you did in labour. It may be of some comfort to know that these cramp-like contractions or "after pains" prevent blood loss after birth and will eventually make your womb shrink to its pre-pregnancy size.

The early feeds will go best if you are comfortable and relaxed and your baby is calm and awake. It is essential that your baby attaches to the breast correctly, and the majority of babies do this spontaneously. Your careful attention to this in the beginning will help to prevent nipple soreness and frustration, and will enable your baby to feed well, making the experience enjoyable and fulfilling for you both.

POSITIONING FOR FEEDING

No two women are the same shape or size, so a position that works for one woman, may be impossible for another. You will have to experiment to find the way that works best for you and your baby. Many mothers do not need "how to" instructions for this personal and intimate relationship. However, if you do have difficulty in the beginning, you may find these suggestions helpful. But don't feel restricted by them; you should feel free to be led by your intuition and to discover on your own what feels and works best for you and your baby. After a few weeks your baby will be able to breastfeed with ease in a variety of positions that suit almost any situation, and you won't even need to think about how to hold him.

GETTING STARTED

It can be best to start by simply sitting upright in a chair or on the bed with your back well supported. Make sure that your feet are flat on the floor and your lap is horizontal. If necessary, raise your feet on a stool or pillows, so you can really relax your legs. When feeding in bed, you may find it easiest to sit cross-legged with your knees and back supported by pillows. In the cradle position (below), you can hold your baby with the arm on the

POSITIONING TIPS

❀ If the baby's arm closest to you is getting in the way, use your free hand from underneath to gently bring it down toward your waist. Or try swaddling the baby before feeding.

❀ Make your breast more accessible for your baby by cupping it gently, fingers around the base and thumb up, as pictured below.

Cradle hold

Place one or two pillows across your lap to lay the baby on, so that she is at the right height to approach the breast comfortably from just below. Lay your baby facing you, belly to belly, on her side with her head resting in the crook of the elbow of the arm on the same side as the breast. Her shoulders and spine can be supported by your forearm with your hand around her buttocks. Head, neck, and spine will then be in line. Avoid holding your baby's head; it should be free to tilt back slightly, so that the chin and mouth reach the breast first. This will also make it easier for her to breathe.

Underarm position

In this position, your baby lies belly toward you, on her side, with her head at the level of the breast and her body tucked under your arm. Lay her on a pillow so that her body is supported, while her head is in front of the breast. Make sure she can approach the breast from just below. You can use the arm on the same side to support her back and neck while the opposite hand is free to cup the breast. It may be helpful to put a footstool under the foot on the side you are feeding to elevate your thigh a little. This position is especially useful if you have large breasts or you have had a caesarean.

side from which he is feeding or with the other arm. In this case, place your palm behind the baby's shoulders with your fingers just supporting the neck. Whichever arm you use to cradle your baby, the other hand can be used to support the breast from underneath, if necessary. At night or while resting in bed try half-lying on one side with your torso supported by a beanbag or some big cushions. Position your baby beside you with his belly facing you and his head level with your breast. In this position you can doze while your baby feeds.

LATCHING ON

When the latch is correct, the baby's bottom lip curls under and the nipple is drawn to the back of the baby's throat. Large areolae may still be visible while the baby is feeding, whereas small areolae may disappear almost completely into the baby's mouth.

When your baby has latched on correctly, the nipple is drawn in to the back of his mouth and the movements of the jaw and tongue massage the milk down the baby's throat as it lets down and ejects. When your baby is feeding well you can see the rhythmic movements of the jaw around his temples quite distinctly. You may also be able to see his ears moving. The first rapid sucks stimulate the let down and, as sucking deepens and slows down, the baby will swallow the milk after every two or three sucks. When positioning is right, breastfeeding is not usually painful. Your nipples may be tender in the early days, causing discomfort as the baby starts sucking. However, this should pass as the feed progresses. Seek advice from your midwife or breastfeeding counsellor, if it persists.

The gape
Your baby will open her mouth or "gape" as she approaches the breast. You can encourage this, by touching her lips with the nipple. Mimicking the gape yourself while you say "open", will help your baby to open her mouth really wide.

Latching on
As soon as you see your baby's mouth open, bring her in toward you by bringing the arm that is supporting her closer to your body, rather than leaning forward over her. Make sure that she approaches the breast from just underneath and that a good part of the areola is drawn into her mouth.

STEPS TO COMFORTABLE POSITIONING

❀ Get really comfortable yourself first.

❀ Start feeding when your baby is calm.

❀ Hold your baby close so that his belly is turned in toward your body.

❀ Position your baby's nose in front of the nipple.

❀ Wait for the gape.

❀ Bring your baby toward the breast, not the breast toward your baby.

❀ Relax your shoulders and breathe deeply.

NIGHT FEEDS AND FEEDING LYING DOWN

For minimal disturbance to your sleep, acquiring the art of feeding while lying down is invaluable. This is best learnt once the breastfeeding relationship has settled, as most newborns are not ready to feed this way, with the occasional exception. Feeding lying down on one side, is often the best position to use when you are resting and for night feeds. Start by lying down on your side as described on the facing page and progress to lying down flatter when you feel ready. When a baby is born by caesarean section or is premature, reclining breastfeeding positions can be the most suitable. Be sure to use plenty of pillows as needed. When feeding lying down, try to ensure that your baby latches on correctly as described on the facing page.

AFTER A CAESAREAN

Breastfeeding can begin within an hour of a caesarean birth. If you have had epidural anaesthesia, you will continue to have pain relief for a few hours after the birth and this is an ideal time to bond with your baby. It takes 30 to 60 minutes to come around after a general anaesthetic. You are likely to feel groggy at first, but breastfeeding is possible as soon as you are ready to receive the baby. You will need to take pain-relieving medication, and even though these drugs may enter the breast milk, they are necessary after surgery. Homeopathic treatment, which does not affect the baby, can reduce your need for medication and promotes rapid healing.

Feeding lying down or in a semi-reclining position (see above) are the best positions to use immediately after a caesarean. It is easiest to start with a pillow covering your belly so that the baby doesn't kick the incision. In the next day or two you will be encouraged to feed sitting up and the underarm position will probably be

Feeding lying down on one side supported by pillows is often the best position to use when you are resting. Position your baby so that his belly is toward you, with his mouth at the level of the nipple. A young baby may need to lie on a pillow and may need time to get used to this, while an older baby will easily find the breast and latch on in this position. Once your baby is feeding well, you can put a pillow under your head and relax until he has finished the feed.

Once breastfeeding is working well in an upright or semi-upright position, you are ready to try feeding while lying down flat. Lie on one side with a pillow or two under your head. Hold your baby facing you on her side, body turned toward you and very close, with her mouth facing the nipple. Your arm can support her back, just as when feeding sitting up. The other hand can be used to cup the breast if necessary. To feed on the other side, you can lay your baby on your chest and roll over. In time you will be able to simply lean over the baby and offer the opposite breast without moving her. With practice, feeding lying down enables you to "sleep feed" so that you are barely aware of the night feeds and feel much more rested.

most comfortable for feeding. While you are recovering full mobility, ask your midwife for help when you need it, or contact a breastfeeding counsellor, who will have plenty of experience helping mothers after a caesarean. It is a good idea to have your partner, a friend, or a member of your family with you in the post-operative days to help to position the baby when feeding. Feeding your baby frequently and other forms of loving physical contact are the best way to establish the normal hormonal balance and closeness with your baby.

PREMATURE BABIES

A premature baby may need to spend time in hospital in a special care baby unit. In these cases, it is especially important for the mother to maintain as close contact as possible (see also page 159). Sometimes breastfeeding needs to begin with feeding expressed colostrum and milk through a nasogastric tube. You may need to express your colostrum and milk at first, starting by hand and then using a special electric pump. It is important to ensure that the milk is properly expressed, to contain the rich hind milk and meet all the baby's energy requirements. Even babies born after only 30 weeks can learn to breastfeed successfully, so try to start breastfeeding as soon as possible.

Breast milk of mothers of premature babies is specially adapted to their unique needs and has higher concentrations of specific nutrients, digestive enzymes, and immune factors. Premature babies need a great deal of sleep and rest so take your

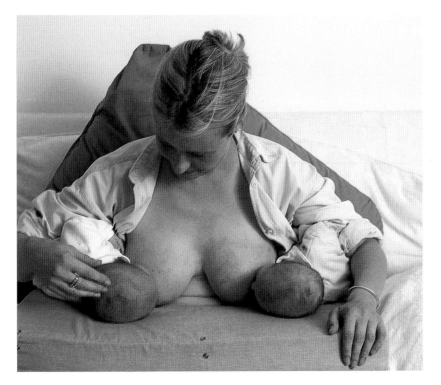

One way to feed twins at the same time is with one baby tucked under each arm, using a special support pillow (available by mail order). You can also breast-feed two babies at the same time in the cradle hold without the pillow (called the criss cross or V hold) or have one baby in the cradle hold and the other under one arm.

Some mothers make a point of rousing both babies when one wakes up for a feed. You can wind one baby while the other is still feeding.

time and be patient. If your baby's sucking reflex is weak you may need to use a syringe or an infant-feeding cup at first. This method is preferable to bottle-feeding. The midwives and specialist paediatric nurses will help you learn how to breastfeed in this special situation. Alternatively, contact a breastfeeding counsellor (see Organizations, page 186)

BREASTFEEDING MULTIPLES

Nature ensures that mothers of twins or triplets have enough milk for all their babies, and many mothers of multiples manage successfully to breastfeed fully or partially. Multiples are more likely to be premature, so the advice above may apply. With multiples you will need to evolve a pattern of care that works for you, taking account of the support available. The first twin to wake can be fed first, or if both are awake they can be fed at the same time. With triplets, the third can be fed while the other two are settled by someone else. Knowledgeable support and help will enable you to find a way of feeding your babies that works best for all of you.

The first few days

In the colostrum of the first hours there are millions of immune-active cells per cubic millimetre...These... neutralize and digest the most dangerous of germs. The most copious antibodies, called IgA, cannot be made by the newborn itself and are not brought by the placenta...Colostrum is, in fact, an army able to suppress any kind of infection.

Dr. Michel Odent, *The Nature of Birth and Breastfeeding*, Bergin and Garvey 1992

PROMOTING HEALTH AND NATURAL IMMUNITY is a priority, and ensuring that your baby receives as much colostrum (first milk) as possible is especially important. A full intake of colostrum gives your baby's immature immune system a healthy start and prepares the digestive system for optimum absorption of the mature breast milk.

Some babies are born hungry and will feed vigorously immediately. Others are happy to take their time before settling into feeding. Occasionally this can take a few hours or even days. Once they get started, newborn babies can breastfeed many times over 24 hours. Feeds take longer in the beginning and can last from half an hour to an hour, although some babies may feed faster. Most new mothers are surprised by the amount of time they need to spend feeding in the beginning. It is really more or less continuous during your baby's waking hours. This is because your baby is used to being fed continuously in the womb and needs constant nourishment to grow. It is also for comfort and security in a new and sometimes overly stimulating environment. There are many benefits to feeding your baby as much as possible at first. The milk supply will be stimulated so that the mature milk comes in sooner, jaundice is less likely, soreness and engorgement may be reduced.

THE IMPORTANCE OF COLOSTRUM

Frequent feeding in the first few days ensures that your baby gets plenty of the first milk called colostrum. This is a kind of concentrated "super milk" produced primarily in the first two or three days following the birth. It is usually yellowish and has the consistency of liquid honey. Colostrum is highly nutritious. Among other nutrients, it contains a high proportion of essential fatty acids (see page 39) It is also rich in antibodies and other immune factors that the baby cannot yet make himself.

Colostrum helps to establish the right balance of microorganisms in the gut (intestinal flora) to protect the baby from potentially dangerous invaders. The steady trickle of concentrated colostrum that the baby consumes gently expands the baby's stomach, which

FIRST BREASTFEEDING AFTER BIRTH

Successful breastfeeding is more likely when the first sucking occurs soon after birth. Nature ensures that:
✿ The newborn instinctively searches for the nipple and may find it as early as the first hour after birth.
✿ The mother, under the influence of the birth hormones, has an instinct to breastfeed.
✿ The earlier you breastfeed, the earlier your milk will come in.
✿ If you can't breastfeed in the first hour, a strong commitment to breastfeeding will soon make up for lost time.

is about the size of a walnut at birth, and prepares it for the much larger volume of milk that will come in a few days. Colostrum also stimulates the bowel into action, helping to clear the meconium (first stools) from the baby's bowel. In addition, it lines the whole digestive tract and prepares it for absorbing milk.

The behaviour of other mammals in the first few hours after giving birth gives an insight into how we can maximize the intake of colostrum in a human baby. A mother cat, for example, will rest undisturbed in a dark and protected corner with her newborn kittens, who spend all the time snuggled close to her body, feeding more or less continuously. New human mothers need to behave in a similar way. Even though "rooming in" with your baby beside you in a bassinet is now favoured in hospitals over keeping the babies in a separate nursery, there are usually regulations that prevent mothers sleeping and resting around the clock in bed in body contact with their babies. This separation is likely to reduce the amount of colostrum that the baby consumes. Babies are sometimes offered a bottle containing glucose water or formula to allow the mother to sleep following the birth. This is a very poor substitute for colostrum.

Your newborn baby needs only your milk, with no supplements at all, and will feed many times through the day and night, getting plenty of colostrum.

WHEN THE MILK COMES IN

Sometimes the baby can get frantically hungry on the second or third day just before the milk comes in. If this happens, rest and drink a lot yourself. You can give the baby a teaspoon or two of spring water or cooled, previously boiled water if he seems thirsty. It is most important to keep breastfeeding frequently to stimulate the milk to come in as soon as possible. Try to ensure that both breasts are stimulated evenly.

The transitional milk will come in on the second or third day after the birth. Expect to feel emotional, vulnerable, weepy, and possibly very uncomfortable when this happens. Both breasts may be over full and engorged. They may be hot, hard, and swollen. Sometimes this swelling extends right into the armpits. Your baby may have difficulty latching on to the distended nipple and this can lead to soreness. This problem should ease within about 24 hours.

TIPS FOR EASING ENGORGEMENT

❁ Feed your baby frequently. You needn't be afraid to wake your baby if you need relief.

❁ Soften the breasts before feeding by applying heat with warm compresses or soaking your breasts in a warm bath or shower.

❁ Gently massage the breasts toward the nipple from all around the breast to take off a little milk.

❁ Apply warmth while feeding to help the milk flow and cold ice packs wrapped in a towel, between feeds, to reduce swelling.

❁ Say no to all visitors and try to avoid going home from hospital on this day.

❁ Improvise a halter-style support with a long scarf to use instead of a bra, or wear a T-shirt and knot it under the breasts to create a soft support.

❁ To absorb heat and reduce swelling, place one or two cold white cabbage leaves around the breasts. Keep a few cabbages in the refrigerator and replace with the outer leaves periodically.

❁ The homeopathic remedy Belladonna 6 can be taken hourly. Stop taking the remedy on improvement.

Baby-led feeding

HUMANS ARE MAMMALS, and by definition this means that we feed our young from special mammary glands, or breasts. In fact, we belong to a specific group of mammals that carry their young and feed them frequently or continuously, as opposed to other types of mammals that leave their young in a nest or cache and come back periodically to feed them. Mammals that leave their babies have a more concentrated milk, which sustains their young for long periods while they are away, whereas human breast milk is designed for more frequent feeding, both during the day and night.

Early humans were hunter-gatherers, who carried their babies around with them, tied to their bodies, and fed them whenever they gave the slightest indication that they were hungry. Thousands of years of this way of nurturing our young is still deeply imprinted in our genetic makeup and is still the way that babies are cared for in traditional societies. While I am not suggesting that we go back to the Stone Age, by looking at how our ancestors nurtured their babies, we can get clues as to what "natural" can mean in the context of caring for a baby in the contemporary world.

Your baby needs a certain amount of milk in order to grow and develop. If your baby is denied milk at night, he will try to make up for the deficit during the day. But the only way you can be sure that your baby is being properly nourished is to be led by his requests for feeding both during the day and the night, throughout his first year at least. Hunger is an urgent need and your baby will certainly let you know when he needs a feed. If in doubt as to what your baby needs when he appears unsettled or fussy, it is always a good idea to try feeding first. You can't overfeed or "spoil" a breastfed baby by letting him feed whenever he wants to.

FEEDING RHYTHMS

Breast milk is digested within about two hours, whereas the protein in cow's milk used to make formula takes three to four hours to digest. A breastfed baby may feed frequently around the clock and is not likely to feed on any regular schedule. Probably the length of time between feeds will vary within each 24-hour period. There is likely to be one longer gap between feeds in the day, often in the mornings, when, after a night's rest, the milk is richest and most satisfying for your baby. In a young baby almost continuous feeding and comfort sucking is common in the evenings when many newborn babies tend to be a little unsettled. Be

YOUR BABY'S WEIGHT

Your baby's weight tells you a lot about his overall health and that's why babies are weighed when they have a check-up. Steady weight gain tells us that a baby is feeding and absorbing nutrients well. If your baby is obviously thriving and growing and seems contented, it is not necessary to watch the weight gain pattern too precisely.

Your baby will be weighed soon after birth. Many newborns lose 115–170 grams (4-6 oz) in the first few days after they are born. Weight gain should begin after about five days and is quicker when the baby is kept in close body contact with the mother day and night in the first few days and takes in the full amount of colostrum. Some babies naturally gain more slowly and as long as their nappies are wet every three hours or so and their weight is increasing slowly, there is no need for special action – just keep feeding as often as possible. Medical attention may be needed if your baby loses weight. (See also Slow weight gain, page 167.)

Your breastfed baby can go along with you wherever you need to go, and breastfeed whenever she is hungry. If you feel shy, choose clothes you can feed in discreetly and it is likely that nobody will notice.

guided by your baby and offer a feed whenever he indicates the need by increased activity, mouthing, or rooting for the breast. You don't need to wait for your baby to cry before you start feeding or to worry about getting your baby into a routine. Your baby needs to double his birth weight by five months and this means feeding a lot. A baby knows when he has had enough and will let the nipple go by himself – usually as he falls blissfully asleep. Restricting feeds to a time limit on each side will discourage optimal nutrition.

HAVING ENOUGH MILK

It isn't always easy to believe that our bodies are really capable of producing enough milk to completely nourish a baby. As we don't actually see the volume of milk produced, doubting the milk supply is a common worry. In fact it is very rare for a mother not to have enough milk. When breastfeeding follows the baby's cues, the stimulation to the breast ensures that there is just the right amount of milk for the baby. When a baby is not gaining weight, a careful assessment of the situation needs to be made with expert help. There is usually a breastfeeding solution. A genuine problem with milk production that necessitates supplementation with formula feeding is very rare. One way of reassuring yourself that your baby is getting enough milk is to keep an eye on what is coming out at the other end. By the fifth day a newborn should urinate at least six times in a day and three to four bowel movements daily is quite normal. If your baby is thriving and growing you can leave the rest up to nature.

GROWTH SPURTS

Every three weeks or so a baby's growth rate accelerates. At these times, your baby will want to feed more frequently both in the day and at night. This is the way your baby stimulates and increases the milk supply as he gets bigger and needs more milk. Often this signal from the baby is misunderstood and mothers are told that their milk supply is low and may be recommended to introduce a supplementary bottle or solids. In fact, the best thing to do is to cancel your arrangements and cuddle up with your baby, feeding almost continuously until the milk supply increases, eating and drinking a lot yourself, and sleeping while your baby sleeps. Within a day or so, milk production will increase and your baby will need to feed less often.

Solving problems

FOR SOME WOMEN, THE EARLY DAYS and weeks of breastfeeding are not easy. Soreness, pain, and difficulty feeding can be very distressing, and it is easy to feel like giving up. However, most problems with feeding do have a solution that involves continuing with breastfeeding. Most difficulties can be overcome with perseverance and patience. Sometimes it only takes a day or two – occasionally longer – to find a solution. Usually mothers feel very proud and pleased that they persisted when they are breastfeeding successfully in the end.

Encouragement and support from a breastfeeding counsellor can be invaluable. It is always a good idea to telephone her as soon as you become aware of the prob-

Make sure you get good food, plenty of fluids, and enough rest. Keep some unsweetened fruit juice or water handy at all times so you can have a drink while your baby feeds. If you get hungry between meals eat nutritious snacks rather than cakes or sweets.

lem. Often telephone support is enough, but sometimes a home visit is a good idea, to be sure that your baby is attaching to the breast correctly, as this can sometimes be the underlying cause of initial difficulties. Sometimes the cause of breastfeeding problems is emotional and you may need to talk to someone who understands and can help you to deal with the issues. If problems worsen, then further help should be sought from your midwife or doctor. Always try to continue feeding and look forward to the months of trouble-free and rewarding breastfeeding ahead.

SLEEPY NEWBORNS

Newborns need to feed about 8 to 12 times a day. However, some babies are very sleepy and uninterested in feeding after birth. Your baby may not be feeding enough if he is slow to regain his birth weight and is not producing enough wet and or soiled nappies (diapers). Your baby will become more alert in due course, but in the meantime try to rouse him if more than four hours have passed since he last fed. Change will stimulate him so he stays awake long enough to feed, try changing his position, changing his nappy (diaper), wiping his face, or giving him a gentle massage. When feeding make sure he is properly latched on. If he falls asleep after a few sucks, remove him from the breast, change him, wind him, and offer him the other side.

It's easist to wake a sleepy newborn when you notice her eyes moving under the eyelids, little sucking movements of the mouth, or restlessness. You can pat her chest, gently sit her upright, and lay her down again several times or change her nappy (diaper) to wake her up for a feed if she is sleeping for more than three hours at a stretch during the day.

POOR FEEDING

It is upsetting and worrying when a baby is not feeding well, and because, in rare cases, not feeding well can be a sign of illness, it is wise to see your doctor to rule out this possibility. Some babies find it difficult to latch on at first and feed ineffectively or refuse to feed altogether. This may be because the baby is recovering from the birth or the effects of drugs given during labour. If your baby is still not feeding well enough after three to four days, you may need to supplement feeds with expressed breast milk (see page 57). Kept in the refrigerator in a boiled, sealed container, breast milk will stay fresh for up to 24 hours, and can be warmed and fed to your baby in small amounts after breastfeeding. To do this hold your baby on your lap and use a previously boiled premature baby feeding cup, a syringe, or even a dropper. You can also give a small amount just before a feed to calm an agitated baby, who may then eventually take the breast.

WINDING, POSSETTING, AND VOMITING

Babies often swallow some air as they feed. This is particularly likely in the early days when the milk flow can be very fast. Bubbles of air in the stomach can cause your baby discomfort, so it is worth trying to get rid of them, but don't worry if your baby doesn't seem to need a burp; some babies always have wind to bring up while others do only rarely. If your baby seems windy, after feeding on one side, you can hold him over your shoulder, as pictured below, and stroke down his spine or pat gently to help bring up any wind. Two alternative winding positions are also shown below. Use the winding position that seems to work best for your baby. There is no need to thump his back vigorously. After winding, your baby may not complete the feed on the second side and may drift off to sleep. It is usually not necessary to wind him again, so you can relax with him and have a rest yourself. Start the next feed on the breast you ended with last time in order to ensure both breasts receive equal stimulation.

It is normal for young babies to spit up a little after feeding; this is also known as possetting. If your baby takes too much milk he will bring it up. Similarly, if your baby has swallowed too much air, some partially digested milk may come up with the air bubble when he burps.

Over the shoulder
Hold your baby upright, placing a cloth over your shoulder in case your baby possets. You can gently pat or stroke her back and walk her around a little and you may be rewarded with a burp. Breastfed babies generally need winding only when they are very young, but bottle-fed babies may swallow more air and need winding for longer.

Tiger in a tree
This position works really well for some babies, especially if they are colicky. Hold your baby face down with one hand between the legs, palm over the belly and thumb close to the hip. Support your baby's head and trunk on the other arm so he can relax in your arms like a tiger lying on the branch of a tree. The warmth and gentle massage of your hand may soothe and relax a crampy belly and bring up wind.

Sitting up
Another way to wind your baby is to sit her up on your lap. She will flop forward in the newborn sitting posture, so support her chest with one hand under her chin. You can use the other hand to gently pat her back. This is a useful position to wind your baby midway through a feed, before offering her the other breast.

Vomiting, in which larger quantities of milk are thrown up, is a reflex designed by nature to prevent choking or to expel irritants from the stomach. The occasional vomit is nothing to worry about, but if vomiting is recurrent, contact your doctor. Repeated vomiting can be a simple infection or upset. In rare cases, it can be a symptom of a condition called pyloric stenosis. This can be corrected by a simple operation and then breastfeeding can continue. (See also page 168.)

BREASTFEEDING AND WORKING

Ideally it is best to delay returning to work until your baby is at least six months old, but this is not always possible. However, if you can manage three months of full breastfeeding, you will have given your baby a good start in life. You can continue to breastfeed when you are not working, whether full or part time. The milk supply will be maintained and adjust to the amount of feeding you are able to do. Nutritionally, it is best to feed your baby your own expressed breast milk. However, babies also do well on a combination of breast milk and formula. You can talk to your employer about what you intend to do and arrange for a private place to express your milk and facilities to wash the equipment and refrigerate your milk.

EXPRESSING MILK

If you intend to express milk either for the occasional feed or if you plan to leave your baby for a length of time, it is best to start learning how to do this after the milk supply has settled down. This takes at least six weeks. Expressing milk is easiest to do in the morning when the milk supply is most plentiful, or by collecting small amounts throughout the day.

Using a breast pump

There are a variety of breast pumps available, including hand pumps and electric or battery-operated varieties that are reasonably priced. The best fully automatic electric pumps are expensive to buy and can be rented for less money than a day's formula milk would cost. Directions for using and cleaning breast pumps come with the manufacturer's instructions.

Expressing from both breasts takes 15 to 20 minutes. The key to success is to encourage the natural let down reflex and to imitate the rhythm of a baby's sucking. Remember that the release of breast milk is hormonal, so do this at a time when you can relax and trigger the let down by stimulating the nipples, massaging the breasts, and/or thinking about your baby. Leaning forward and shaking the breasts also helps promote milk flow. You can repeat this ritual a few times throughout the session and change breasts a few times in one session.

Storing expressed milk

You can store milk in special plastic bags, or clean glass or hard plastic containers that have been washed in hot soapy water, rinsed well, and sterilized. Breast milk has anti-bacterial properties and can be kept at room temperature for several hours and in the fridge for up to five days. Breast milk will also keep in the freezer compartment of a refrigerator for two weeks, in a separate freezer unit for three months, and in a deep-freeze for six months or more. However, recently expressed milk, that contains nutrients appropriate for your baby's age, is best.

Before feeding, warm the milk by standing the container in a pan of previously heated warm water. Shake the container to mix the contents before testing the temperature. You can keep thawed, previously frozen milk in the refrigerator for a maximum of eight hours. Never refreeze it. Don't warm breast milk in a microwave or directly on the stove, as this can destroy some of its valuable components.

Bottle-feeding

MANY WONDERFUL MOTHERS completely or partially bottle-feed their babies using expressed breast milk or formula feeds, and this does not detract in any way from the quality of love and attention the baby receives. The last thing I want to do, in my enthusiasm for breastfeeding, is to make you feel guilty or inadequate if you choose or need to bottle-feed your baby. Some women find breastfeeding difficult for emotional or psychological reasons and, although there are solutions to most breastfeeding problems, in some cases the best option is to bottle-feed.

Always hold your baby to bottle-feed. Just as with mothers who breastfeed, this time is about far more than nutrition. Your baby thrives on the physical contact and love that you give him while he feeds. As he gets older he will learn to hold his own bottle, but closeness is still important to him.

MEDICAL REASONS

Babies with certain medical conditions may need to be formula fed. Sometimes this is the best option when the mother has to take medication that may not be safe for newborns. If the medication is needed only temporarily, then you can express your breast milk to keep up the supply, while your baby feeds on formula. You can then resume breastfeeding later. With some medications, the length of time that the drug remains in the breast milk is known and feed times can be planned to minimize the baby's intake of the drug. Your physician should be able to provide this information.

Mothers who test positive for HIV are advised not to breastfeed, as it is thought that the virus can be transmitted in the milk. Many questions remain unanswered about this and the research remains inconclusive regarding the actual risks to the baby. While the recommendation for HIV-positive mothers to formula-feed in some countries (including the UK) is mandatory and has been legally enforced on occasion, there is controversy about whether this should be the case or whether the parents should decide.

MIXING BREAST AND BOTTLE

Bottle-feeds may contain expressed breast milk or formula. Some babies are exclusively bottle-fed and many breastfed babies are occasionally or partially fed with a bottle. Many breastfeeding mothers choose to introduce a bottle of expressed breast milk or formula occasionally or when another person is caring for the baby. The occasional bottle-feed is best given to the baby by someone else, often the father, as the breastfed baby will probably associate his mother with breastfeeding. This is an option many working mothers choose. Mothers of twins or multiples may find that mixed feeding, using a combination of bottle- and breastfeeding, is a workable solution for feeding more than one baby. However, many excellent mothers of multiples make the decision to bottle-feed exclusively as a way of staying sane in the face of the inevitable extra demands they face.

When bottle-feeding you can encourage bonding through close contact and intimacy, which will promote the secretion of "love hormones" (see page 20). You and your baby can still benefit from some of the breastfeeding principles. So if you are bottle-feeding – either partially or exclusively – much of the advice on breastfeeding in the first part of this chapter is still relevant. Above all, it's essential to be confident in your choice and to enjoy feeding your baby!

One of the benefits of bottle-feeding is that fathers can be involved. Sometimes it's lovely to take off your shirt, hold your baby, and let him get used to your smell, the feel of your skin, and the sound of your voice while he is feeding. These intimate moments are important and pleasurable for both of you.

FORMULA FEEDS

Feeding a baby with organic infant formula is an acceptable alternative to breast milk and will ensure adequate nutrition. While commercial formulas cannot duplicate the special properties of breast milk, they are designed to be as close to human breast milk as possible and do form a reasonable substitute. There is no alternative to colostrum, however, so it is beneficial, if at all possible, to breastfeed for the first few days even if you ultimately intend to bottle-feed. (See also page 50.)

Infant formula comes ready constituted or in powder form. When mixing formula powder with water, use pre-boiled, preferably filtered or bottled water. Follow the manufacturer's instructions precisely and avoid adding more or less formula than recommended. Infant formulas are made from processed cow's milk, goat's milk,

BOTTLE-FEEDING GUIDELINES

✿ Respond to your baby promptly when he signals or cries to let you know he is hungry. Just as with breastfeeding, let your baby determine his feeding schedule. Bottle-fed babies tend to have longer intervals between feeds than breastfed babies.

✿ A newborn will take up to about 85ml (3fl oz) per feed fairly frequently. As he grows older he will feed less often and take more milk at each feed. Babies know when they have had enough and it doesn't matter if they don't empty the bottle. Throw away the leftover milk. As they get older, babiesmay need a little more than one bottle if they still seem hungry after a feed. Let your baby guide you as to how much he needs.

✿ Cradle your baby while you feed in a similar position to that recommended for breastfeeding but hold him a little more upright to make it easier for him to swallow.

✿ Begin feeds by stroking the baby's cheek closest to you to elicit the rooting reflex and then introduce the teat (nipple) slowly and not too far back in the baby's mouth.

✿ You can minimize air bubbles by tilting the bottle while you feed to ensure that the teat is full of milk and not air.

✿ Pause from time to time. Change sides halfway through the feed, holding your baby with the other arm.

✿ Maintain skin contact by bottle feeding your baby undressed to his nappy (diaper) at times, and holding him against your naked body. Stroke, caress, and cuddle your baby, express tenderness with eye contact and smile, talk, or sing to your baby while feeding.

When bottle-feeding your baby, close contact will promote the secretion of mothering hormones.

soya beans, or contain other specialized ingredients. Several brands of organic formula milks for babies from birth to four years are available from health-food stores and also by mail order. The same brands may also produce follow-on formula for use with weaning cereals from the age of six months. Such products should not be used for younger babies as they are more difficult to digest.

COW'S MILK FORMULAS

One benefit of cow's milk formulas is that they have been shown by scientific studies to contain virtually no pesticides. However, they do contain some other pollutants. Although the protein in cow's milk formula is hydrolyzed and partially pre-digested, it does not have the special digestive enzymes that are found in breast milk, and therefore takes longer for the baby to digest. Additives include vitamin D and iron which are both low in breast milk, so formula-fed babies do not generally need vitamin or mineral supplements. Check that the formula you choose for your baby is enriched with essential fatty acids similar to those found in breast milk. The label will state that the formula is supplemented or enriched with LCPs (long-chain polyunsaturated fatty acids). These are needed for optimal brain development (see page 39). A few babies are allergic to cow's milk formula, so observe your baby carefully for possible signs of this (see page 38).

SOYA-BASED FORMULAS

Soya-based formula is mainly used by vegans and vegetarians or for babies who have been found to be lactose intolerant. It is made from protein derived from soya beans and contains sucrose rather than lactose. It takes a little longer to digest than cow's-milk formula. Because soya beans are a source of plant oestrogens or isoflavones (also known as phytoestrogens) there is some concern about high levels of these substances in babies fed on soya-based formula and their potential effect on the endocrine system. UK government guidelines recommend that babies for whom this type of formula has been advised for medical reasons should continue to use it, as there is no convincing evidence as yet of any risk to babies. Allergic reactions to soya are almost as common as those to cow's milk products. If you observe possible symptoms of intolerance then you will need to consult a specialist in infant nutrition or your doctor (see page 162). After three months babies generally have a higher tolerance for soya-based formulas.

COW'S OR GOAT'S MILK

Unmodified cow's or goat's milk should not be given to babies under a year old. They are suitable for calves and kids and not humans and have a higher protein and mineral content and lower levels of fatty acids than human milk. Full-fat milk (preferably organic) can be given after one year.

ORGANIC CHOICES

❁ If you are using a cow's milk formula, if possible, choose an organic product, which may contain fewer pollutants.
❁ If you have been advised to use a soya-based formula, try to obtain a brand made from non-genetically modified soya. The long-term effects of GM foods are not yet known.

EQUIPMENT TIPS

❁ Choose glass bottles or a type of plastic that is less likely to leach chemicals into the feed.
❁ Sculpted silicone teats (nipples) are preferable to latex, and "anti-colic" teats are available. Make sure the hole is big enough to release several drops per second when the bottle is inverted.
❁ Wash bottles thoroughly in warm soapy water with a bottle brush. Use salt to clean the teats (nipples) and rinse thoroughly.
❁ An electric steam sterilizer is chemical free. Alternatively, boil equipment for 15 minutes in a covered pan or use a dishwasher.
❁ Warm bottles just before use, by standing in hot water. Don't carry a pre-warmed bottle when going out. Test the temperature of the milk on your wrist before feeding.

Weaning

When your baby is sitting up confidently, you can give her finger foods to chew. This will introduce her to new tastes and help her teeth to come through. Long pieces of lightly steamed carrot are good to start with. Keep an eye on her. Take away the food if it breaks or starts to disintegrate.

BREASTFEEDING IS THE IDEAL NUTRITIONAL SUPPORT for optimal growth for babies in the first six months. No other food or water is needed by a healthy fully breastfed baby (or thriving formula-fed baby) during this time. While solid foods may begin to be a part of your baby's nutrition up to his first birthday, milk remains the mainstay of his diet.

Weaning is a natural process that happens gradually when your baby is ready to move on to include new foods in his diet. Considerable muscular and nervous coordination is needed before a baby is ready to move from sucking and swallowing liquids to eating more solid foods. Before four months of age, babies do not have the skills to move the food around the mouth or the coordination to swallow at the right time. A reflex to thrust the tongue forward will push solid food out of the baby's mouth and the gag reflex is easily stimulated. Their digestive system and organs are not yet sufficiently mature at this age to deal with a diverse diet or solid food. A baby's nervous system also needs to mature to the point whereby he can recognize a spoon, coordinate swallowing, and signal when he is hungry or full.

SIGNS OF READINESS

The appearance of the first teeth is a natural sign that your baby is getting ready to chew rather than suck. Readiness for weaning usually coincides with the time that babies can sit upright in your lap or on a high chair. They usually let you know they are hungry by getting very interested in what you are eating, following your food longingly with their eyes as you eat, and reaching out to grab the food on your plate! For most babies this point is reached at around six months. However, some babies are ready as early as four months, while others may not be really interested for most of the first year. Breastmilk or formula (or a combination of both) contain all the nutrients your baby needs throughout the first year, so there is no need to be anxious if your baby takes his time to start eating other foods.

A natural approach to weaning is to continue breastfeeding until the child no longer needs or wants it, while simultaneously introducing other foods gradually. When weaning is sudden, it is often emotionally traumatic for the baby and upsetting for the mother, who is likely to have some physical discomfort from engorgement as well as feelings of sadness and loss. Unless the situation leaves no alternative, it is always best to wean progressively over a period of several months in accordance with your baby's development.

NATURALLY ORGANIC

Ideally your baby's first solids should be organically grown foods, freshly prepared at home. There are many compelling reasons to give your baby only organically grown produce. The first is to prevent your baby from consuming the residues of chemicals used in non-organic farming. An excess of organophosphates (a group of chemicals used in pesticides) has been shown to cause long-term damage to the developing brain and nervous system. Another disadvantage of eating non-organic produce is the use in non-organic farming of nitrogen, potash, and phosphates to encourage plant growth. These rob the plants of nutritionally important minerals such as zinc, chromium, and selenium. Organically grown foods are nutritionally superior and provide a healthy mineral and vitamin balance.

DRINKING

At six to seven months your baby can be introduced to drinking from a baby cup with a spout and handles. By about 12 months, most babies can hold a cup independently and feed themselves. Bottle-fed babies can hold the bottle at this age, too. Exclusively

Messy play with food is an important part of your baby's development. Learning to feed herself is a skill that takes practice. In the beginning, most of the food will go everywhere except in her mouth. A useful tip is to feed just before bath time and spread newspapers all over the floor.

FOODS TO AVOID

Avoid before 12 months
✿ Cow's milk and cheese
✿ Salt, sugar, spices, and unpasteurized honey
✿ Nuts and nut pastes (before six years old)
✿ Egg whites (hard-boiled yolks can be given after seven months)

Avoid before seven months
All of the above plus:
✿ Wheat cereals, wheat pasta, bread
✿ Soya products (except soya formula, if lactose intolerant)

Avoid before six months
All of the above plus:
✿ Yogurt

breastfed babies will usually happily drink from a cup, which makes feeding easier when you are not around. Dentists recommend that bottle-feeding should be discontinued after about a year in favour of a cup to reduce the risk of tooth decay. There is a natural progression to drinking from a cup as sipping and swallowing replace sucking. Teaching your baby to drink by himself from a cup may seem messy, but is an important skill to develop.

GETTING READY FOR FEEDING

Weaning your baby is going to be messy, so prepare an easy to clean area around the high chair, protect the floor, and lay in a good supply of bibs and an apron for you or a towel to spread over your lap! As your baby learns to accept and swallow solids and then later to feed himself, a good deal of what happens is about play, rather than nutrition. This includes banging spoons on the table to enjoy the sounds, throwing things onto the floor to see how far away it lands and who will pick it up, and other antics. Squeezing, poking, and prodding food are important part of food exploration. Try to relax and accept the chaos – your baby needs to be messy to learn about eating. There will be plenty of time for learning table manners later on!

As your baby learns to use utensils, most of the food will be spilt or dropped, a good reason not to invest too much time in food preparation. Around 12 months your baby will gain more control and self-feeding skills will increase, but expect mess well into toddlerhood.

You can sit your baby on your lap and use a baby spoon or your finger for feeding. Introducing the tastes and textures of food to your baby is fun. It is a whole new experience for him to accept something more solid into his mouth, to learn to swallow and digest. You will enjoy watching his reactions as he encounters these new and interesting sensations.

FIRST FOODS

From about six months babies begin to chew, but these skills need to develop. As your baby has been used to a liquid diet, you could start with no more than a teaspoon of organic baby cereal (a gluten-free cereal such as rice is ideal) mixed with a little breast- or formula milk. Alternatively, try a puréed organic fruit such as apple or pear. Offer first tastes from a small spoon or with your fingertip. Remember that these early tastes of solid food are less about providing extra nutrition than about your baby learning a new skill, so the amount he takes is unimportant. Always feed your baby in an upright position either on your lap or in a high chair. It will be difficult for him to swallow lying down or semi reclining.

PREPARATION

When preparing first foods keep the consistency very liquid at first and use cooking methods such as steaming or gentle stewing for fruit and vegetables. Do not add salt, honey, sugar, or spices to your baby's food. The new tastes will be very interesting to him just as they are. Salt in particular is not recommended in the first year because a baby's kidneys are not able to excrete salt effectively.

One solid "meal" a day is enough to begin with and it is best to stick to the same food for a week or so. This will enable you to discover if your baby has an unusual reaction to that food. There are no rules about when you give your baby his meal, or whether you do it before, during, or after the main milk feed. Let your baby be your guide.

WHEN BREASTFEEDING ENDS

Many mothers continue breastfeeding in addition to a mixed diet throughout toddlerhood. This can only benefit your baby with additional immune support and comfort. Breastfeeds gradually reduce to brief comfort feeds. However, when your child is fully weaned onto a mixed diet and is drinking from a cup, you may want to gradually bring breastfeeding to an end. If so, it is best if you are there to set the limits firmly and kindly, rather than going away. Drop one feed at a time and progress slowly, offering plenty of enticing distractions and cuddles, so that love and comfort remain consistent while your baby learns to let go of the breast in gradual stages.

PROGRESSION

When your baby indicates that he is ready, you can introduce solids twice or three times a day at mealtimes. Don't worry, however, if your baby continues to prefer his milk feeds. There are plenty of thriving babies who don't eat three meals a day until after they are a year old, while others will eat a variety of foods with relish very

Go along with your baby's rhythms, taste, and appetite, so that eating is always pleasurable.

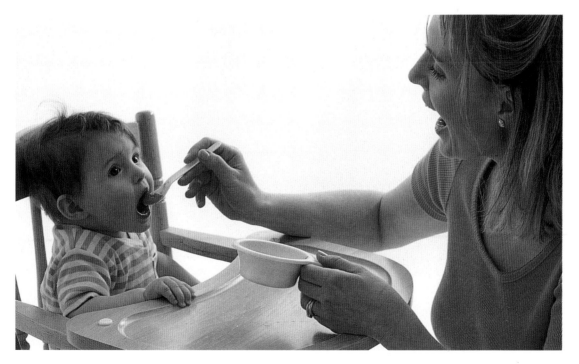

IDEAS FOR FIRST FOODS

✿ Rice or barley cereal mixed with breast or formula milk
✿ Mashed banana
✿ Stewed apple
✿ Blended pear
✿ Mashed avocado
✿ Blended peach
✿ Puréed potato (baked or steamed)
✿ Puréed carrot (steamed)
✿ Puréed sweet potato (baked)
✿ Puréed squash or pumpkin (steamed)

FAVOURITE FOODS

The yellow vegetables, such as pumpkin or squash, sweet potato, sweet corn, and carrots, are usually accepted easily by babies and these can be followed by green vegetables, such as green beans, cabbage, peas, courgettes, spinach, and broccoli. These are good sources of iron and are the foods least likely to cause an allergic reaction. Iron absorption is helped if your baby eats foods rich in vitamin C , such as small amounts of citrus fruits, kiwis, or tomatoes in the same meal, when his menu expands.

Mashed ripe bananas or avocados are often baby favourites You can try blending mashed ripe avocado with either lightly cooked green vegetable purée, banana, or cooked apple. Since your baby will only be eating tiny amounts at first, keep it simple. You can freeze excess cooked food on the day of preparation in ice cube trays in the freezer.

soon after you start to offer them. By seven to nine months your baby will be much more dexterous at picking up small things between his thumb and forefinger and will be fascinated by tiny bits of food. Absolutely everything he discovers goes into his mouth (see page 103) Hard finger foods, such as apple slices or carrot sticks, can be introduced around this time and will help with teething.

As your baby's interest in food progresses, you can gradually introduce new textures and tastes from the wide range of foods included in your family diet. You can give your baby foods with a thicker consistency, until he is ready to chew and eat food in small pieces.

You will notice your baby's chewing and swallowing ability progress. When you can see clearly that your baby is getting much better at chewing, you can start to introduce foods such as little pieces of steamed vegetables, puréed boneless fish, chicken, hard-boiled egg yolk, plain yogurt, or fromage frais blended with ripe banana or one or two soaked apricots, oatmeal, barley, and rice cereals, rice cakes, and plain tofu. You can also mix tahini (sesame paste) into food blends and add well-cooked whole rice, lentils, beans, or chickpeas. Wholegrain noodles, spaghetti, and peas are baby favourites. By 12 months you should be able to offer puréed mixtures made by adding water or salt-free vegetable stock to plain foods from the family meal. The consistency can be quite thick and contain little pieces of solid food.

BABY PREFERENCES

Babies have likes and dislikes when it comes to food just like everyone else. Some babies are fussy about what they like and don't like from the start and others will enjoy a variety of foods. When you start weaning, observe your baby's signals and if he doesn't seem to like a taste, try something else next time. If he sticks his tongue out, closes his mouth, or turns his head away it means he's not interested in eating right now and don't try to force him. On the other hand if he eats it with curiosity or relish, then you can gradually increase the quantity in the next few weeks and begin to experiment with a greater variety of foods.

Make weaning enjoyable for you both by adopting a relaxed and casual attitude. Expect the process to take time. Observe your baby's signals around mealtimes and let him show you the way. Take it slowly, ideally choosing foods that are part of your normal family diet. So long as your baby is still enjoying his milk, it really doesn't matter how long it takes him to learn to eat solids. It may take weeks or even months. Eventually he will be eating regular small meals. Milk may remain the favourite food for quite some time, with solids being treated more as fun than as a way of satisfying hunger. Or your baby may lose interest in breast- or bottle-feeding and rapidly move on to a varied diet of solids.

KEEP IT NATURAL

✿ Read labels on all foods.
✿ Avoid chemical additives.
✿ Buy organic foods where possible.
✿ Avoid non-organically reared meat and non-organically farmed fish.
✿ Avoid irradiated or genetically engineered foods.
✿ Don't use aluminium foil or plasticized food wrap. Instead use greaseproof (wax) paper to wrap foods and stainless steel, glass, or ceramic containers for storage.
✿ Use ecological products for washing dishes.
✿ Don't use a microwave oven.

FINGER FOODS

Finger foods need to be able to dissolve in the baby's mouth or to be mashed by the gums into a swallowable consistency. Cut food into manageable chunks, pea size for harder foods and about 1cm (1/2in) cubes for softer textures. Put just a few pieces onto your baby's feeding plate or tray and replace as he eats them. Vary the choices regularly.

For teething make your own rusks by baking firm wholemeal toast fingers in the oven or try strips of dried organic fruit such as mango.

✿ Cooked pasta pieces
✿ Wholegrain toast or bread
✿ Salt-free rice cakes
✿ Scrambled or hard-boiled egg yolks
✿ Bite-size steamed vegetables
✿ Chunks of soft ripe or cooked fruits
✿ Cooked peas or lentils
✿ Chunks of plain tofu or cheese
✿ Cubes of soft French toast made with egg yolk only
✿ Slices of wholegrain pancake
✿ Organic ready-made cereal pieces
✿ Flaked poached organic or free-range ocean fish (check carefully for bones!)
✿ Soft, well-cooked and slightly mashed pulses

Caring for your baby

Taking care of your baby involves plenty of fun and games, quiet peaceful times, as well as delight in your baby's emerging personality. It is also hard work, especially in the beginning when your baby is getting used to life outside the womb and you are finding your way as a new parent. Most parents underestimate the challenge of the early weeks, but life does get easier as your baby settles and your confidence grows. The key to coping is to slow down and relax. Let being with your baby be your main priority. Confidence comes with experience and you will find your way by trial and error. So long as your baby has a sense of being cared for, it really doesn't matter how you achieve this practically.

It's helpful to know that babies aren't nearly as fragile as they look. Although they are very sensitive, they are also quite strong and resilient. They like to be handled slowly, with gentle firmness rather than in a delicate, hesitant way. As your baby gets more communicative and interested in the world around her, changing, bathing, and dressing your baby become wonderful opportunities for interaction and play. This first year with your child will only happen once. The time and attention you give to her now lays the foundation for a secure and trusting relationship in the months and years that lie ahead.

Approaches to care

W HEN CARING FOR A NEW BABY, the best way to proceed is to follow her lead. Like many new parents, you may feel unsure at first about how to understand what your baby needs or how to communicate with her. Babies understand far more than most people realize and express themselves in a variety of ways which include facial expressions, eye contact, gestures, movements, and body language. All their expressions are meaningful. When you talk to your baby, smile at her, and engage her in "conversations", she is learning the basic elements of speech and verbal interaction. You can tell her just before something new is about to happen and acknowledge what she is expressing in words – for example, "Oh, do you want me to pick you up?" or "Are you hungry now?". The first thing to learn is that you need to slow down when communicating with your baby. Babies are easily overwhelmed if transitions from one activity or situation to another happen too fast. Take your time and be guided by your baby's responses. You will soon learn exactly what she needs and the best way to interpret her messages.

Once he enjoys being naked, take time when changing and dressing your baby to play. Your baby will delight in funny sounds and expressions and at the same time will be learning to socialize from these interactions.

A SENSITIVE APPROACH

A sensitive way to care for your baby is to respond to her signals immediately, both during the day and at night. Contrary to what some people may tell you, this will not "spoil" your baby, but will make her feel satisfied, secure, and loved. It will give her a positive sense of herself and trust in other people, making her more contented in the short term and more independent later on. There will be times in the coming year when you will need to gently introduce some boundaries into your baby's life. This happens naturally when your baby reaches for an unsuitable object or when she becomes more mobile and needs your help to avoid danger. The key to successful, attachment parenting is to slow down and relax with your baby so that your life falls into place around your baby's needs. Very soon the chaos of the early days will take shape, as family life with your baby settles into place.

SHARING CARE

As a mother, especially if you are breastfeeding, you share a strong physiological bond with your baby. You are the central person in your baby's life. However, in most cultures, mothers are not the sole carers of a baby. Parenting works best when both parents support each other and take turns to look after their baby, or when another trusted person is there to help you.

As your baby starts to initiate communication and learns to play, your relationship will really take off. Expect to have a lot of fun when you care for him, as well as warm and tender moments of shared affection.

Fathers love their baby in a different way, and may also have a strong protective instinct and desire to share in practical baby care from day one. Don't hesitate to hold her, to lie down with her close beside you, sometimes including direct skin-to-skin contact. Your familiar smell and the sound of your heartbeat will rapidly become very recognizable to your baby. You will learn to handle her confidently in your own way. This "hands on" practical care of your child will greatly enhance your relationship with her. Babies don't care whether you carry out these tasks perfectly, they just like to have you there taking care of them.

Other people in her life will also love her and can provide good alternative care when the parents cannot be there all the time. Because mother and father teams are the most common, I will refer mainly to them, but the information applies no matter who is caring for your baby.

Holding and carrying

Your baby loves to view the world from the safe vantage point of your warm body. When she is tired she will fall asleep on your shoulder.

MOTHERS HAVE AN INSTINCT to hold their baby from the moment of birth. Your baby feels loved and protected when held in your arms against your warm body. This lies at the heart of practical baby care and makes your baby feel secure and contented. A very young baby thrives best with almost continual holding, simulating the continuous holding in the womb. This need to be held continues throughout infancy. Gradually, as your baby becomes more independent and enjoys looking about, sitting up, crawling, and walking, the need to be held is reduced, but is still a vital part of your baby's wellbeing. Close body contact also helps your baby's digestion, and strengthens the immune system. When others care for your baby they are essentially standing in for you. Good carers are the ones who are warm and loving and don't hesitate to hold and cuddle your baby just as you would yourself.

BABY WEARING

In traditional cultures all over the world, mothers carry their babies using a cloth sarong, blanket, or special baby carrier, so that the baby has continuous body contact for a substantial part of the day. This is a natural parenting style that allows you to continue your normal daily activities, while providing an optimal environment for your baby. It is infinitely better for your baby's health and development than being transported exclusively in car seats or strollers. Don't worry if a baby carrier feels awkward to use at first. Once you get used to "wearing your baby", you will be surprised how much more contented and happy she will be. You will also be able to pick up her signals sooner – often before she needs to cry.

Using a baby carrier is a skill that needs to be learned as most new parents have not had the opportunity to carry a baby in this way before. So persevere through the initial awkward phase and keep trying until practice makes you more confident. Once the carrier is in place, your baby will probably settle down and be very happy in it. Both mother and father can carry the baby this way for quite long periods of time and it is a great aid to attachment parenting in the early weeks and months.

A baby who is carried a lot will not become clingy or demanding. On the contrary modern research reveals that the benefits of baby wearing encourage children to feel secure and content with a solid sense of self-esteem. A baby carrier is an essential first purchase and there are several types to choose from.

Side slings (right) are invaluable in the early days. These are good for newborns, because they allow an even pressure along the length of the baby's spine, which curves into the fabric, replicating the fetal position in the womb. They give the mother the added possibility of feeding the baby in situ.

BENEFITS OF USING A BABY CARRIER

❀ Baby wearing provides an intimate connection between you and your baby.

❀ Held close to your heart, your baby feels safe and secure and is more contented.

❀ Helps to prevent postnatal depression.

❀ In the carrier your baby will be in a quiet-alert state or asleep most of the time, and seldom in a state of distress.

❀ Being carried a lot in the early months helps her to develop good muscle tone and posture. Sitting, crawling, and walking may happen sooner. Babies who are carried a lot in the beginning often display enhanced balance once they are walking.

❀ Regular carrying may stimulate brain development and learning ability.

❀ Being carried is good for digestion, helping to reduce colic and reflux.

❀ It is easy to feed your baby promptly because she is right there next to you.

❀ With a well-fitting baby carrier you can carry your baby in a variety of positions without back strain.

Front carriers can be used with the newborn facing inward toward your body, or, when she gets older, outward (as shown) so that she can see the view. Once your baby is able to sit unsupported, you can also use a back pack.

Comforting your baby

YOUR BABY HAS A WIDE RANGE OF EMOTIONS and they are real and intense. They may include happiness, joy, bliss, sadness, anger, love, grief, and fear. The times when your baby is upset are just as valuable to her development as the times when she is happy. She depends on you to understand what she is experiencing. She will learn to feel valued and loved through your responses when she cries.

Your baby will let you know by fussing or crying when she is hungry or uncomfortable and wants to be picked up or held. Crying is most often about something happening in the moment. As urgent as your baby's cries may seem, as soon as the need is met, the crying will usually stop. Sometimes babies just need to cry as a way of releasing pent-up feelings. Your baby may also react in other ways when she is uncomfortable or overstimulated by making jerky startled movements, arching her back, turning her attention away, looking dazed, or even falling asleep.

The most essential parenting skill is to listen to what your children are telling you and this starts from the moment of birth. Sometimes it is appropriate to respond with an action and other times your baby just needs you to be present and understanding.

One of the first parenting challenges is to learn how to interpret your baby's signals and how to respond to her crying. You may feel confused or even panicky at first when your baby cries. After a few weeks, you will be able to understand your baby's "language" and interpret very quickly whether she wants to be fed, is tired, needs her nappy changed, is too hot or too cold, or simply wants to be held and walked around.

RESPONDING WHEN YOUR BABY CRIES

It is always best to respond to crying as soon as possible, before your baby gets too worked up and becomes really distressed. Her cries are meant to get your attention and to ensure her survival. Babies are not capable of manipulation and you will not "spoil" your baby by reacting immediately and picking her up. Research indicates that babies whose parents respond at once to their cries are likely to cry less after the age of six months than babies whose parents ignore their cries.

It is very hard, if not impossible, for most mothers to ignore a crying baby. A baby's cries stimulate an increase in the secretion of one of the mothering hormones, prolactin, and make you naturally want to pick

WHY BABIES CRY

Hunger

The most common reason that young babies cry is because they are hungry. These cries build in intensity and are generally accompanied by rooting movements of the mouth and head searching for the breast, or sucking her hand. A prompt response will help prevent your baby from becoming frustrated, when it may be more difficult to latch on properly. If your baby does not want to feed she will refuse the breast or bottle and you will need to try something else.

Hot or cold

She may be too hot or too cold, or her nappy may need changing. A hot baby is often sweaty and her tummy will feel hot rather than warm. She may look flushed or have a red prickly rash on her face, neck, and upper torso. Babies' hands and feet are normally cool. If she is too cold her lips may look bluish and she will shiver and may not cry.

Wind

Your baby may cry because she has digestive discomfort and needs winding. This is more common in bottle-fed babies, who may swallow air along with the the milk when feeding. This rarely happens with a breastfed baby except in the early days when the milk flows very fast.

Pain

If your baby is in pain, her cries will be loud and insistent and will probably be accompanied by agitated body movements. Her mouth will be wide open and her body tense (see also Colic, page 170). If you think your baby is in pain, try soothing her with some of the suggestions on page 77. If your baby can't be soothed when she cries, then it is best talk to your midwife or doctor to make sure that there is no underlying problem.

Unwell

When babies don't feel well they often whinge and fuss. There may be frequent, but not necessarily continuous, bouts of crying.

Tired, overwhelmed, or overstimulated

Short bouts of crying that may be accompanied by rubbing or patting her ears, eyes, or head tell you that she has had

Whatever the cause of your baby's distress, when she cries she is asking for your attention.

enough and needs to be somewhere quiet or is ready to be settled with a feed. Check out the environment and see if something is too much for her such as music that is too loud or too many people around.

Bored or lonely

Babies usually like to be near to other people, especially their parents. Sometimes babies cry because they want a change of scenery, or are ready for play and interaction.

Expressing feelings

Sometimes a long or difficult birth may make the baby disoriented and unsettled. Cranial osteopathy and homeopathy can be very helpful treatments for a baby who cries a lot after an assisted or difficult birth. Consult a practitioner as soon as possible after the birth. Massaging your baby daily can help in the long term. There may be other reasons why your baby needs to release her feelings. If you think that this is the case and have tried everything else, there is nothing wrong with holding her lovingly and letting her cry.

up and comfort your baby. Nature, has designed us to respond in this way for good reason. When left to cry, a baby will soon learn that no one comes and will stop. They may even sleep through the night. While this is convenient for the parents, and is the main "selling point" of sleep-training methods, I believe that leaving a baby to cry breaks down trust, may make the baby feel helpless and hopeless, distances mothers from their babies, and is bound to diminish their relationship.

BABIES WHO CRY A LOT

Some newborns adapt to life after birth quickly and easily, while others are more disoriented at first, will cry a lot more, and will need almost continual soothing. Most young babies have a patch in the day when they are fretful and want to be held or to feed almost all the time. This usually occurs in the evening when you are more tired and have been active all day, but can also happen at other times,

When your baby cries, follow your instincts and pick her up. This will help you to find out if she simply wants to be held or whether there is another reason she is crying.

including in the middle of the night. Most babies settle within about 12 weeks. However, some young babies are fretful and restless a lot of the time and this can go on for several months.

The paediatrician Dr William Sears, in his book *The Fussy Baby* (see Resources) has used the term "high need" to describe babies who cannot get used to being separate from their mothers and need a lot of physical contact throughout the day and the night to feel secure. Dr Sears stresses how important it is not to be judgmental or to create a negative feeling about either mother or baby or to label a high-need baby as "difficult", "bad", or "demanding". Having a high-need baby is very challenging for both parents. It is easier to cope if you are able to work as a team to meet your baby's demands to enable each of you to get little breaks.

GETTING HELP

You may have feelings of helplessness, panic, and a loss of power, when every effort to calm your crying baby fails. When you are very tired, this can take you close to despair. While parents should never act on them, many loving, caring people have quite violent thoughts and feelings when a baby screams and screams and can't be soothed. Such feelings are a clear signal that you need someone else to take over for a bit, but be reassured that most other parents get to feel that desperate occasionally. If no one is around and you feel like this, put the baby down in a safe place. Calm yourself with some Rescue Remedy, get your breathing smooth and even, maybe put on some soothing music, and then try again. Acknowledge that you are doing your best in a trying situation. This may help you regain your composure. Do not hesitate to contact an appropriate support organization for advice (see Resources).

CALMING YOUR BABY

The key to calming your baby is to find the cause of the problem. Once you know that you can try one of the following soothing suggestions.

❀ Respond as soon as you can when your baby shows the first signs of distress.

❀ Always pick up a crying baby. Body contact is very comforting.

❀ Try feeding her, she may just want a comfort suck, even soon after a feed.

❀ Swaddle your baby in a flannel sheet or shawl or put her into a baby carrier. Being closely confined may comfort her.

❀ Take turns holding and walking your baby. Let your partner explore his own strategies without interfering.

❀ Try movement, rocking, or cuddling your baby.

❀ Check that she is comfortable. Change her nappy (diaper) or make sure she is not too warm or too cool.

❀ Reduce visual stimulation by holding your baby close in a darkened room to simulate the darkness of the womb.

❀ Continuous monotonous sounds such as humming or even a recording of "white noise" from a household appliance or running water may help.

❀ Remove her from a stimulating environment if she seems overloaded.

❀ If you think she may be bored, change her position so she can see something interesting such as a light or mobile. Or go out for a change of scene; a walk outdoors or a car ride may help.

❀ Try bathing and massaging her just before the time she is usually unsettled.

❀ Sleeping with your baby will comfort her at night and help you to pre-empt her crying (see page 122).

❀ Consider cranial osteopathy treatment (see page 156).

Elimination

URING PREGNANCY YOUR BODY TAKES CARE of the elimination of waste products for your baby through the placenta. After she is born your baby begins to eliminate urine and faeces independently for the first time. The baby's digestive system does not function in the womb, and a substance called meconium accumulates in the bowel. Meconium is dark green, almost black in colour, and has a thick, mucus-like consistency. The colostrum and the first breast milk help to stimulate the bowel and to clear the meconium. within the first few days after the birth.

The best time to change your baby's nappy (diaper) is when he has a full belly – halfway through or after feeding. You will probably need to do this at every feed including during the night at first, so keep some changing supplies beside your bed.

BOWEL MOVEMENTS

Over the first few days, your baby's bowel movements gradually become a browny green and thinner in consistency until all the meconium has been passed. Then you will notice the characteristic sweet-smelling, squidgy, mustard-coloured faeces of a breastfed newborn. In the early weeks it is common for a bowel movement to occur at every feed and there are likely to be up to 12 bowel movements a day. After this bowel movements become far less frequent and its not uncommon for a day or more to pass between them. So long as the bowel movement that is eventually produced has the usual colour and consistency, this is simply a sign that the baby is absorbing a lot of nutrients and needs to defecate less often. A baby's bowel movements are often "explosive" and the sounds are very noticeable, but this is no cause for concern.

The bowel movements of a formula-fed baby are different from those of a breastfed baby. Formula-fed babies tend to have less frequent bowel movements, which are firmer in consistency, darker in colour, and have a different smell. Whether you are breastfeeding or giving your baby formula milk, the form and frequency of your baby's bowel movements are likely to develop a pattern within about six weeks. The frequency decreases throughout the first year to once or twice a day at around 12 months.

URINATION

In the first week after birth the urine is clear at first although orange-coloured spots are common in the first few days. After this the colour of the urine deepens slightly. Urination normally occurs 20 to 30 times in a 24-hour period. Seek medical advice if your baby's nappy is dry for longer than six hours. This could be a sign of dehydration or urinary retention. If the urine appears dark or has an unpleasant smell, there may be an infection and medical help should also be sought.

CONTROL OVER URINATION AND DEFECATION

In the first year of life the processes of elimination are totally involuntary and the baby is physiologically incapable of control. A discussion of toilet-training is therefore outside the scope of this book. However, a relaxed and commonsense response to your baby's elimination patterns now, will establish the basis for you to follow her lead when she makes the natural transition to self-control.

THE NAPPY (DIAPER) DEBATE

You are going to have changed a lot of nappies (diapers)– one study estimated 5,000 – by the time your child can use a potty. There are a range of options available when choosing the best system for you and your baby. Your choices include standard disposables, environmentally friendly disposables, and a wide range of washables, which can be laundered at home or by a nappy (diaper) service. In deciding what type to use, you will need to consider your baby's comfort and health, your convenience, and also the environment.

STANDARD DISPOSABLES

There are some disturbing facts about standard disposables, which now account for at least 80 per cent of the market. They are made from wood pulp, plastic, and an absorbent powder or chemical gel. While they are convenient and absorbent, standard disposables are potentially toxic to the baby and their disposal creates problems for the environment.

None of the chemicals used in standard disposable nappies (diapers) is regulated, and there is little research into their effects on babies. Beads of the chemical gel (sodium polyacrylate, AGM, or absorbent gelling material) used in disposables are sometimes found on the baby's skin and it is thought that the powder in its dry form could also potentially travel up the vagina in girls and urethra in boys. Nonylphenyl ethoxylate (NPE), used in the stay-dry lining of disposables has oestrogen-like properties, which could potentially cause reproductive disorders. It has been associated with sex changes and a low sperm count in fish. There is concern that it could be absorbed if the baby had an open sore such as nappy (diaper) rash. Recent research done on mice revealed that exposure to

ENVIRONMENTAL CONCERNS

✿ Millions of trees are felled every year to provide wood pulp for disposables.

✿ One cup of crude oil from non-renewable sources is used to manufacture each nappy (diaper).

✿ In Britain, 8 million disposables are used every day, (approximately one tonne per baby through infancy), representing 4 per cent of household waste.

✿ It is estimated that it can take a disposable nappy (diaper) 200–500 years to decompose fully. None of them has decomposed yet!

✿ Decaying paper pulp produces methane gas contributing to global warming.

PRACTICAL SOLUTIONS

Many mothers who mainly use washables, also use disposables occasionally. Disposables may be more convenient in the first weeks, when travelling or going out, and when leaving the baby with someone else. Choose environmentally friendly disposables, if possible (see page 80).

NATURAL LAUNDERING

After flushing any solid waste down the toilet, presoak used nappies (diapers) in a bucket. Add one of the following natural deodorizing and disinfectant solutions to the water:

❀ 5–6 drops tea tree oil, or
❀ 2–3 tablespoons of white distilled vinegar, or
❀ 2 tablespoons of baking soda.

Machine wash in very hot water, using an enzyme-free, ecological detergent. Avoid products that contain perfumes and brighteners, which may irritate your baby's skin. Boiling is not necessary. A cup of distilled vinegar can be added to the rinse instead of fabric conditioner.

some types of disposables caused respiratory symptoms. The study concluded that there may be links between asthma-like symptoms and chemical emissions from disposables. Chemicals are also used to deodorize and scent disposables.

ENVIRONMENTALLY FRIENDLY DISPOSABLES

These are free from chemicals and are made from unbleached cellulose in a similar design to standard disposables. While they do use raw materials and energy in production, they have less impact on the environment and have no known health risk for babies. Mothers tell me that they are not quite as effective as the standard disposables, but work well when changed often enough. They may not be available in newborn size.

WASHABLES

Made from natural fibres, washable, cloth nappies (diapers) allow the skin to breathe and contain no chemicals. There are plenty of styles and sizes to choose from to suit all tastes and budgets, including some that are made from entirely organically grown, unbleached cotton, wool, and silk. Most suppliers offer a trial pack so you can try them out before you invest. The favourite style of the parents

Washables may involve a two-part system that includes a washable cotton pad placed inside a fitted cover which generally has ties, poppers (snaps), or velcro tabs. Some types are "all-in-one" and made to resemble disposables. While convenient to use, all-in-ones tend to be bulky and take much longer to dry.

RASH PREVENTION TIPS

Nappy (diaper) rash can generally be prevented with a few simple precautions .

✿ Change your baby's nappy often and avoid the use of plastic pants. Let your baby go without a nappy (diaper) as much as possible.

✿ Make sure that the nappy (diaper) is the right size for your baby.

✿ Use washables rather than disposables. Select a style that has no irritating edges on the outer wraps.

✿ Avoid commercial baby wipes; these remove the natural oils which protect the skin in a moist environment. Use moist cotton-wool balls or simply dip your baby in warm water and wash with your hand.

✿ Avoid routine use of chemical barrier creams (see page 175 for natural alternatives)

✿ If you are breastfeeding, pay attention to your diet and eliminate possible irritants such as spicy or acidic foods. Take antibiotics only when they are really necessary, because they increase the risk of thrush (page 173). Try a homeopathic or other alternative treatment first. If you need to take antibiotics, take Lactobacillus acidophillus supplements afterward to restore your intestinal flora.

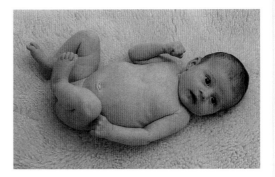

In a warm room, expose your baby's skin to the air for a while at each nappy (diaper) change

I have talked with, has a rectangular cotton nappy (diaper) that folds into three to make a soft absorbent pad. A disposable liner is placed over this to catch the solid waste, which can then be thrown down the toilet. The folded nappy (diaper) and liner, is placed inside a waterproof outer wrap and secured like a disposable with velcro fastenings. Washed carefully, they can be used up to 200 times and will probably last through two children. Many parents find the laundering easier than they expected. But some find it more convenient to use a specialist laundry service that collects and delivers.

GETTING PREPARED FOR CHANGING

You will need a safe surface on which to change and dress your baby, but it isn't necessary to buy a special baby changing table, since you are unlikely to use it for very long. You can use a table or desk-top, large enough for you to lay out essential equipment. This can be covered with a washable padded surface for the baby to lie on and an improvised "roll guard".

All you need at first when changing a nappy (diaper) is some cotton wool and a bowl for warm water. With these items in place, you will be ready for immediate action when you arrive home from the hospital or when you are on your own after the midwife leaves, if you are having a home birth. Later on, when your baby becomes more active and starts rolling, it is safer to change your baby on a wide bed or on the floor.

It is best to prepare a changing table ahead of time with everything you need on it. Have a spare set of clothes ready, and a container to put the soiled nappy (diaper) in nearby. The best time for nappy (diaper) changing is usually midway through or after a feed when your baby is contented and likely to have had a bowel movement recently. Make sure that the room is very warm. You may find that your newborn baby doesn't like having her warm nappy (diaper) removed and may cry while you do this at first. Later, this will become a time for leisurely interaction with your baby and she will enjoy it. The best strategy is to keep calm and work continuously and methodically, even if your baby is crying.

When you change your baby, you are building a trusting relationship. Smile and talk to her while you work. She will learn to enjoy this special time of contact with you.

CHANGING TIPS

❀ There is no need to remove the clothes from your baby's upper body unless they need changing, but pull them out out of the way. Undo your baby's nappy (diaper), remove the liner if you are using one, and use the clean part to wipe her bottom, holding both ankles in one hand. Put one finger between the ankles to protect them.

❀ Use plenty of warm water and cotton wool to clean your baby's bottom.

❀ Always clean girls from front to back to avoid getting germs into the vagina or urethra. Only clean the parts you can see and don't separate the labia or try to clean inside.

❀ Boys should be cleaned around the penis and testicles. Never pull back the foreskin when cleaning the penis. This area is self-cleaning.

❀ Dry thoroughly, going right into the folds, by patting gently with a soft towel. For extra dryness, sprinkle a very small amount of homeopathic calendula powder or cornstarch in the creases and rub in with a finger to dry thoroughly.

❀ Put a clean nappy (diaper) under her bottom, fold it up between her legs and close securely, but not too tightly. Once your baby enjoys changing times it is a good idea to wait a while before you put on the new nappy (diaper), to give the skin regular exposure to the air.

Check carefully for any sign of redness around the anus and in the groin.

Keeping your baby clean

WHEN THEY ARE VERY YOUNG babies usually dislike being exposed. Unless your baby is happy being naked, it is a good idea to keep her undressed for as short a time as necessary. Some newborns like water, especially if they had a water birth, but most babies take at least a few weeks before they enjoy bathing. It is not necessary to bath your baby every day. You can "top and tail" your baby instead once a day and bath her every two or three days. This will allow you to clean the most vital areas with minimum fuss.

TOPPING AND TAILING

Before topping and tailing your baby or bathing her, always make the room very warm, and ensure that it is draught free. Undress your baby down to her vest and nappy (diaper) and wrap her in a soft bath towel. Place her on her back on a changing surface. Have some cotton balls and a bowl of clean warm water (this should have been previously boiled for a newborn) nearby. Hold her head with one hand and start with a fresh piece of cotton for each eye, wiping from the inner to the outer corner of the eye. Then wipe her mouth and nostrils. After this remove the vest and wash around her neck, outside and behind the ears, and under the arms. Then clean each hand and each foot carefully. Pat dry thoroughly and make sure her that the folds in her neck and under her arms are dry. You can apply a tiny amount of cornstarch or calendula powder with one finger into the folds after drying. Never use cotton buds to clean the inside of your baby's ears or nostrils; these areas are self-cleaning. You can then put on a clean vest. Change the nappy (diaper) as usual, before fully dressing your baby.

BATHING

Once they are familiar with bathing, bathtime is enjoyable, calming exercise for babies. They usually relax in the water and can move their limbs freely and release muscular tensions. This is a special time to relax and play with your baby. When a baby seems afraid of bathing, it may be helpful to swaddle the baby lightly in a small towel until she is immersed and then slowly take it off in the water. If your baby doesn't seem to like bathing, continue with topping and tailing and try again in a few days.

BATHING WITH YOUR BABY

An easy and enjoyable way to bath a baby is to fill the bath tub and get in with her and you can do this from the early weeks. Until you get used to bathing with your baby, it is best to have someone to help, as it can be tricky to get in and out of the bath while holding the baby. Prepare the

---

SAFETY

✿ Fill the bath, to a maximum temperature of 29°C (85°F). Judge the temperature by putting your elbow in the water – it is just right when it feels neither hot nor cold. Protect hot taps or sharp edges with a washcloth.

✿ Never leave a baby or young child alone in the bath, even for a second.

✿ Use a large non-slip mat beside and in the bath.

Bathing with your baby is a great way to make getting clean fun. It is also a great preparation for swimming (see page 114).

the bath and everything you need first. Place a non-slip mat in the bath and one next to it. The water needs to be warm (see Safety, page 83), and the room should be well heated.

When everything is ready, undress yourself first, then undress your baby slowly and hold her close to you. Get in carefully, holding her against your body all the time, and ease into the water slowly. Once in the bath, you can lie back, bend your knees, and lay her on her back on your thighs facing you, with her body immersed and head out of the water. This is also a good position to wash her hair. You can do this using your hand at first and just let her head release back a fraction, supported by your knees. You can simply use water at first, but after a few weeks you can use a little baby shampoo once a week and a washcloth to rinse it out. Don't be afraid to massage the scalp gently when you shampoo; you won't damage the fontanelle. Another way to hold her is to let her lie on her belly on your chest, body immersed and head out of the water. As you both become more confident you can support her chest in the water so she can kick freely in the water.

A baby seat that you put directly in the bath provides secure support for your baby during bathing and leaves you with both hands free.

If she wants to feed, breastfeeding in the bath can be very relaxing for you both. When its time to get her out, your partner can sit beside the bath with a warm towel ready to receive the baby. Keep the baby in body contact as you pass her over, and avoid standing up with her and climbing out.

USING A BABY BATH

If bathing with your baby does not seem right for you, there are a variety of baby baths on the market that you can use. Some have their own stand, others are designed to straddle the bath and there are some, for the older baby, are like little seats that go directly in the bathtub. You only need to fill the baby bath with 10 to 12 centimetres (4–5 in) of water.

It is a good idea to wash your baby's hair before the bath, or even on a separate occasion over the sink. Wrap her in a towel, arms inside and hold her securely under one arm, head slightly lowered close to the water. Support the back of her neck and her head with one forearm and hand, while keeping the other hand free to rinse her head. Pat her head dry. Then, keeping the towel nearby, lower her into the bath gently. Support her shoulders with one hand, your fingers tucked under the armpit. Hold her lower body with the other hand and once she is relaxed in the water, you use that hand to wash her. Support her securely but lightly so she enjoys the buoyancy of the water. Lift her out gently and wrap her immediately in a towel to cuddle and dry her.

SKIN CARE

Generally the less you put on your baby's skin the better. You may not need anything other than warm water for cleansing. Sometimes environmental factors such as dry air, central heating, wind, and sun, as well as dribbling and moisture in the nappy (diaper) area, may cause dryness. If you notice that your baby's skin seems dry, you can rub your baby all over, including in the creases, with a light moisturizing lotion daily after bathing.

Choose skin-care products that are as natural as possible, avoiding perfumes, foaming agents, or soaps. Babies can occasionally react quite strongly to these agents by becoming fretful. If you want to avoid preservatives, then you can use an organic grapeseed or sunflower oil on your baby's skin instead. Grapeseed oil is a light oil that is ideal for allergy-prone babies. Pure sunflower oil (not as generally sold for culinary use), which has a lovely non-greasy feel, leaves the skin smooth. You can obtain organic base oils from a health-food store or aromatherapy supplier. If your baby has very dry skin, a thicker baby cream may be necessary.

SUN PROTECTION

Babies' skins burn easily in the sun and those under six months should generally be kept out of the sun. All children should be kept in the shade between the hours of 11am and 2pm, when the sun's rays are strongest. You will still need to take sun protection measures outdoors on overcast days.

✿ Shade your baby from the sun wherever possible.

✿ Dress her in a sun-protective lycra suit. Ordinary fabrics do not offer the same degree of protection.

✿ Make sure she wears a hat that protects the face and neck area.

✿ Consider buying a UVA-proof tent if you will be in strong sunshine for any length of time – for example, on the beach.

✿ Always use a hypoallergenic sunscreen lotion made for babies that protects against UVB and UVA rays. Choose a product of factor 30 or above. Apply liberally every one to two hours and after swimming, even if you are using a waterproof product.

First clothes

Tops with wide necks make for easy dressing.

YOUR BABY NEEDS TO BE KEPT COMFORTABLY WARM, but take care not to let her get overheated by putting too many clothes on her. Her body temperature controls are not yet working properly. Comfort and convenience are key considerations when selecting your baby's clothes. Newborns can be dressed in the same clothes during the day and the night. You don't need too many clothes in newborn size, as your baby will soon outgrow them. But bear in mind you will probably need to change your baby's clothing more than once a day and may not have much time for doing laundry. The following suggestions are not intended to be a complete list of necessary baby clothing, but are simply to give some general guidance.

For easy changing it is hard to beat all-in-one suits with poppers (snaps) down the front. When your baby's all-in-one suits start to become a bit tight, one way of getting an extra few weeks wear is to cut off the feet and use socks instead. A couple of soft, knitted shawls or cellular blankets will be useful in the early days for loosely swaddling your baby. They generally like this, as it makes them feel secure. Babies lose a lot of heat through their heads, so a hat is essential when going out in cooler temperatures. In a warm environment it is good for babies from birth onward to have their hands and feet exposed so that they can explore the feel of the different textures that surround them.

Natural fibres are not only more comfortable and hard wearing, they are also made from renewable sources. Choose 100 per cent natural soft fabrics, such as brushed cotton, which allows your baby's skin to breathe. Read labels carefully as cotton is often blended with synthetic fibres to make it stretch. Wool may irritate some babies and should not be worn next to

FOOT CARE

The bones of your baby's feet are soft and pliable so it is very important not to let her wear stretch suits, socks, or leggings that are too tight. Shoes are not needed until the baby is walking outside and soft shoes are preferable at first.

TIPS ON BUYING CLOTHES

❀ Invest in at least six changes of top clothing.
❀ Make sure that everything you buy is machine washable.
❀ Choose soft, natural fibres such as cotton when possible.
❀ Make sure the "feet" of all-in-one suits are loose and not constricting.
❀ Choose vests with wide "envelope" necks that pull over the head easily, and snap fastenings under the nappy (diaper).
❀ Hats for use in windy or cold weather should cover the ears.

the skin. Untreated organic fibres are often best for babies who have especially sensitive skin or suffer from allergies.

When dressing your baby, take your time, allowing your baby to relax tense limbs before gently easing them into the clothing.

DRESSING YOUR BABY

Newborns often cry when you dress and undress them as they are not used to being exposed and handled. Try not to let this phase upset you and calmly get on with the job. Make sure that the room is very warm and draught free. It is safest to dress a wriggling older baby on your lap, on the floor, or in the middle of a double bed. Be careful not to turn your back for a second, as babies can move incredibly quickly. Have everything you need at hand before you start.

Crawling babies often need to be dressed on the move. By this time you won't need to learn how to dress your baby and will find ways that work best for you.

Newborns often feel more secure when swaddled in a shawl, light blanket, or flannel sheet in the early weeks. Fold this into a triangle on your bed first. Then when your baby is dressed place her in the centre, shoulders level with the folded edge. Fold up the bottom first and then cross over the sides one at a time and tuck in. It can help a baby who is having trouble with positioning and latching onto the breast to be securely swaddled in this way before feeding.

Baby massage

YOUR BABY'S FIRST SENSATIONS came from the rich sense of touch and movement on the skin surface in the womb, and touch continues to be a primary source of comfort and wellbeing throughout infancy, childhood, and beyond. Baby massage has been practised in different cultures all over the world for centuries. It helps your baby to be comfortable with her body and enjoy an intimate and close connection with you.

I have had the pleasure of working with Peter Walker, the pioneer of baby massage in Britain, for almost two decades. With Peter's kind permission, I have based the massage sequence in this book on his recommended routine. You can learn more about this and about movement for the older baby from his book and video (see Resources).

MASSAGE OIL

It is best to use a plain organic sunflower or grapeseed oil when massaging a very young baby. Make sure the oil is comfortably warm before application. Once your baby is three months old you can continue using a plain plant oil or you could introduce a ready-blended pure aromatherapy baby massage oil which gives the additional benefits of essential oils.

Give your baby plenty of verbal encouragement as you massage her and be aware of her responses. Continue as long as she seems to be enjoying the experience. During the massage focus on the pleasure of communicating with your baby through touch and eye contact.

PREPARING FOR MASSAGE

Make sure the room is very warm, with low lighting or soft daylight and that it is peaceful and quiet. You may like to put on some tranquil music. You can also massage your baby outside. Be sure to stay in the shade, if the sun is shining. It is safest to work on the floor. Choose a comfortable sitting position, perhaps on a cushion or with your back supported against the wall, legs crossed or extended. Alternatively kneel with your knees apart and then sit back on your heels. If being on the floor doesn't work for you, prepare a safe surface at waist height. You need a soft surface for your baby such as a thick folded towel or a towel over a baby fleece. Place the massage oil beside you in a bowl or non-spill bottle and make sure your hands are clean and warm.

BABY MASSAGE ROUTINE

When your baby is approaching two months old, you can massage her more formally once a day. Once she begins to crawl, it will be harder to get her to stay still for long enough and she will prefer massage combined with movement. The massage sequence should last no longer than 20 minutes, as babies have a relatively short attention span. So perform each stroke for only about 20 seconds or for four or five repeats and then move on.

Choose a time of day when your baby is awake and in a playful mood, never immediately after a feed, or when your baby is hungry. The best time may be immediately after bathing in the late afternoon or early evening. This can help to settle a fretful baby and induce more restful sleep. It is good to massage at more or less the same time every day so your baby looks forward to it. Let your baby be your guide and if she cries or doesn't soon relax into the massage, then don't persist. Try again on another occasion. Always stop when your baby lets you know she has had enough and don't massage your baby when she is unwell.

With the room well prepared (see above), undress your baby so she is completely naked. Put plenty of oil on your hands and keep replenishing it so your hands glide smoothly over your baby's skin. Relax your hands as you work and begin gently, working very slowly and rhythmically. Over time as your confidence increases, the pressure you are using will naturally become a little stronger. It may surprise you eventually how firmly you can work and how utterly relaxed your baby will become by the end of the massage. Every massage session should end with a cuddle and then, usually, a feed.

MASSAGING A NEWBORN BABY

You can start massaging a newborn through clothing. When your baby is happy to be undressed, you can start working directly on the skin. Warm a little massage oil in your hands first before applying. Massaging a newborn is no more difficult than stroking a kitten or puppy. Holding your baby close to you in whatever position seems secure and comfortable for you both, work over your baby's body using gentle stroking or circling movements. Trust your instincts and respond to your baby's signals and you can't go wrong.

STEP-BY-STEP MASSAGE

Step one

Place your baby on her back. Begin by massaging one foot, concentrating on the tops and soles, and gently massaging each toe by rolling it gently between your thumb and forefinger. Repeat with the other foot.

Step two

Starting from the top of the thigh, pull the leg downward with a smooth "hand-over-hand" movement, to include the ankle and the foot. Repeat with the other leg. When you have finished, hold both legs at the ankles and gently "bicycle" them a few times, bending one leg while you straighten the other.

Step three

Clap your baby's feet together gently so that her knees roll outward. Use your right hand to take her right foot to her navel. Keep it in this position while you massage the back of the right thigh and buttock with your left hand for about 30 seconds. Then holding the ankle, softly shake the leg straight. Repeat with the other leg. Do a few more "bicycles" and then hold her feet with the soles together with one hand and gently push them down onto her belly so that her bottom lifts up. Massage around the base of her spine for about 20 seconds.

Step four

Gently shake the legs. Then lay your hand lightly on your baby's belly until you feel it soften and relax. Then, using the weight of your relaxed hand, massage clockwise in a circular movement. Repeat a few times and then stroke from side to side across the belly, your hands moving between the ribcage and the hips.

Step five

Place both hands on your baby's chest. Stroke up and outward over the shoulders a few times. Now stroke from the centre of the chest outward to the sides. Repeat a few more times and then cup your hands slightly and tap lightly across the top and sides of your baby's chest.

Step six

Work with both hands from the chest, up and out over the shoulders and down the arms, gently pulling them downward through your palms, along the sides of her body.

Step seven

As she relaxes, you will be able to open out her arms sideways in line with her shoulders.

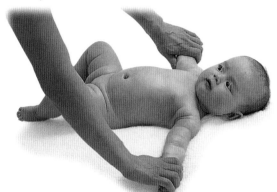

Step eight

After giving the arms a gentle little shake, you may be able to take them up over her head, but don't force this.

Step nine

Lay your baby on her front with her chest and shoulders supported by a cushion. You can stop using the cushion once she is used to lying on her front. Use long firm strokes and, keeping your hands relaxed, work hand-over-hand down her spine several times. Then cup your hands slightly and pat her quite firmly all over her back and shoulders and down the length of her spine. Stroke down the back of her legs from the hips to the feet, gently pulling the legs and feet through your palms.

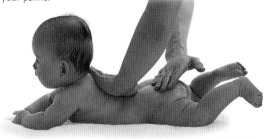

Step ten

When your baby is old enough to rest her weight on her arms, you can work from the chest around the shoulders and then draw the arms down the sides of your baby's body, keeping the arms down low beside her torso. When she naturally lifts her chest in this position you can gently aid the movement as far as is comfortable by pulling the arms down through the centre of your palms from the shoulders to the wrists. Repeat a few times taking care to keep her arms low down beside her hips.

Step eleven

Finish the session by sitting her on your lap and gently massaging her head all around its contours. Start with fingertips and then use your whole hand. Continue for a minute or so and then support her chest with one hand and use the other to massage the back of her neck and shoulders.

Development and play

Your baby starts learning the minute he is born. He will soon become increasingly interested in what is happening around him. In the weeks and months to come, he will learn to lift his head, grasp, and hold objects, to roll over, to sit up, to crawl, stand, and begin walking and talking. Life becomes a new adventure as you engage in your baby's discoveries and share his excitement.

In the early days his vision and hearing focus primarily on his mother. He senses and explores her body through skin contact and touch. From this secure place, he begins to discover the light, colours, sounds, textures, smells, and tastes of the wider world. He will also soon readily accept his father or other close person as someone with whom he feels secure. He needs you to be there to help him feel safe, to provide new challenges, and to explore his ever-expanding world with him through play.

For convenience, in this chapter I have looked at the average progress in development that you can expect over two to three month periods. However, there is a wide range of variation and every baby will reach the expected milestones in his own time. Heredity, environment, personality, and most of all, your involvement all play their part in the progress of your baby's development.

Discovering the wider world

ALL THE TIME YOUR BABY IS AWAKE AND PLAYING, he is learning about the world around him. Play is a vital activity and is a child's most important work, laying the foundations for both physical and mental development. In the year to come your baby will be finding out about things that are smooth, rough, textured, pointed, hard, cold, soft, warm, big, small, solid, or liquid. He will be endlessly fascinated by shapes and by how things behave, balls that roll, feathers that float on air, soap bubbles that burst, objects which fall or float, water that sprays, trickles, or

Babies are fascinated by the simple things around them. Part of the fun of having a baby is your own rediscovery of everyday miracles. Hold your baby up close to interesting objects so she can see and touch them and delight in watching them move.

splashes, leaves and flowers that sparkle in the sunshine. Your job will be to introduce him to these simple yet extraordinary things and to give your child the space to explore and experience the natural textures and objects around him.

THE PLACE OF TOYS

The world as it is, is a very interesting place to a baby. In our culture we tend to overestimate the value of toys. Even very young babies these days will have an array of toys strung across the stroller, pushchair, pram, or car seat. While the right toy at the right time can really enhance development, it is best not to overstimulate or clutter your baby's life with too many of them. In fact, babies and children very soon get bored with too many toys and will ignore them, whereas a well chosen, small selection will continue to be enjoyed in new and different ways as your baby develops. You can also invent many of his toys yourself from simple materials around the house that have no sharp edges and that are not swallowable, breakable, or toxic.

Engage with your baby sometimes when she plays with toys. Wait for her to make her own discoveries without helping and praise her when she achieves something new.

Select any toys you buy carefully, offering him those that are appropriate to his stage of development and the skills he is currently acquiring. Choose toys made of natural materials wherever possible and read the labels to be sure that they are non toxic, safe, and designed for his age group. Tasks that are too complex will confuse your baby, so avoid giving him toys that are meant for an older child.

Remember that no matter how interested he becomes in the world of objects, people are his preferred toys. Even though he will also play by himself at times, he will always prefer playing simple interactive games with you. Toys will come to life for him when you use them to play with him.

Simple toys like a colourful beach ball allow opportunities for plenty of interaction with your older baby. He will enjoy simple games such as patting or rolling the ball between you.

THE VALUE OF SONG

Babies love music and are fascinated by sounds. Songs and nursery rhymes or nonsense rhymes you make up yourself, will enrich your baby's life and stimulate the development of speech. Experiment with different sounds and types of music to see which he likes most. Singing lullabies to soothe babies to sleep is sadly a lost art these days. Whether you are good at it or not, your baby will love your singing. You can find recordings of lullabies and nursery rhymes for inspiration in most good toyshops and bookshops.

DAYTIME IS PLAYTIME

When your older baby is awake and ready for fun, keep him engaged and entertained in the day. This will help him to learn that nights are for sleeping. This does not mean that you need to make a special point of playing with him all the time. It's important to find the right balance between stimulation and quiet time so that your baby also learns to enjoy silence and his own company when he is awake. He will thrive on being included in your everyday life and activities and will nap when he gets tired, wherever he is.

FAMILY AND SOCIAL LIFE

Babies are not meant to be cared for by only one person. In an extended family or tribal community, there are plenty of people around to entertain a baby and new mothers do not have to care for their babies on their own. Fathers can establish a baby's trust early on and siblings can also play a big role in a baby's world. Children usually communicate, stimulate, and play with babies very naturally. Older brothers and sisters are often very gentle and affectionate with a new baby, but be warned that this may be spiced with a little normal sibling rivalry!

However, in our society one parent is often the sole carer of the baby for hours on end and this can be both lonely and exhausting. If you find yourself in this position, try to plan a variety of activities into your day. These can include a walk outdoors, an expedition to the shops, or a special activity for parents with babies, such as a baby massage, movement, or swimming class (see Water babies, page 114). Getting together with other parents and babies is essential. You need adult company and babies also benefit enormously from the company of other babies. In their first year babies tend to play side by side rather than interact directly. They are fascinated by other babies and usually enjoy social occasions. They love to be with older children or siblings.

Babies love to be together while you enjoy the company of other parents. In good weather it is preferable to be in the open air in a natural environment.

OUT AND ABOUT

Start with short, easy trips to places where you will be able to feed and change your baby with no problem. Local mother-and-baby groups, visits to relatives and friends, or to a baby-friendly café are ideal early outings. It may surprise you how communicative people can be when you have a baby with you. Avoid smoky and overcrowded places. In the early months the essentials you need for going out with your baby are a baby carrier, changing bag, and a car seat if you will be driving or travelling by car. Information about the practical aspects and benefits of "wearing" your baby can be found in Chapter 4. Many parents use a baby carrier or back pack throughout the first year, but if this doesn't suit you or your baby begins to feel too heavy to carry, there are a variety of different types of stroller to choose from.

It is a good idea to have a prepared changing bag, ready packed with nappy (diaper) changing kit and a spare set of clothes. Babies often feed more than usual when you go out; feeding is a refuge when it all gets a bit too much. If you are bottle-feeding, you will need to take sufficient supplies with you to last for the time you are out. Keep made up bottles of formula cool in an insulated bag.

DEVELOPMENTAL CHECKS

Assessment of your baby's development will be made when he has his routine checks at the baby clinic or from your physician or paediatrician. The purpose of this is to ensure that development is progressing normally and to give you an opportunity to discuss any concerns you may have.

ENCOURAGING YOUR BABY'S DEVELOPMENT

The way you touch, handle, and play with your baby is just as important to his physical development as verbal interaction is to the development of speech. Throughout this chapter you will find suggestions for physical play. These are not really exercises as such, but they will help you to be confident in handling your baby in a way that will encourage his development as it unfolds naturally.

Many of the activities are based on everyday handling – for example, when you sit or lie your newborn on your lap, you are helping his development. Before your baby can sit or crawl he depends on you to lay him down, prop him up, or to hold him upright. Later he will benefit from your encouragement to explore and extend his physical skills. In these panels you will find out how to do this safely and appropriately. For more information, read Peter Walker's book (see Resources).

Physical play with your baby builds trust, increases flexibility, balance, and motor development and is great fun. When they are developmentally ready, babies love to move in space, to balance, to be held upside down, or swung safely up into the air. You can expect smiles of delight and peals of baby laughter.

Make sure your baby is in the mood for play and is not hungry or tired. Let him know what you're going to do, wait for a minute or two and then move slowly, confidently, and gently. Always watch your baby's reactions carefully and stop as soon as there is any indication that he has had enough or isn't enjoying the game.

From about four months, the "baby bounce" is a great way to entertain your baby while you relax.

Sensory awakening

URING THE FIRST EIGHT WEEKS your baby's major achievement is to adapt to life outside the womb. These early weeks are all about establishing the natural attachment between mother and baby. At first your baby will spend most of his time sleeping or feeding with short wakeful periods when his attention is focused on you. Then you will notice that your baby seems to be awake more often and increasingly aware of his surroundings.

Social and emotional

The dreamy little smiles that pass across your baby's face when he sleeps are not wind. They let you know that he feels good. His facial muscles are already learning to display pleasure.

Some newborns settle easily in the early weeks, while others may cry and be wakeful more often (see Babies who cry a lot, page 76). Sensations that are similar to those he experienced in the womb are comforting to him, which is why all newborns like to be held and contained (see Baby wearing, page 72). Within a few days of birth, your baby's hearing has become highly sensitive. Babies tend to prefer higher-pitched, softer tones. Adults often seem to know this and will intuitively raise

and soften their voices when talking to a baby. Young babies often startle from sudden loud noises, but will usually sleep through everyday household sounds. It is a good idea to get your baby used to napping in a room in which normal family activities are happening. Being near to you is where your baby feels happiest and safest.

Within a few days after they are born, newborns can recognize familiar faces. Their focal range enables them to see the people who love them more clearly than anything else.

Communication

Your baby is learning to trust and to feel comfortable in the world. Plenty of body contact during the day and also at night will maintain his sense of safety and security. Babies are born with an innate sense of connection to other people. Communication with your baby takes place constantly and becomes increasingly distinct in the early weeks. His behaviour will become more interactive and engaging, revealing more of his emerging personality. During the early weeks you will be rewarded by your baby's first real social smiles accompanied by expressive twinkling of the eyes. It will become easier to distinguish his different moods. He will express his delight in your presence and show you clearly that he recognizes you.

Senses

The newborn's senses are geared to focus on his main protector, his mother. When awake he maintains persistent eye contact with her, as if for reassurance. While this continues during the first few weeks, there is a gradual awakening of the senses to the new sights, sounds, sensations, and smells of the wider environment. Your baby's eyes may not focus effectively during the early weeks, giving him a slightly cross-eyed appearance temporarily. Nevertheless, his eyes are soaking in information as he gazes at your face and his focal range increases every day. His eyelids begin to blink defensively at around six weeks when he is overstimulated by light or startled by a sudden sound. By the end of the second month he will have learnt to follow movement with his eyes.

Vocalization

Your baby will make a variety of noises, beginning to coo, gurgle, and imitate the sounds that you make, as he learns to coordinate his breathing with the movements of his lips and tongue. As he discovers that he can use his vocal cords he will experiment increasingly with his ability to vocalize.

By the end of the second month your baby will respond to the sounds you make with sounds of his own and he will smile back when you smile at him.

PLAY

Babies are fascinated by human faces, round contours, distinct patterns, and moving objects. They soon get bored, so change the objects around your baby regularly.

✿ As your baby turns to look toward the light, you can stimulate his ability to follow objects with his eyes with a squeaky toy or rattle.

✿ Introduce soft soothing sounds to your baby.

✿ Place a few boldly coloured toys, a textured mural, or a picture of a woman's face on the changing table.

✿ Give him safe, clean objects to feel and grasp.

✿ Take your baby from room to room with you, using a baby carrier to keep your hands free. From about four weeks he may enjoy being placed for a short while in a bouncing cradle, or on a bean bag where he can see everything that is going on.

✿ When he can lie on his belly and lift up his chest, supporting himself with his arms, place an interesting toy in front of him.

✿ Once he is comfortable bathing, let him kick and splash and enjoy being in water.

A black-and-white mobile is a good first toy. Young babies like these bold, high contrast designs.

Motor development

The newborn reflexes fade away in the early weeks, although instinctual primary reflexes enable your baby to breathe, feed, swallow, and eliminate waste. His arms will seem more active than his legs and his movements will be large and jerky. When you hold him up as if standing, he will make reflexive stepping movements as his feet touch the ground. This reflex will disappear within 14 days. Held sitting, his back will curve and his head will lag at first, lifting momentarily. Very soon the body opens out from the foetal position, with movement of the arms and legs becoming smoother. He will lose the grasp reflex and his hands will relax. He will grip your finger when you touch his palm. Lying on his tummy, he will start turning and lifting his head to look around him. He will then progress to lifting his head and chest while lying on his tummy.

Held sitting on your lap, your baby will soon learn to support her head independently as the neck muscles strengthen.

Hold your baby facing you. Smile and talk slowly and softly or sing her a song, making different facial expressions to stimulate vision and hearing. Give her time to register and respond.

When you lay your newborn baby on her tummy her arms and legs will be flexed in the newborn "crawl position". Lying on her tummy or on her back, she will turn her head to one side.

ENCOURAGING YOUR BABY'S DEVELOPMENT

❁ Vary her position and lay your baby on her belly for short periods when she is awake. This encourages her to use her neck and back muscles.

❁ Sit on the floor with your back supported and legs together, slightly bent at the knees. Lay your baby on her tummy on your thighs with her head close to your knees, then very gradually lower your knees. Progress to laying her on the floor with her upper body on a cushion. Once she is used to this, let her experience lying on her belly on a flat surface without a cushion. Try putting her on different textures, such as a lambskin, towel, or blanket.

❁ Hold her up sometimes as if standing, with your hands around the chest, so she can stretch out her legs and put her feet down, but don't rest her full weight on her legs.

❁ Lay her on her back and very slowly and gently "bicycle" her legs, singing or talking to her softly at the same time.

Social baby

IN THE THIRD AND FOURTH MONTHS your baby is likely to be awake more of the time and will clearly enjoy the company of close family members. You will find yourself making funny noises, pulling faces, and engaging in baby talk as you delight in your baby's responses. Physical development progresses rapidly. Your baby learns to support his head well and he begins to touch his hands and feet and to explore things with his mouth.

Social and emotional

He initiates social exchanges himself, clearly recognizing people he sees often. People are far more interesting to babies of this age than objects. The time you spend smiling and cooing to your baby contributes to ongoing bonding. Your baby now identifies you as his parents. His smiles express his love and are specifically for you.

Communication

His sense of humour begins to emerge and he sometimes laughs out loud if he finds something especially pleasurable. He also expresses frustration and cries lustily when he is uncomfortable. By now you will find it much easier to understand your baby. Even though he begins to take an interest in the objects around him, he still likes interaction with people best.

Hold your baby upright to help her develop a sense of gravity and space.

Your baby learns to socialize from the intimate exchanges that happen between you naturally every day.

Senses

Your baby's senses are becoming sharper and are used to investigate his surroundings. By the end of the fourth month both eyes are focusing together. He is able to follow a moving object accurately with his eyes and he can see things at a much greater distance. This is a good time to start carrying him facing outward in his sling, so he can see the world.

Vocalization

Vocalization is more expressive now. Your baby engages in "conversations", enjoying rhymes and any baby talk you find yourself inventing. He babbles a lot making new, more rounded vowel sounds and you may begin to hear a few consonants such as "n", "d", "p", and "b".

SAFETY

You need to be very careful not to put your baby on a high surface and turn your back, as he could roll off in seconds. If you haven't done so yet, you will soon need to "baby proof" your home (see page 183).

Motor development

By the third month your baby has full control of his neck and turns his head sideways when he hears a familiar sound. As his spine and upper chest muscles strengthen, he lifts his head, shoulders, and chest higher when lying on his belly, supporting his weight on his forearms. This progresses to reaching out, balancing on one elbow, then using both arms and resting only on his belly briefly as if he were swimming. When lying on his back he kicks vigorously and waves his arms around bringing his hands to the centre of his chest. By the end of this period, his head is steady when you hold him sitting up, and his back seems less floppy, although he still needs support. When supported standing on your lap, he begins to bear weight on his legs. He instinctively pushes up when his feet touch a surface, and although his legs are getting stronger, they will tend to buckle at the knees.

When lying on his tummy a three-month-old is able to hold his head up for a minute or two.

Around the fourth month he discovers that he can roll from his back to his side.

PLAY

✿ Hold your baby close and let him explore your facial features, hair, or body.

✿ Stimulate his ability to track through sight and sound with a moving rattle or bell.

✿ Give him brightly coloured toys that are easy for him to hold and shake. Toys that make sounds or have interesting textures to chew help your baby to explore and develop good hand-eye coordination.

✿ Lie him on his back under a baby gym toy with objects within reach of his hands or feet. Hold it over him so that he can bat or kick. Toys that move or do something when he hits them teach him about cause and effect.

✿ Put him on his tummy on a play mat with objects of different colours and textures to stimulate his senses.

✿ Lay your baby on his tummy and roll a little ball, just out of reach in front of him. This will encourage him to play with one or both arms and to lift his head and strengthen his chest.

✿ Place a toy about 30 centimetres (12 in) away to one side of him to encourage him to reach for it and roll over.

✿ When lying on his tummy, let him push with his feet against your hand to encourage the beginnings of crawling.

Anything that makes an unusual sound, such as a rattle, will be appealing to your baby and he will look at it intently and follow or "track" its movements with his eyes.

Hand-eye coordination

Your baby will be fascinated by his own hands and feet. He will gaze intently at his fingers and put his hands in his mouth to suck on them.

At this time your baby will learn to grasp. Although you can see that he wants to get an object, his movements may not be coordinated enough to do so. As his vision improves, reaching for objects becomes more deliberate. Once he can grasp, he will try to take the object to his mouth. However, until these movements become more purposeful, things reach his mouth by accident rather than design.

A rattle will go straight into her mouth as soon as she has sufficient coordination to do this. Oral exploration is an important part of her development.

ENCOURAGING YOUR BABY'S DEVELOPMENT

Once your baby can lie on his tummy with his head held up in line with his chest, his spine is strong enough for supported sitting and the legs are becoming much stronger. Continue to vary your baby's position, lying on the front and back, encouraging rolling, and also experimenting with supported sitting and standing. You can gently introduce these movements for short periods of time as you play with your baby. Keep checking to be sure that your baby is enjoying the game and stop at any sign of discomfort.

Sit your baby on the floor with the soles of the feet together and the knees spread out to the sides to create a stable base. Support his chest with one hand and lower back with the other. Hold for a few moments and then give him a cuddle.

Support your baby standing up on your lap or on the floor to develop strength in the legs. Hold her around the chest with your hands and let her face toward you and also face her outward sometimes. Her weight rests only partially on her legs.

Sitting baby

You can try this game once your baby is sitting. Kneel behind your baby. With your arms under your baby's arms, hold her feet together securely in the tailor position by the ankles (see page 107). Come up slowly into a kneeling position and swing your baby gently from side to side three or four times.

BY THE FIFTH AND SIXTH MONTHS your baby's birthweight will have doubled and he will be starting to learn to sit up unsupported. This enables him to look round him more widely and easily. When he no longer needs his hands for support he will enjoy reaching for things, holding them, and exploring them first with his mouth and then by pulling, prodding, and squeezing. He will be able to play on his own for a short while, surrounded by a few of his favourite toys.

Social and emotional

Your baby chuckles and laughs a lot and but may howl loudly if annoyed or upset. He starts to find other children very stimulating. Although he enjoys company, somewhere between four and seven months he may go through a phase where he is unsure about strangers and it can be difficult to leave him with someone else. It may help if your babysitter arrives early and starts to communicate with your baby in a very gradual unthreatening way while he is sitting on your lap.

Communication

His ability to remember is growing and he will be just starting to learn that when you leave the room you also come back. He recognizes familiar people and enjoys getting their attention. His facial expressions are more varied, letting you know more clearly how he is feeling. Body language is also becoming more expressive and he will wave his arms around when excited. He is also likely to react to his name being called and to the presence of family pets.

Senses

He looks at everything around him with lively interest, his eyes moving in unison. He is fascinated by dropping objects and delights in watching where they fall. Whenever possible, he puts objects into his mouth to be explored, including his own feet. He enjoys toys that allow him to produce a result, like a squeaky toy, things that move when he bats them, or that make a noise when he bangs them together.

Vocalization

He has a whole repertoire of noises and takes a keen interest in your reactions to the sounds he makes. His babble includes both single and double syllables and little words such as "baba", "dada", and "mama" may appear, but he won't yet use them with meaning. Even though your baby can't speak yet, listening to adults talk is a vital part of learning to vocalize.

ENCOURAGING YOUR BABY'S DEVELOPMENT

Your baby has a natural drive to sit. You will notice him lifting his head and shoulders and craning his neck as he attempts to sit up from lying on his back, or pushing up with straight arms when lying on his front. However, he is dependent on you to give him the opportunity to practise. Establish good posture from the start by sitting him up with the soles of the feet together and knees open. Stroke with alternate hands down his back, gently grounding the base of the spine and the pelvis. He will support himself with his hands at first and then gradually his spine will strengthen so that, in the next month or so, he will be able to sit upright without help.

At first, place cushions over his legs to support his torso.

Later remove the cushions and hold his pelvis to steady him.

Feeding

Sitting on your lap at meal times, your baby may be interested in the food on your plate and may reach out for it. This usually coincides with teething and a desire to bite on things. These are signals that he is ready to try solid food (see page 62). He is able to hold a spoon himself and may put it near or in his mouth. Soon he may be ready to start using a high chair and to have his first finger foods.

When your baby can sit comfortably, put him in the tailor position (see page 107) and place a toy or two just out of reach to encourage crawling.

Motor development

The major achievement is learning to sit independently. At first he will lunge forward and need your support or use his arms for support on the floor in front of him. This will progress to unsupported sitting, usually in the sixth or seventh month. He still enjoys rolling over and his spine, chest, and back muscles are much stronger, allowing him to balance on his tummy for a short while, with both arms free to hold an object. He might skim around the floor a bit on his tummy. Some babies start the basics of crawling by coming up onto the arms and knees. His back is

Once the spine has fully strengthened, your baby will sit independently with a lovely straight back and relaxed open hips.

PLAY

Knocking down comes before building in the normal sequence of development. Build your baby a tower of blocks and then let her enjoy destroying it.

❀ Give her hard things she can chew on or teething rings.

❀ Games like "peek-a-boo" and hide and seek with toys are favourites. This type of play teaches your baby that things (and you eventually) don't disappear permanently when temporarily out of sight.

❀ Your baby is ready for songs with actions such as "pat-a-cake", "this little piggy", and other nursery-rhyme favourites.

❀ Noisy toys, simple nesting, sorting, or posting sets, stacking rings, wooden blocks, pots and pans with a wooden spoon are all appropriate. Games such as building a little tower and letting her knock it over or hiding a block under a cup will be fun. She will also like playing by herself with a variety of toys around her that challenge her exploration of shapes, spatial relationships, and sounds. This two-handed play helps to sharpen her co-ordination and new motor skills.

❀ Support her sitting up in the bath and give her some bath toys to splash around with.

❀ Playing at mealtimes is an important part of getting used to the textures, colours, and tastes of solid foods.

now strong enough for you to use a high chair and back pack instead of a baby carrier if you wish. Supported standing is not balanced yet, but he can take more weight onto his feet and may come up onto his toes as his feet strengthen.

Hand-eye coordination

Your baby is becoming more dexterous, reaching accurately for objects with both hands and rotating his wrist to inspect them. His finger movements are finer and he can pick things up and can also pass things from hand to hand. He has yet to learn to let go and release things he has grasped.

Not yet able to put the pegs into the holes, this baby rotates her wrists to inspect them. She still doesn't know how to let go of objects.

Some babies love to be held upside down. Lay your baby on her back on your thighs with her head at your knees. Hold her securely by the hips. Come up onto your knees and lift her up gently for a few seconds and then lower her carefully back onto your lap, head first.

ENCOURAGING YOUR BABY'S DEVELOPMENT

Once your baby is able to sit confidently, sit behind her with your legs wide apart and gently place the soles of your baby's feet together with knees spread in the tailor position.

Then gently encourage your baby's legs to open wide, first one at a time and then both together. Holding the knees softly, "bounce" and massage them, without forcing, to gradually relax the knees.

Once your baby is confident with supported standing, you can try this first assisted somersault. Kneel on the floor and lay your baby on your lap facing you. Cuddle him in close with his legs close to your body, his head by your knees.

Hold him securely with both hands on the shoulders. Then come up slowly onto your knees, until he is upside down.

Now, still holding the shoulders gently let him roll over until his feet touch the floor and support him in the "standing" position.

Crawling baby

UNLESS YOUR BABY IS ONE OF THOSE who goes straight from sitting to standing, around this time most babies start crawling. He will be very curious and interested in the world and will explore every nook and cranny of your home. You are about to have a baby on the move, so make sure your home is baby proof. At this stage your baby will be learning to be aware of the difference between himself, others, and the world. Up to now he simply tuned in to whatever was within his sight, soon forgetting about things that disappear. Now he will notice when someone or something special is missing and will learn to look for hidden objects.

Social and emotional

He may develop strong affectionate bonds with people he knows well, such as his grandparents. Being more independent seems to go hand in hand with feeling more insecure at times. Your baby may become anxious and reserved when meeting strangers and may be upset by new surroundings. He needs to get used to new people gradually, from the safety of your arms. He will "parallel play" beside another child his age, but at this stage they will each be absorbed in their own world and any sharing that takes place will be accidental.

Communication

He can signal by raising both of his arms that he wants to be picked up, and chuckles and squeals when you play with him. Make a point of naming objects that you give him. He turns toward you when you call his name, remembers familiar words, and responds to simple requests. As he becomes more mobile and independent, he begins to learn about boundaries as the word "no" inevitably is needed occasionally to help him to avoid danger.

Senses

All senses function actively as your baby explores the world. He is visually insatiable, his head and eyes moving in all directions to scan the environment. His mouth and tongue are very sensitive and he will still put everything in his mouth. He looks at objects with intense concentration.

He will enjoy the sound of his own voice and will be amazed at the increasing variety of sounds he can make.

Vocalization

The sounds your baby makes now may be quite tuneful, almost like singing at times and will include his whole repertoire. He may play with his fingers in his mouth while vocalizing and will imitate sounds he hears. Spend lots of time chatting to him. Speak slowly and your baby will listen carefully to everything that you say and will babble constantly, just beginning to associate sounds he makes with meaning.

Feeding

He may be enjoying a variety of tastes now, although the main part of his nutrition still comes from breast milk or formula. He is able to feed himself solids with a spoon and enjoy

Sitting confidently now, your baby will be fascinated with objects he can pick up .

experimenting with different foods. He can drink from a beaker or cup with assistance.

Motor development

Your baby has an impressive range of physical skills. He sits up without support, turns to reach for things, and he still loves holding his feet and putting his toes in his mouth. He can also roll all the way over from side to side and may come up onto all fours. This rapidly leads to the start of crawling. A few babies skip the crawling stage and sit or shuffle around on

Some babies crawl like crabs on their hands and feet.

Others go on their hands and knees. Lots of babies start crawling backward or drag one leg.

PLAY

✿ Spend a little cosy time each day looking at first picture books.
✿ The games and toys you introduced in the sitting phase continue to be amusing and to develop motor co-ordination. "Out of sight is not out of mind" games such as "peek-a-boo" are still important. Introduce a few toys that roll or do something as a result of your baby's action.
✿ Encourage your baby to grab, reach, and crawl. Put a favourite toy a short distance away from her to stimulate her to reach out and move toward it.
✿ Position her in a crawling position and place your hand against her feet so he has something to push against to propel herself forward.
✿ Babies this age continue to love building block towers and knocking them down. Mirror play is another favourite.
✿ When she stands holding onto the furniture, offer her a toy in the other hand to develop balance. Balance will increase when standing in preparation for walking, so continue to support her in standing positions.

Choose colourful, indestructible first books. Your baby will enjoy "reading" the pictures while you name the objects in them.

their bottoms until they rise up on to their feet. Pulling up to standing, stepping on alternate feet, and then sitting down again may become a favourite pastime.

Hand-eye coordination

He can pick up small, even tiny objects precisely with two fingers (pincer grip). He learns to let go of objects and especially enjoys dropping things, watching attentively where they fall. This is a way of exploring distance and space and is an important part of his development.

Your baby will begin to pull himself up onto his feet holding on to the furniture.

Hand skills develop along with crawling. Now your baby can pick up tiny objects and will study them with intense concentration.

Your baby's spine and muscles are strengthening. In this natural "swimming" position he can lift both legs and arms off the floor.

ENCOURAGING YOUR BABY'S DEVELOPMENT

At this stage your baby will still enjoy all the physical play she has learned so far and will continue to do so until she is a toddler. Her sense of space and distance is developing and she will enjoy games that involve movement through the air. Her body is now both strong and flexible. You can sit on the floor with your legs extended and lay your baby on her back across your thighs so she can safely extend her spine into an arch. She is likely to enjoy this and it is an excellent way to encourage flexibility of the spine. The games below are father and baby favourites.

Hold your baby securely and whizz her around, or lift her up and down in the air. Stop if she isn't enjoying it.

Carry your baby on your shoulders, holding her around the hips or by the arms.

Walking, talking baby

A S HE APPROACHES THE END of his first year, your baby may begin walking and talking. The normal range for both of these skills is between 10 and 16 months. All his senses are fully functional. As your baby takes his first steps, he will need your help to practise. On his own, he will totter and fall until the great day arrives when he starts to walk forward. At 12 months his vision is almost fully developed. He still loves to explore distance and space by dropping and throwing objects, and enjoys copying the things you do such as playing with the telephone or pulling his clothes over his head. Try to accept a degree of chaos as your child gets more adventurous. A somewhat untidy household is far more interesting and stimulating for your baby.

You are still the centre of your baby's world when he begins the transition from baby to toddler. As he takes his first steps into the world, he will still need plenty of cuddles, reassurance, and close body contact. His expressions of love and affection are especially endearing.

Social and emotional

He is interested in everything that goes on around him. He confidently recognizes familiar people and loves going out, watching people, cars, and animals. Babies at this age readily show their affection for family members. He still likes to be within sight or sound of his mother or a familiar adult, but has a clearer understanding that you will come back when you leave the room. His increasing independence goes along with the need to reinforce his security and he is likely to be both more independent and more clingy while he learns to walk.

Communication

Your baby is beginning to share your view of the world. He can increasingly imitate and remember your actions. He can also let you know precisely what he wants with a range of gestures. Your baby will learn to point to things and to look at things you point to. He will look for your reaction when he comes across something new and will draw back if you seem

Feeding

He is able to drink from a cup by himself (and fling it onto the floor!). Self-feeding becomes more assured and accurate.

He will still love to see his own image in a mirror but may not yet realize it's him. Tell your baby who he's seeing, pointing out and naming his facial features.

Your baby needs to experiment with different foods and drinks and to develop the skills to feed himself.

to disapprove. Let him discover and explore things himself, while setting the essential limits to avoid danger.

Vocalization

Soon your baby will call you "dada" and "mama", often saying "dada" first, as this is an easier sound for babies to make. He increasingly associates specific sounds that he makes with their meanings such as the names of objects, parts of the body, and so on. He will respond to simple instructions such as "give to Daddy" and "wave bye-bye".

ENCOURAGING DEVELOPMENT

Your baby may be ready for walking around this time, although this should not be hurried. First he will stand up briefly unaided and fall quickly down onto his bottom. When he takes his first tentative steps you will know that he is ready to practise walking.

Stand behind your baby and support him gently by the wrists or hands when he takes his first steps.

PLAY

Attention span at this age is short, so you always need to be ready to provide new stimulation when she gets bored.
✿ Play games with a big ball.
✿ Provide your baby with banging spoons or hammering

Your baby will learn that squatting is the best way to come down and up from standing and will also play comfortably in this position.

Motor development

Your baby has probably mastered the art of fast, well-coordinated crawling. Many one-year-olds are intrepid climbers, so you need to be continually on your guard. He will love pulling himself up, holding on to the furniture and cruising along, picking up his feet one at a time, and moving hand over hand. Eventually he starts standing unsupported and walks forward while holding your hands. As his balance improves, the great moment comes when he takes his first few independent steps. At first he falls down after a few quick steps, but progresses in his own time to squatting, standing, and walking.

It is a good idea to have a box or cupboard full of unbreakable household objects that are safe for your baby to discover.

toys, stacking blocks to build and knock over, simple "take apart and put together toys", nesting cups, an easy posting box, and musical toys.

✿ Push along toys will help to develop his walking. A heavy wooden wagon with a hand rail is ideal. These are preferable for safety and development to baby-bouncers or sit-in walkers as they allow the baby to go at his own pace.

✿ Spend a time each day reading first books with bold and brightly coloured illustrations.

✿ He may make his first scribbles if you give him some (non-toxic) crayons.

✿ He will love crawling through tunnels, clambering over low objects. You can create an exciting play environment for him using cardboard cartons with the bottoms cut out or a blanket thrown over a small table.

✿ Outside in fine weather let him play in a bowl of water or shallow paddling pool with a few plastic containers or corks that float and some sand with a shovel or a spoon. Never leave him unattended in the water.

✿ Respond to any games that your baby initiates. A small ball is a good toy for this.

Water baby

SWIMMING AND WATER PLAY are great fun for babies and are excellent activities to build the bonds of love, trust, and communication between you. Because new-born babies have spent nine months in the amniotic fluid of the womb, they are perfectly at home in warm water. In fact they are born with an instinctive ability to move under water. They generally have no fear of water and, if you are not anxious, your baby will soon learn to swim with you confidently. Swimming is just as good all round exercise for babies as it is for adults. It allows freedom of movement, makes the heart and lungs strong and the body athletic. Most importantly, your baby will learn to be buoyant and float from an early age – important safety skills that every child needs to acquire.

Swimming is wonderful, liberating exercise for babies. Long before they are fully mobile on land, babies are instinctively agile and independent under water. Joining a water baby programme can give you the confidence to develop your baby's natural water skills.

THE DIVE REFLEX

Up until they are about four months old, babies have an instinctual "dive reflex", which prevents them from inhaling when under water. This is why they can learn to swim so easily. When the brain matures, the dive reflex is lost and then babies need to learn how to hold their breath under water.

INTRODUCING SWIMMING IN THE BATH

When someone is there to help you, you can start to familiarize your baby with floating in the bath at home. Make sure the water is warm and deep enough and have some towels ready to wrap your baby in as soon as you get out.

✿ Cuddle your baby against your body on his front, head on your chest with the rest of his body submerged to teach him to relax in water (see the photograph on page 84).

✿ When he is used to this, sit up and support him on his tummy in the water with your hands holding his chest, head out, and body submerged. Let his chin rest on your wrists and let him float. Then gently and slowly draw him toward you and away from you.

✿ Then try laying him on his back on your body and cuddling him.

✿ Cup your hands around his head and let him float away a little so he feels relaxed in the water. Still holding his head, gently move him forward and back in the water.

WATER BABY PROGRAMMES

Learning to swim takes time and is best done over several months by attending a weekly parent and baby swimming session. You may find these in your local leisure centre. Before starting the programme, make a few visits to the pool with your baby and practise the same things you were doing in the bath at home in the shallow

end of the pool. Get into the water slowly, holding your baby close to you in a relaxed way. Bring along some of your baby's favourite water toys and maybe observe a class or two first before you enrol for a full course of lessons. When teaching your baby to swim, focus your full attention on your baby. If he swallows water or unexpectedly goes under for a second or two, reassure him with a relaxed cuddle.

Most babies take easily to swimming lessons, but if your child doesn't seem to respond, or is anxious or afraid, then don't force the issue. Just have fun in water together, until he is ready to try again. The priority is to keep up his confidence and enjoyment in water. Lessons can be reintroduced later on. Take it very slowly and make sure you are relaxed when playing with your baby in water. Hold your baby firmly and gently, keeping up eye contact and communication. If you are nervous in water, or are unable to swim yourself, then stay in the shallow end and focus on playing with your baby in a relaxed and comfortable way. Keep the activity enjoyable for both of you.

SAFETY

✿ It is best to introduce your baby to underwater swimming with expert guidance from a specialist baby-swimming instructor.

✿ Never leave your baby alone in or near water, no matter how shallow.

✿ A lifeguard or swimming instructor should be present to supervise the pool or class.

✿ The water temperature should not be below 33°C (92°F) before your baby is six months old. Your baby may be put off by water that is too cool.

✿ Special swim nappies (diapers) are available in stores and supermarkets.

✿ Some pools have a filtration system which does not use chlorine and this is preferable. Always rinse your baby in clean water after being in the swimming pool. Dry your baby's ears well on the outside, hold him on each side to drain the water from inside the ears.

✿ Don't go swimming if your baby is unwell or has an ear infection.

✿ Wrap your baby warmly after swimming – especially in cool conditions.

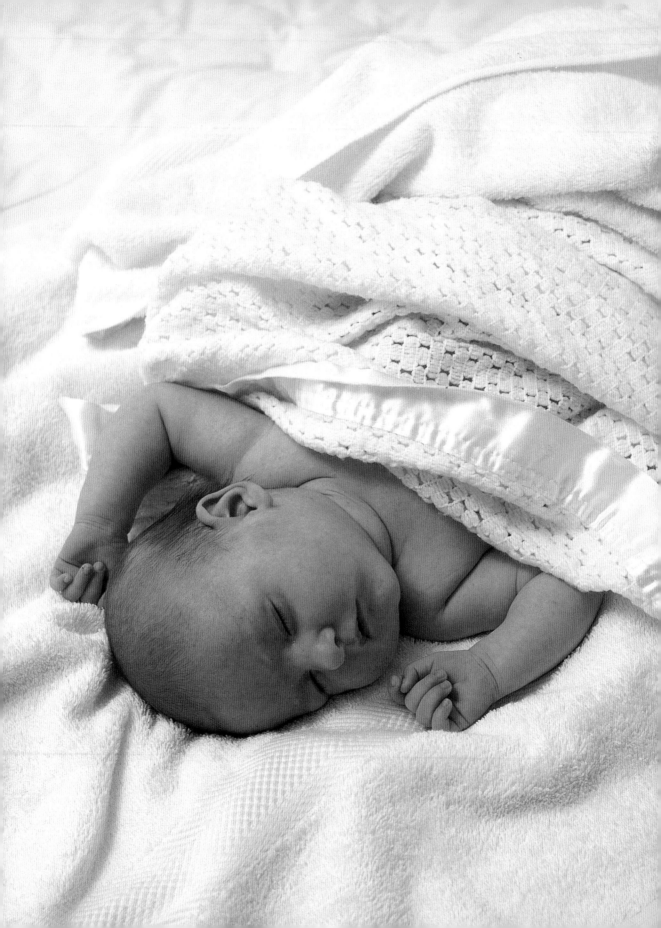

Nighttime baby

Babies need their parents at night just as they do during the day. Most young babies wake up and need feeding several times between bedtime and morning. At first, the disruption of your usual sleep pattern by the arrival of your baby may be the hardest part of being a new parent. However, in time you do get more used to waking at night and effective ways of maximizing sleep can be found so that nighttime parenting does not become a "sleep struggle" with your baby.

Babies' sleep patterns change as they develop, and while infant sleep follows a general trend, there are variations within this, depending on individual physiology and temperament. Some parents have unrealistic expectations and may struggle for months to get their baby into a sleep pattern that does not suit her physiology or stage of development. Some babies are naturally more wakeful than others. Many babies with a normal pattern of frequent waking at night are inaccurately labelled as having a sleep problem, or being "difficult" at night. It is important to find a way of parenting your baby at night that takes into account your baby's natural sleep patterns and that also works for you. This chapter explores ways to achieve this.

How babies sleep

Parenting your baby at night is easier if you understand how babies sleep and how their sleep patterns differ from those of an adult. Both adults and babies sleep in alternating cycles of deeper and shallower sleep. While adults have three different types of sleep: light, deep, and rapid eye movement (REM) sleep, in the first year of life babies have two types of sleep: active sleep (the equivalent of REM sleep), which accounts for about two thirds of total sleep in the newborn, and quiet sleep. By the time a baby is six months old the proportion of active sleep has usually fallen to about one third of total sleep time.

Dr William Sears, in his excellent book *Nighttime Parenting*, describes how babies move more frequently between sleep states than adults do, especially in the early months, when this can happen as much as once an hour. The baby is more likely to wake up when making the transition between sleep states. This ensures that they feed frequently and get their nutritional needs met at night. Research has shown that a breastfeeding mother's sleep cycles actually change to match those of her baby when they sleep together and are physically close at night.

It is safest for babies to sleep on their back in a room where adults are breathing. It is thought that the sound of the parents' breathing reinforces the baby's breathing rhythm.

Once a baby is deeply asleep, her body seems limp and totally relaxed. Her breathing is regular and her face is calm. You can put her down or move her without

waking her up. This type of sound sleep does not usually occur until about 20 minutes after your baby first falls asleep. This explains why she may wake up if you try to move her too soon after she has fallen asleep.

Like adults, babies dream during active sleep cycles. Dreaming is thought to be the way consciousness processes our inner experiences. Sometimes, when you watch a sleeping baby's facial expressions, you can tell that she is dreaming. Often she will seem to be recalling some blissful pleasures of baby life. However, even a baby may have frightening or disturbing dreams occasionally and wake up crying. Usually a quick response from a parent with sound or touch, a cuddle, and a feed will comfort and soothe her. If your baby seems to have been upset by a dream, it may be a good idea to take her into bed with you for the rest of the night.

INCLUDING YOUR TODDLER

Nighttime waking with your new baby can be especially trying if you also have a toddler who is still waking at night. Toddlers often revert to more babyish habits when a new baby arrives, and may want to sleep with you too if you are sharing a bed with the new baby. Some parents cope with this situation by having an extra large family bed that accommodates the toddler as well as the new arrival. An alternative way of including your toddler at night is to place a child's bed or futon beside your bed. When all members of the family sleep in the same room, sleep patterns tend to become more harmonious and this may reduce your toddler's night-waking. Once your toddler is sleeping through the night, he can then be encouraged to sleep on his own, if this is what you want.

EVOLVING SLEEP PATTERNS

Newborns cannot distinguish between day and night and don't yet have the cyclical body rhythms of an older child or adult. They wake up when they are hungry and fall asleep when they are full, at any time of the day or night. They may remain asleep for periods lasting from about 20 minutes to five hours. Between sleeps, they are awake or feeding. Individual newborns vary, but most sleep about 60 per cent of the time, but some naturally sleep more than others. Newborns cannot be trained to sleep at the times that we want them to.

At around six to eight weeks, most babies begin to sleep more at night than in the day and the overall amount of time they spend sleeping gradually decreases. Some babies may sleep for as long as eight hours at night. However, this is very much the exception, and very few babies sleep for longer than four hours at a stretch before the age of four months. Many wake several times in a night. As your baby gets older, more regular sleep patterns will emerge. By about three months she is likely to have one longer wakeful patch in the day, usually in the afternoon or evening.

By the age of about six months, your baby may be content with three main feeds a day, plus an early morning and late night feed so that you get a good stretch of uninterrupted sleep through the middle of the night. Sleeping through the night is more realistically defined as a five-hour stretch. However, many babies still wake frequently at night at six months and research shows that about 25 per cent of babies wake up regularly at 12 months.

A baby-centred approach

IT CAN BE HARD TO PREDICT how the sleeping arrangements you plan before the birth, will work out in practice. Both parents need to be comfortable with the arrangements and need to be open to change if the initial plan doesn't work. This topic can be emotive and can become an area of conflict between a couple. So after you have both read this chapter, spend some time listening to each other and sharing your feelings, doubts, and views on the subject. If you have different ideas, try to reach agreement about which approach you feel most comfortable with, and be ready to review your decision together, as your baby's sleep rhythms emerge and evolve through the first year.

Many parents enjoy sharing sleep with their baby. The warmth and closeness of your bodies will help your baby to drop off to sleep sooner. Then you can lay her on her back between you and settle back to sleep yourselves.

The attachment parenting approach that I recommend is designed to work along with a baby's physiological and emotional needs at night, as much as in the day. This involves staying close to your baby at night and is called "co-sleeping". It is based on evolutionary and historical precedent. Babies throughout the ages and all over the world have slept close to their mother, shared her physical environment and body heat, breastfeeding spontaneously through the night. When this works well, the mother's sleep rhythms attune to the baby's, making night feeds much less tiring. Whatever sleep style you choose, no approach is problem-free and no single solution is right for every family. It is essential to choose what works best in your family, for your baby, regardless of what other people recommend or do. The goal is to find arrangements for your family that respect your baby's needs, maximize sleep for the whole family, and foster nighttime harmony.

Mornings in bed with your baby can be a delight. Playing with your baby after she wakes up and when she is alert and ready for fun, is a great way to start the day.

CO-SLEEPING

Co-sleeping essentially means sleeping in the same room as your baby. It is beneficial for your baby to sleep with you for a minimum of six months and possibly for a year or more. This can be done either by sharing a bed with your baby, sleeping with your baby within touching distance, or by placing your baby in a crib or cot in your bedroom, or a flexible combination of these options. This approach is not only about where your baby sleeps, it means accepting that your baby has needs at night, as much as she does in the day. It involves a full commitment to respond to your baby at night, just as you do at any other time. My confidence in this approach comes from my own successful co-sleeping experiences with my four children and the observations I have made over the years, of how well co-sleeping works in numerous other families. A baby who sleeps with her parents has a positive first experience of sleep. She feels safe and secure and this helps to establish a pattern that encourages good sleeping habits.

OPTIONS FOR CO-SLEEPING

If sharing a bed with your baby doesn't work for you, alternative co-sleeping options include having your baby sleep in close proximity alongside your bed, or in a cot in the same room. What is not co-sleeping is when a baby sleeps in a separate room with an electronic monitor in place as a substitute for the mother and father's senses. Babies need to hear their parents at night too and monitors are a one way system only, so the baby is isolated from human sounds.

Some parents start out sharing a bed with their baby in the beginning, and make the transition to another form of co-sleeping after a few weeks or months. One solution many parents like is to use a cot (crib) with a removable side beside their bed "side-car style", so your baby sleeps at touching distance and can easily be brought into bed with you for a cuddle or a feed. If you don't mind getting out of bed for your child at night, then having a separate cot (crib) in your bedroom may be an appropriate co-sleeping choice for you. You can also have your baby in a cot (crib) for part of the night and in bed with you at other times – for example, for feeding, or in the early morning.

SHARING A BED

In the dark, babies predominantly sense through touch, body contact, and smell. Therefore they benefit from having their mother physically close at night when they cannot see. Sharing a bed with your baby is a normal, natural, and practical way to meet a baby's nighttime needs. It facilitates breastfeeding, provides more time for body contact, and the extra touch and tactile stimulation help the baby to thrive, both physically and emotionally. In many cultures, sharing a bed is the norm and it would

THE BENEFITS OF SHARING A BED WITH YOUR BABY

Most early studies on infant sleep were carried out with babies sleeping in isolation from their parents. It is only in the last 15 years that the sleep patterns in babies who sleep with their parents have been compared with those who do not. In the attempt to reduce the incidence of cot death (facing page), serious investigation has taken place on both sides of the Atlantic into the sleep environment of babies, including bed-sharing. This has revealed distinct benefits when babies share a bed with their parents, compared to when they sleep in isolation, and has also provided guidelines for safe co-sleeping in all its forms.

Breastfeeding benefits

The physical closeness of your baby at night promotes increased secretion of the hormone prolactin (see page 40) in the mother. This encourages the production of breast milk. The physical proximity of the breast enables your baby to feed easily at night and this will promote optimal nutrition and healthy development.

Attunement to your baby's needs

Research has revealed that mothers respond more quickly (within seconds) to babies in the same bed than to babies in a cot or crib, even when they are in the same room. Being physically close to your baby at night sharpens your intuition, making you more responsive when your baby is in need.

be considered very strange indeed for mother and father to sleep together, while their baby sleeps alone.

Sharing a bed with your newborn baby gives her security and warmth. Provided both parents are comfortable with the idea, bed-sharing with your baby can make nights more peaceful and restful for everyone. It is much less tiring to roll over and breastfeed your baby, quietly dozing and resting as you do so, without having to actually get out of bed. The older baby finds the breast herself in the night and her mother may not even remember waking up. Over the months, sharing a bed can become so relaxed, that eventually you may not even remember how many times your baby woke in the night and will feel almost as refreshed in the morning as if you had an uninterrupted night's sleep. You can go on sharing a bed with your baby for as long as you are all comfortable with the arrangement without doing her any harm. Some parents continue co-sleeping beyond one year, while others wean their baby into a separate bed or room much sooner.

CO-SLEEPING AND COT (CRIB) DEATH PREVENTION

The Foundation for the Study of Infant Deaths (FSID), recommends that babies sleep in their parents' room for at least the first six months. This has been shown by research to reduce the incidence of sudden infant death syndrome (SIDS, cot – or crib – death), because the parents are more aware of abnormal levels of activity, noises, snuffles, etc. When co-sleeping, the parents' breathing rhythm reminds the baby to breathe, even in sleep, and babies who sleep beside their parents are less likely to stop breathing while asleep. In cultures where women routinely sleep with their babies, SIDS is virtually unknown. For further information, see page 161.

Sound sleep

Babies tend to sleep better and are less likely to wake up when another person is in touching distance. The comfort and security from co-sleeping helps your baby to make the transitions between sleep stages more smoothly without waking up. Maternal sleep cycles adapt to those of their baby, with more frequent light sleep cycles. It is therefore easier for you to respond to your baby and then go back to sleep, than it would be to be roused out of deep sleep to deal with a crying, more distressed baby.

Temperature regulation

The closeness of your body heat is the natural way to ensure that your baby is warm enough at night and helps to avoid the depression of the baby's breathing that may occur if she is too cool. Equally if it feels too warm for you, you will notice and your baby is less likely to be overheated. Research has shown that babies are more likely to overheat when sleeping on their own than when bed-sharing, even when they have a fever.

Emotional security

Close body contact, warmth, and touch at night help to promote your baby's optimal physical and emotional development. Because her need for comfort and security is met at night as well as in the day, she will be less likely to form an attachment to a transitional comfort object such as a dummy (soother), bottle, blanket, or soft toy. Being fully satisfied at night will help your baby develop into an affectionate child with a strong sense of self-worth. This helps your baby to form intimate loving relationships more easily in later life.

Benefit to parents

If you work during the day, sharing a bed allows you to enjoy more contact with your baby and helps to alleviate anxiety about absence during the day. Fathers who are absent all day at work, benefit from the physical closeness and skin contact at night, and the daily satisfaction of the strong protective instinct they may have for the baby. Less frequent crying gives both parents a better night's sleep.

Despite logic and global historical precedent, in our culture there is still a widespread taboo against bed-sharing today, which you will no doubt encounter among your friends, relatives, and even some health professionals. The British author and co-sleeping mother Deborah Jackson goes into detail on the subject. Her book *Three in a Bed* (see Resources), is regularly updated to include the latest research. I highly recommend that you read this to fortify you when faced with a bed-sharing critic.

BED-SHARING GUIDELINES

There is no recipe for how to share a bed with your baby. Most families swap around, even within one night, so that sometimes the baby is in the middle, at other times on the mother's side or next to the father. Many families also use a Moses basket, bassinet, cot (crib), at different times. Whatever arrangements you make, follow a few simple guidelines.

❀ Make sure that your bed is big enough for all of you to have enough space and that the mattress is firm and fits tightly to the frame. Water-beds are not suitable.

❀ Position your baby so that she will not fall out of the bed and will not be smothered by pillows or bedding. Place her on her back to sleep, without a pillow.

❀ Make sure that your baby is not dressed too warmly or over-wrapped.

❀ Use several lightweight blankets and

Close body contact will help settle a wakeful baby at night. Remember that it takes about 20 minutes for a baby to enter deep sleep. Then you can put her down more easily without waking her up.

sheets rather than a duvet or use a baby sleeping bag (see page 126).

❀ Sleep naked or wear light nightclothes yourself.

❀ Don't fall asleep with your baby lying on you.

❀ Do not smoke, drink alcohol, or take recreational drugs.

WHAT YOUR BABY SHOULD WEAR AT NIGHT

When your baby sleeps in your bed she also shares body heat and will need to wear less clothing than a baby sleeping separately. Cotton bedclothes are best as they "breathe", allowing air to circulate. Unlike synthetic fibres, they absorb moisture and keep your baby warm. Nightclothes should fit loosely, but not be too big. Avoid ties or ribbons, which could strangle. Babies can sleep in the same all-in-one suits they wear during the day. Newborns can be loosely swaddled in a light cotton wrap at night. In hot weather your baby can sleep just in a nappy (diaper), perhaps with a vest. If she is too warm, her skin may feel hot and sweaty and she may appear to be flushed. She may let you know she is uncomfortable by crying.

COMMON QUESTIONS ABOUT SHARING A BED WITH YOUR BABY

Will I roll over and accidentally smother my baby in the night?

Mothers who share a bed with their baby are usually both physically and mentally aware of the baby at all times. When you breastfeed your sleep pattern corresponds to that of your baby and excludes the deepest sleep, so that you maintain a constant awareness of your baby. A healthy baby also has a built-in alarm system and will soon let you know if she is uncomfortable. It is important that neither you nor your partner has reduced responses as a result of drinking alcohol or taking recreational drugs.

If I sleep with my baby, will I ever be able to get her out of my bed?

While it is beneficial to sleep with your baby throughout infancy, the early months are the most essential. You can choose to gently "wean" your baby to sleep separately, when you feel she is ready to sleep without you or if you feel that bed-sharing is no longer working. In any case, your child will eventually leave your bed of her own accord.

Will sleeping with my baby make her more dependent on me?

Sleeping with your baby will not make her more dependent on you in the long term. When she is ready, the deep feeling of safety and inner security she will have gained, from having you there when she needed you at night, is likely to make her fearless of the dark, have fewer nightmares, and develop into a confident child.

How will co-sleeping affect our sex life?

If you feel uncomfortable making love in the same room as your sleeping baby, then you can create a comfortable place to make love in another room, if available. Alternatively, if your baby has a daytime napping place such as a Moses basket or a bassinet, you can also let your baby sleep in another room for a short while, to give you some privacy. It is not appropriate to make love with your baby in the room while she is awake.

Will the baby come between us?

When you sleep with your baby it's a good idea to vary her position so that she does not always sleep in the middle. It may be best to position the mother's side of the bed next to a wall, so that when the baby is placed on that side, there is no danger of her rolling off the bed. If you are feeling distant from your partner, this could mean that there are problems in your relationship that are unrelated to where your baby sleeps. Remember, you will have plenty of time to be alone in bed when your child is older.

Nighttime environment

ANEWBORN OR VERY SMALL BABY will not yet be able to regulate her own body temperature. In the early days soon after the birth, make sure that the room temperature remains at a fairly constant 20–21°C (68–70°F). Once your baby has started gaining weight, if the temperature is comfortable for you, it will be fine for your baby. You do need to ensure that your baby is warm enough and not over-or under-wrapped and that the room temperature remains more or less the same all through the night. If heating is left on at night it is a good idea to use a humidifier in the room where your baby sleeps to keep the air moist, especially if your baby has a stuffy nose.

The best way to assess if your baby is warm or cool enough is to observe her and feel her skin. Look for exactly the same signs about temperature that you would see in an adult or child. Hands and feet are usually cooler than other body parts on a baby, so it is better to feel the back of the neck, and the skin under her vest and on her thighs to check if she feels cold.

Babies who are very cold do not cry, as they are conserving energy to keep warm. If your baby feels very cold, then undress her to her nappy (diaper); clothes may keep the cold in. Take her into bed with you to warm her up with body contact. More serious chilling needs urgent medical attention.

A sleeveless cotton sleeping bag that encloses the feet is idea for babies who sleep in a cot or crib, but may be too warm if you share covers with your baby. Laying your hand on her chest may help her to settle down before sleep.

YOUR BEDROOM

You will be spending a large percentage of your time in the first weeks of your baby's life in your bedroom and it is worth making this a healing and restorative space with a restful atmosphere. If you intend to sleep with your baby, having a bed that is large enough to accommodate you all comfortably is essential. Choose a bed with a fairly firm, well-fitting mattress. A king size is best for bed-sharing. A good low-budget solution may be to use an extra thick king-size cotton futon on a low base.

As in the rest of the house, natural materials and textiles instead of synthetics and chemically treated materials are best for use in the bedroom. Good ventilation and soft lighting are essential. It is also soothing to diffuse natural light with soft curtains or blinds. Pure cotton sheets with layers of cellular blankets are best if you sleep with your baby. Choose washable mattress and pillow covers that are designed to reduce dust mites.

COTS, CRIBS, AND MATTRESSES

Many parents who share a bed with their baby never need to buy a cot or crib. Instead, a single futon on a low base can be the ideal transitional bed as it can be used in the parents' bedroom at first and then easily moved to the nursery. It also allows the versatility of lying down with your baby or toddler to settle her to sleep. If you intend to follow this style of parenting, you may find that your baby can progress directly to a child's bed.

If you decide to buy a cot (crib), choose a sturdy one, preferably made of natural unpainted wood, with bars no more than 6.5 centimetres (2½ in) apart. A removable side with an adjustable base is ideal, so that the mattress can be placed flush next to your bed for easy breastfeeding at night. The sides should be adjustable and fasten securely. The mattress should fit snugly, so that your baby can't get a hand or foot down the side. Make sure that the mattress follows the latest safety guidelines and that it has air holes and does not contain flame-retardant chemicals.

A waterproof cotton-lined mattress cover and fitted sheet are ideal on the bottom. At a room temperature of 18°C (65°F) a baby sleeping alone may need 2 to 3 cellular blankets, whereas at 27°C (80°F) only a sheet is necessary. Once your baby starts kicking off the covers, a baby sleeping bag is a better solution to prevent your baby getting cold at night. Don't use duvets, sheepskins, or baby nests for your baby, as they may make your baby too hot. Some babies are allergic to synthetic fibres used in bedding. Choose 100 per cent cotton or natural fibres.

Placing a cot (crib) "side-car style" is a practical solution, especially if you have twins, who can be placed to sleep beside each other across the width of the mattress when they are small. With this arrangement, you can easily reach your baby (or babies) without getting out of bed.

Settling your baby for sleep

A S SOON AS YOU FEEL YOUR BABY IS READY, it is a good idea to introduce a consistent bedtime, using similar rituals each day to guide your baby into parent-friendly sleep patterns. Make bedtime the best part of the day with your baby, and allow time to be with your baby before sleep. This is especially important if you work or plan to work during the day. It is a good idea for both parents to learn to soothe their baby to sleep in a variety of different ways. Each family will develop its own bedtime rituals, but here are some ideas to help your baby settle at night:

❀ Give your baby a warm bath, followed by a massage.

❀ Give her a long relaxing feed and let her fall asleep while feeding.

❀ Babies sleep best on a warm surface especially in cold weather. Use body contact or warm your baby's bed first with a hot-water bottle (be sure to remove it before putting your baby to bed). Flannel sheets feel warmer than other fabrics.

❀ After feeding, let her nestle up on her dad's chest to fall asleep.

❀ Carry your baby in a sling during the evening and gently put her down when she is sleeping deeply.

❀ Lie down with your baby as she drifts off and have a little rest yourself. However, do not fall asleep with your baby lying on you.

Lying on your chest, your baby can hear your heartbeat. The warmth of your body and familiar movements of your breathing will soothe her to sleep. Once she is sleeping soundly, be sure to put your baby down before you fall asleep yourself.

✿ Being in a darkened room can help some babies to sleep.

✿ Household sounds, soothing music, and lullabies can all help to soothe babies to sleep. However, some babies need a quieter environment.

✿ Steady slow rhythms are comforting. Try carrying her and rhythmically swaying or bobbing up and down, rocking her, wheeling her, or even driving her around in the car when desperate!

✿ Lay your warm hands on your baby's body or head to calm and settle her. Keep them softly in position or pat or stroke your baby gently while singing to her.

LEARNING TO FALL ASLEEP BY HERSELF

Some parents I know recommend teaching an older baby to learn the skill of falling asleep herself without feeding. This is distinct from so-called "sleep training" that is sometimes imposed on younger babies (see page 130). Either parent can start to do this from about four months old. Make sure that your baby has been fed, changed, and is due for a sleep. Soothe your baby in your arms first by walking, rocking, chanting, singing, or any other method that works, until she is very relaxed and sleepy, but not yet asleep. Then put her down softly and stay with her until she falls asleep. Don't pick her up again, but do sit with her quietly. If she wakes up and cries, go back to her and try soothing her again by calmly laying a warm hand on her head or chest, or continuing the song you were singing, without picking her up and see if she settles. Some babies will take to this approach very well. If your baby isn't able to settle like this, she is just not ready yet or it doesn't suit her temperament. You could wait a few weeks and try again.

JUGGLING SLEEP

You can expect that your older baby will go about four hours between feeds at night at the most and will inevitable wake up hungry at least once in the night. If your baby is hungry and you delay feeding her and try to comfort her some other way, it will take longer and be more exhausting to settle her down. Giving water or juice is not likely to help either, as they will not satisfy her for long and she will wake up hungry again soon. Sometimes parents are advised that giving a baby extra food in the evenings or adding cereal to the formula will encourage better sleep. In my experience this doesn't usually help and may even give the baby indigestion.

You can, however, work toward juggling your baby's feeding habits so that you get a longish stretch of uninterrupted sleep at night. You can do this by waking your baby up for a good feed in the late evening, when you are ready for bed. Change her nappy (diaper) to rouse her fully and then settle down for a long, relaxing feed. This should satisfy her for at least four hours. If you sense her stirring in the night, you may lose less sleep if you give her a little suckle immediately, before she fully wakes up. Feeding your baby frequently during the day will also help her to sleep longer at night.

DAYTIME SLEEPING

By about two months babies are starting to become more wakeful in the day and sleep more at night, although their daily body rhythms may not yet be fully established. Babies need a certain amount of sleep in each 24 hours and daytime naps are essential for your baby's healthy development. If possible, it is a good idea to try to rest or catch a nap yourself whenever your baby does in the day.

Somewhere between 6 and 12 months, she will probably settle into two fairly predictable nap times in the morning and afternoon. With an older baby it often works well to encourage a nap around noon. She may then sleep till around 2pm and only need one daytime nap. You can gently steer your older baby in the direction of sleeping more at night by filling her days with interest and activity so that she sleeps less during the day. If you are leaving your baby with a carer, make sure that you are aware of nap times in the day.

"SLEEP TRAINING"

Some much-publicized approaches to nighttime babycare are designed to train babies to accommodate their sleep patterns to fit the demands of adult life. Parents with a time-pressured, career-oriented lifestyle may be attracted to a "sleep-training" method that promises uninterrupted sleep at night. Generally, such methods go against a baby's physiology. Sleep training may be convenient for adults, but there are some strong objections you may wish to consider, before you go down that route.

Sleep-training methods generally involve systematically ignoring the baby's cries and withholding feeds at night, letting the baby "cry it out". For practical reasons, these methods require the baby to sleep separately from the parents. Some methods are marginally kinder than others, proposing a transitional period in which the baby is left to cry for five minutes the first night, ten minutes the second night, and so on. While some babies respond to this training according to expectations, others may simply not be able to do so. The fact that some babies seemingly cooperate so quickly may not be as desirable as it seems.

Waking up and crying is the only way a baby can tell us if she is uncomfortable or needs our help. One very important reason babies wake up at night is to feed. Learning to feed only in the daytime is a slow process that happens when a baby is physiologically ready, just like

learning to sit up and crawl. Some babies may not be physiologically ready to go through the night until they are over 12 months. Nighttime feeding boosts secretion of prolactin, the hormone that stimulates milk production. Consequently, there is a risk to the mother's milk supply if breastfeeding at night is dropped.

Bottle-fed babies may go for about four hours between feeds, as cow's milk formula takes longer to digest than breast milk, but still need to feed in the night when they wake up. A baby fed less than she needs may appear to be fine, but her development will not be optimal. A tiny percentage of young babies are at risk from dehydration if refused feeds at night.

Sleep-training methods in this age group necessarily involve a premature separation between mother and baby. We can't ask babies who have been trained to sleep alone how it feels when the most important people in their lives disappear every night. We need to consider whether sleep training affects their sense of security and trust in their parents, and whether it is possible that short-term convenience may lead to long-term emotional damage. On the other hand, we can be sure that a baby who co-sleeps with her parents feels secure, contained, and safe.

Sleep problems

IT IS NORMAL FOR BABIES TO NEED FEEDING several times at night. About 20 per cent of toddlers still do not sleep through the night or wake up full of energy at 5am! A real sleep problem usually occurs consistently over several weeks. Your baby may be unusually difficult to settle at night, or may wake more often in the night, or may take a long time to settle back to sleep. It is all too easy to feel vulnerable and guilty when this happens, especially if you are working and away from your baby in the day. A mother going through this kind of experience often feels inadequate and this can get in the way of handling a wakeful baby sensibly.

Try to determine the cause of the sleep problem. Frequent waking often coincides with a growth spurt. Your baby may just be taking advantage of the calmer night-time to increase your milk supply. This should cease in a few days, but meanwhile try to make more time for rest in the day (cancel your engagements, if necessary). Babies who are teething, or who are unwell, may be in pain at night. Your baby may be uncomfortable, feel too warm or too cold, or there may be a medical problem. If you suspect the latter, be sure to discuss the issue with your doctor. Emotional upset in the family, such as discord in the parents' relationship, or disruption of the normal family routine – for example, during or after a holiday – may also affect your baby's sleep patterns.

It can be helpful to take turns to get up with a very wakeful baby. Once he has been fed, cuddle and comfort him, but don't make night-waking too entertaining. He will gradually learn that nighttime is for sleeping.

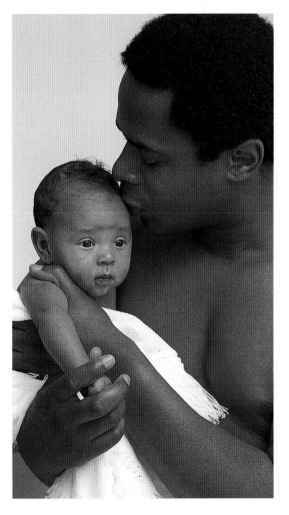

Sharing a bed with your baby is often the most successful remedy for frequent night-waking. Babies who naturally wake very often at night may be helped to make the transition from light to deeper sleep without waking, when you are there to notice the first stirrings. You can help your baby into deeper sleep, by laying on a calm hand or offering a sleepy suckle. In time your baby will learn to make this transition by herself and her sleep pattern will adapt. Occasionally the opposite is true: although most babies bed-share happily, some babies actually sleep better in a cot (crib). There are no rules when it comes to your baby's sleep habits. Above all, do what works best for you and your baby.

Family life

There is no doubt that the arrival of a new baby profoundly changes your life, your relationships, and the dynamics of your family. Even if you are already a parent, you may be surprised by how your interactions with your partner, other children, parents, and friends are affected by the little person you have brought into the world.

Your baby's happiness and emotional development depend on having a harmonious and stable family life. Whether you are a traditional nuclear family, a lone parent, a step family, or same sex parents doesn't matter to your baby. He will thrive in whatever sort of family he is born into. What does count is that everyone from the youngest to the oldest feels valued and cherished and that family members communicate well and respect each other's uniqueness. A baby brought up in such a home will grow up to be a self-confident person who is affectionate and secure.

Family life isn't always easy, but a loving environment is one of the best gifts you can give to your baby. This chapter is all about how to create that and includes – because it is vital to all families of young babies – a section on the health of the mother. For the sake of simplicity, the chapter refers to the more common family unit of mother, father, and baby. If your family differs, please adapt the information accordingly.

Well mother

THE TRANSITION TO PARENTHOOD, though richly rewarding, can be tiring and emotionally draining. New mothers have powerful feelings and for fathers too, the weeks and months following birth are often a time of intense and contradictory emotions. Paying special attention to taking care of yourself emotionally and physically while remaining sensitive to each other's needs will help you to get through this exciting, tumultuous, but often stressful period.

Going out regularly with your baby in the fresh air is healthy for you and is a delightful way to spend time with your baby.

For a new mother your life with a young baby, though generally a happy time, can be all-consuming. You will find that your whole being is focused on your baby and you may have little time or energy left over for anything or anyone else. If you've had an absorbing career or lifestyle the change in your priorities can come as a shock. A sense of loss of the stimulation and indepedence of your former life may vie with the joy, love, and pride you feel for your baby. In time you will become more comfortable and fulfilled by your new role as a mother. In the meantime, treat yourself gently and try not to do too much besides caring for your baby. Life will get easier as your baby becomes more settled and predictable. As a mother it is important to have confidence in your ability to do what is right for you, your partner, and your baby. When faced with conflicting advice, trust yourself and find your own way. Nobody knows your baby better than you do.

PHYSICAL WELLBEING

Throughout the first year of your baby's life, it is essential to rest when you can and to try to take a short break regularly to pamper yourself, while someone trusted looks after your baby. Nurture your body with healthy, nourishing food and, as soon as you can, make time for exercise. It takes about six months for your body to regain its former strength after childbirth. You can support this recovery by taking safe forms of exercise during this time, such as postnatal yoga, pilates, walking, swimming, or modified exercise in a gym. It is best to avoid all forms of strenuous exercise until your body has fully recovered from pregnancy and birth.

NUTRITION

As a new mother, you need to pay attention to your diet in order to rebuild your reserves following pregnancy and to provide for your own needs while looking after a young baby. If you are breastfeeding, you need to be especially careful about diet. The nutrients needed for breast milk come from your body. When nutrients are not available from your diet they are drawn from your bones and fat stores. Loss of calcium and other minerals from your skeleton can increase your risk of

COMMON BREAST PROBLEMS

Some mothers have no difficulties with breastfeeding, but the following problems are common, especially in the beginning. Always consult a breastfeeding counsellor or midwife for advice and support.

Sore or cracked nipples

Soreness usually results from the baby not latching on correctly. See page 46 for advice on latching on. A crack on your nipple (similar to a crack that you can get on your lips when you have a cold) can be very painful, particularly at the start of a feed. It is best to continue breastfeeding if you have sore or cracked nipples. If you stop feeding, the breast may become engorged (see page 51), and worsen the problem. The beginning of the feed, before the let down, is usually the most painful time and this should ease as the milk flow increases. Some slow deep exhalations will help you to get through this pain.

The following treatments and advice may be helpful:

✿ Apply a compress of finely grated carrot on a pad.

✿ Apply a small quantity of pure lanolin or a greasy nipple cream to the nipples and areolae between feeds or try herbal ointments that include calendula or chickweed.

✿ Start feeding on the less painful side and be sure to break the baby's suction carefully with your little finger and never pull the baby off the breast.

✿ Try varying the breastfeeding position and using the underarm hold (see page 45).

✿ Consult a homeopath. Suitable homeopathic remedies include chamomilla, graphites, and sulphur.

Blocked milk duct

This appears as a tender sore lump on the breast and is usually cleared by the baby feeding frequently. It may also help to apply heat to the breasts in the form of warm water (in the bath or shower) or by applying warm compresses.

Then apply a light vegetable oil, massage the breast gently with your fingers and palm from the base of the breast, above the sore spot and down toward the nipple. Continue gently kneading above the sore area while feeding.

Mastitis

This is an infection in the breast, which is most likely to occur in the early months, but can happen at any time while you are breastfeeding. Your breasts may be swollen or engorged, you may notice a tender, hot, red area on the breast and feel achy and feverish. Continued frequent breastfeeding is usually the best cure for mastitis, even if it feels very sore to begin with. Homeopathic treatment is often successful, but you will need to see your doctor for antibiotics if there is no improvement within 24 hours.

✿ Rest and drink lots of fluids. A herbal infusion of cleavers, marigold, mullein, and dandelion root will help to alleviate congestion and inflammation.

✿ Take 1,000mg of vitamin C a day.

✿ While taking antibiotics and for a week or two afterwards, eat plenty of live yogurt or take Lactobacillus acidophilus tablets to replace the natural microorganisms in the gut.

Pain on breastfeeding

Some women experience pain while feeding that has nothing to do with incorrect positioning. This results from vasospasm (contraction of the blood vessels), caused by exposure to cold or emotional stress. If you have this problem, consult a breastfeeding counsellor. Evening primrose oil or fish oil supplements may be effective, but results can take up to six weeks to show. Warming the breasts before feeding, feeding in a warm room, and/or taking deep breaths at the start of the feed may be helpful.

PAMPER YOURSELF

In the early days, there may not be much time to pay attention to yourself or your appearance. Once your baby is a little older, a new outfit, haircut, visit to a beautician, or a complementary treatment, can boost your confidence and self-esteem.

The caring touch of an aromatherapy massage can be wonderfully nurturing. It can lift fatigue, leaving you relaxed and ready to care for your baby.

osteoporosis in later life. While you are breastfeeding it is vital for your energy levels now and your future health, to eat three nourishing meals a day and to drink plenty of fluids. Now is not the time to diet: depriving your body of food can affect your moods, cause low energy, and may contribute to depression. In any case breastfeeding will help you to shed any excess weight, although it may take 12 months or more to regain your pre-pregnancy weight.

To ensure that your breast milk contains a minimum of environmental pollutants aim to eat a well-balanced, mainly fresh, organic diet. Have plenty of fruit and vegetables, wholegrain carbohydrates, and protein (preferably from lean meat and poultry, oily fish, and pulses). Keep greasy, fried, and sugary foods to a minimum. You should also avoid alcohol, nicotine, unnecessary drugs and medications, caffeine (in coffee, tea, chocolate, soft drinks), and artificial sweeteners.

Whether or not you are breastfeeding, you will benefit from a daily multivitamin and mineral supplement specially made for the postnatal period. This can be particularly useful if you are anaemic, emotionally upset, stressed, depressed, or have cravings for sweets. A nutritionist or good supplier of supplements can suggest a suitable one, but remember that supplements are not a substitute for a healthy, well-balanced diet. See Resources for suggested further reading on this subject.

EMOTIONAL WELLBEING

A few days after birth, oestrogen levels plummet and are replaced by floods of the mothering hormone prolactin (see page 24). Secretion of prolactin is stimulated by close contact with your baby and this is the way nature prevents postnatal depression. However, these massive hormonal changes can make you feel very emotional in the first few days following the birth. Separation from your baby due to complications can result in temporary feelings of depression, which may lift when close contact resumes. Throughout the world, childbirth is seen as a rite of passage, a transition from one state of being to another. Sadly, the traditional support given to new mothers in many cultures is often missing in our own.

POSTNATAL DEPRESSION

Postnatal depression (PND), defined as "a profound and consistent lowering of mood" following childbirth, may in part be a reflection of lack of support. It often creeps up insidiously in the weeks and months following birth and may be mistaken for tiredness both by the mother and those around her and by medical professionals. Symptoms include tearfulness, irritability, anger, or simply feeling "flat" and joyless. Sometimes depression can be masked by excessive activity. Often such feelings are worse early in the day when it may be difficult getting out of bed or you can feel "paralysed" and almost unable to do practical babycare tasks. Other indications that you may be depressed include difficulty concentrating and thinking clearly, feeling exceptionally tired all the time, having problems sleeping – for example, waking in the night and being unable to drop off again — appetite changes – for example, eating less or more than usual – feeling hopeless, desperate, or having suicidal thoughts. Often the roots of the depression go back to events in the mother's childhood or early adult life, with issues coming up after birth that may have been suppressed before. This can feel overwhelming, along with the reality of caring for a baby and result in depression. Full-blown puerperal psychosis – in which the mother temporarily loses contact with reality – is rare and tends to begin fairly soon after birth.

Talking with other mothers who face similar challenges is very supportive. You need friends with whom you can share the experiences of new motherhood and enjoy the stimulation of adult conversation.

Some women with mild PND often find relief from counselling or complementary treatments such as yoga, and meditation. Research has shown that baby massage helps to enhance your relationship with your baby and lift depression. However, if depression persists, psychotherapy or medical treatment may be needed to get to the root of the problem and in extreme cases a mother and her baby may need to be admitted to a special hospital for a while, where the staff are trained to help recovery. Whatever route you take, immediate support, comfort, and help with specific problems are vital. If at any time following birth you feel overwhelmed, anxious, or persistently low don't try to struggle on alone. Seek advice from your doctor or other health professional. An appropriate self-help organization may also be able to provide support and and advice (see Organizations, page 186).

FATHERS' FEELINGS

The early weeks have their ups and downs for fathers too. Recent research even suggests that new fathers may experience a hormonal upheaval that parallels that experienced by the new mother. Whether or not this is true, this time is very special but it may come as a surprise how much time and attention a newborn baby needs. Even though you love your baby, you may feel neglected, and excluded from the intense bond that exists between mother and baby. It is natural, especially if you haven't had much contact with babies, to feel apprehensive about your role and the long-term responsibility fatherhood involves. Keeping the lines of communication open with your partner (see page 139) and spending time with other dads or couples with children can help practically and emotionally.

You and your partner

A LOVING RELATIONSHIP BETWEEN you and your partner is the foundation for a strong and secure family. However, the transition from being a couple to being the parents of a new baby presents challenges for most couples. The birth of a baby – however much wanted – can place unanticipated strain on a relationship. Parenthood may bring a revolution in roles, lifestyle, and expectations. The way you think about the world may suddenly become quite different and your priorities may change. In the months following your baby's birth, your relationship will inevitably be different as you adjust to being parents.

Pregnancy is often a time of unusual closeness, but research reveals that once the baby is born, parents' satisfaction with their relationship tends to decrease. The demands of a new baby are pressing and relentless, and mothers and fathers can find their daily lives diverge, perhaps for the first time since they met. It is easy for a situation to develop in which everyone feels that their needs are not being met

You need to be alone together sometimes without your baby. Making the time to talk regularly and to nurture your relationship will help you to work together as a team in parenting your baby.

and for this to fuel resentment and frustration. Your ability to survive and emerge stronger and closer depends on your capacity to work together and to recognize and understand each other's needs.

NURTURING EACH OTHER

Couples who care for each other are sensitive to each other's needs and willing to compromise. Listening, talking, touching, and showing your love for each other are all ways to nurture and sustain your relationship as you grow into your new roles.

The ability to be flexible and to take into account your changed situation is important. For the father this may mean rearranging work or leisure activities to make yourself more available for your new family. For the mother it may mean standing aside and allowing your partner the chance to get involved in caring for the baby, even if he doesn't do things in exactly the way you would. Nurturing each other may also mean accepting that your partner needs to spend time apart from you and the baby sometimes to pursue his or her own interests as well as making time to spend alone with each other doing things you both enjoy.

COMMUNICATION

With a new baby in your life, it's all too easy to fall out of the habit of good communication. The spontaneous intimate moments and conversations that used to occur as you went about your daily lives tend to get put off, because you are both so busy. Planning to spend regular time together talking and listening, just as you would schedule a meeting or a business appointment, becomes a necessity rather than a luxury. You may need to overcome some resistance to such an apparently contrived focus on relating, especially if communication is not your strong point. It is well worth finding a regular time and space to be alone sometimes without your baby, to talk and to take care of your relationship. However awkward it may seem at first, you and your partner need to understand and support each other through honest and intimate conversation. Both of you need to learn to recognize and accept your own and each other's positive and negative feelings.

MIXED FEELINGS

In addition to the joy a baby brings you, there may also be feelings of frustration and guilt that the early days of parenthood are not as you dreamed they would be. The early weeks can be stressful as well as blissful, especially if you have a high-need baby. You need to work through these difficult times together as a team, and help each other to put aside the myths of ideal babies who sleep through the night and "superparents", who get it right all the time.

Maintaining common interests and a shared outlook are the best ways to keep your bond alive. A dinner in a quiet restaurant, so you don't need to bother with

WORKING IT OUT

Researchers Belsky and Kelly in their book, *The Transition to Parenthood: How a first child changes a marriage* (see Resources), define six areas that need to be bridged in the transition from couple to parents:
✿ Developing a joint identity as parents and working together as a team.
✿ Resolving differences about the division of labour and your respective roles.
✿ Handling stress in a way that doesn't impact on your partner.
✿ Learning to manage disagreements constructively and to maintain common interests.
✿ Realizing and accepting that however good your partnership becomes, it is changed forever by the birth of a baby.
✿ Communicating in a way that keeps your relationship alive.

shopping or cooking that day, is an excellent weekly ritual to include in your life. Until he is old enough to leave behind with a babysitter for a little while, if you can find a breastfeeding-friendly restaurant, baby can come too. While your baby is very young, it may be easier to have a luxurious late breakfast alone together at a time when your baby usually naps.

DEALING WITH CONFLICT

Misunderstandings and disagreements are inevitable from time to time in any relationship. Making a real effort to listen to your partner and understand his or her point of view, especially when it is different from your own, will strengthen your relationship. The ability to reach a mutual compromise is crucial. It is easy if you are tired or stressed, to develop a pattern of negative communication. Tiredness can place a huge strain on the relationship and sleep deprivation creates irritability, which sometimes makes good communication difficult. If exhaustion is getting the better of you, take a break either while your baby sleeps, or while someone else takes over for a few hours. You are going through a momentous life change so try to be kind and respectful to each other, rather than getting annoyed if you find it difficult to relate to your partner. One useful tip when dealing with differences, is to make a time to discuss whatever it is you disagree about and then for each of you to talk openly for five minutes in turn about your feelings. During this time all you do is listen without interruption, judgement, or blame. In addition, don't forget to let your partner know about all the things you appreciate about him or her.

Always try to resolve issues and conflicts in private away from your baby and other young children, since they understand far more than most people realize. Avoid talking over your baby assuming that he can't understand. The fact that they can't speak does not mean that babies are not sensitive to what is going on around them. Sort out conflict in private so that you can create a united front and support each other. This is an important parenting skill to develop from the outset.

KEEPING ROMANCE ALIVE

Parents are also lovers and once the early weeks are over and your body has recovered from childbirth, you may need to make more effort than previously to keep the flame alive. Sex is an area of concern for many partners in pregnancy and after birth. Men and women's sexual needs often diverge as new parents. Many (but not all) women temporarily lose interest in sex after childbirth and this can go for several months. When you've been looking after a small baby the very last thing you may feel inclined to do at the end of a busy, tiring day is to make love, although you may still want your partner to hold and caress you. If you are breastfeeding, another factor is that the hormone prolactin, produced copiously during breastfeeding, suppresses the desire for sex. The drop in oestrogen levels following birth can lead to vaginal dryness and, if you had an episiotomy or a bad tear, to pain or fear of pain during intercourse that can make you anxious about penetrative sex.

A man's libido, meanwhile, remains unaltered, and you may feel frustrated, neglected, and rejected. It will help if you are able to understand that it is not that your partner has "gone off sex", but simply that most of her energy and emotions are, for the time being, focused on your baby.

It can be difficult to talk about such personal issues, but it will help to discuss your emotions and to reassure each other that you still love each other. If you are a woman you may need to explain the changes that are going on in your body to your partner and tell him that you still need him and that he is not to blame for your disinclination to make love. If you are a man, you will probably need to take it slowly and to show your partner that you care for and love her by being sensitive to her needs and feelings at this time. Be creative and try to think of other ways to express your loving feelings for each other. Intercourse is not the only way to make love and a sensual massage can be very nurturing. When you do finally make love for the first time after the birth, treat it as a special occasion and take time to woo your partner and make her feel cherished. After a luxurious soak in a scented bath, give your partner a sensuous massage with aromatherapy oils. A new mother may need more time to get aroused and it will usually help to use a lubricant. Be gentle and allow your partner to take the lead. Experiment with positions to find the most comfortable. It is perfectly natural for breast milk to leak out during lovemaking, as the hormone oxytocin that is involved in letting down the milk is also involved in sexual arousal and orgasm. Lying side by side or with the female partner on top is often more comfortable than the traditional missionary position, especially if your partner is still tender from an episiotomy or tear. She may find it more comfortable if you penetrate her before your penis is fully erect. Go slowly and avoid powerful thrusting for the time being.

CONTRACEPTION

Even if your partner is still breastfeeding and hasn't had a period yet, you'll need to use contraception if you don't want to conceive another baby. It is impossible to tell with any certainty when the first ovulation after childbirth has taken place. Discuss suitable contraceptive options with your family planning adviser.

New mothers can feel exhausted afer a day of carrying and feeding a baby. A gentle massage will help to relieve tension in the shoulders, neck, and upper back and make her feel cared for and nurtured.

Sibling relationships

WELCOMING A NEW BABY INTO A HOUSEHOLD when you already have one or more older children is a different experience from having a first baby on whom to focus all your love and attention. The arrival of a new baby completely alters family dynamics and you'll need all your reserves of patience, energy, and insight to make sure that everyone's needs are met. It surprises most parents of second and subsequent children how having a tiny newborn makes their other children suddenly seem huge, even when they are barely more than a baby themselves. It may be hard for you to give your older child the time and attention he is used to, while you are recovering from the birth and taking care of the new baby. However, it is important to make the time to give him some special attention, for example, while the baby is sleeping.

REGRESSIVE BEHAVIOUR

Older children need time to get used to having a new baby in the family. They are bound to have mixed feelings about the new arrival. Excitement and fascination mix with understandable feelings of anger and jealousy. It is common for an older child to revert to more babyish behaviour for a little while. For example, he may start wetting or soiling again or wetting the bed at night. He may want to suckle from your breast or from a bottle (let him have a try to satisfy his curiosity), have a dummy or comfort object, or revert to a more babyish way of talking. It is best not to appear shocked or get annoyed. Instead try to give your older child some

---

COPING WITH SIBLING RIVALRY

Some children react well to the arrival of a new sibling while others become demanding and unsettled. An older child may ask for the baby to be sent back to the hospital, for example, or may become over-boisterous when playing with the baby. Sibling rivalry is normal, but how rivalry develops in your family will depend on how you handle it and on the ages and personalities of your children. There are some steps you can take to minimize problems:

❀ Try to reduce disruption to your older child's life by sticking to his usual routines and making any major changes to sleeping arrangements well before the baby arrives.

❀ Make a fuss of your older child as much as possible and when talking about the baby involve your older child, for example show him photos of when he was a baby and remind him he once had tiny fingers and toes like his new sibling.

❀ Do things alone with your older child away from the baby such as a walk or outing or a game.

❀ Let him know it's all right to feel as he does, by agreeing that babies can be noisy and smelly at times.

❀ If the baby starts crying when you are doing something with your older child don't just drop everything to meet his needs. Take time and apologize for the interruption. Reassure your child that you'll come back and carry on whatever you were doing after you've attended to the baby.

time on your own together. Praise him for "grown up" behaviour and play up the advantages of being "big" such as being able to have friends round to play, go to school or kindergarten (if this is something he enjoys), or stay up later at night.

MAKING TIME FOR ALL YOUR CHILDREN

Even though you feel intensely preoccupied with the new baby, you may need to make a concerted effort to be there for your older children at first, reassuring them that your love for them hasn't changed. As you get to know your new baby and life becomes more settled and predictable, it will came naturally to spread your affection and attention between all your children. In the meantime some of the care of older children can be taken over by your partner, grandparents, or a helper. However, it is also wise to hand the baby over sometimes, so you can be with your older child alone and do things together, without being interrupted by the demands of the newborn. Make a point of including your older child whenever you can by reading a story, listening to a tape, or doing a puzzle, while feeding, bathing with both children together, or going on outings.

DEVELOPING RELATIONSHIPS

Small babies are usually a source of great fascination to older children, and it is important to allow your older child to develop his or her independent relationship with the baby. However, it isn't always easy for siblings to know how to interact with the baby while he is still small and helpless. From soon after birth encourage your child to hold the baby – and play with him. At first this may simply involve showing your older child how the baby will grasp his finger or look at his face. As the baby gets older this will develop naturally to include proper toys and games. Help your older child to play with his new sibling by showing him what the baby likes – for example, shaking a rattle, talking to the baby, holding a mirror for the baby to look in, hiding an object under a cup or cloth and letting the baby "find" it, or playing peek-a-boo. The attention given to a baby by older children can be a source of great stimulation, although you should be on the look out for the natural expressions of rivalry that go along with sibling affection.

Give your baby and older child plenty of opportunities to communicate and trust your older child to hold the baby while seated in a safe place. This will encourage affectionate and protective feelings, while stimulating your baby's development.

Support with parenting

IN MANY PARTS OF THE WORLD new parents are part of a wide supportive network consisting of the extended family and other members of the community. The first weeks after birth are thought of as a time to rest. Special post-birth rituals exist to ensure that the new mother has the time and seclusion she needs to recover from the birth and get used to caring for her baby. The modern nuclear family structure most common in the West can be tough on new parents. This is especially true if one of you is the main carer of the baby, while the other is the breadwinner, trying to combine building a relationship with the baby and going out to work. It is essential to find some support so that caring for your new baby is pleasurable and not overwhelming. The main thing is to develop a stable support network that is consistent with your parenting style.

SOURCES OF SUPPORT

In an ideal world, new parents would get support in the home for at least six weeks after the birth to allow them time to settle down together as a family. If there is any way you can arrange this, your transition to parenthood will be much easier. Grandparents, if they live nearby or can come and stay, can be a wonderful source of support – provided you get on and they respect your privacy and the way you want to care for your baby. Friends and relatives with babies or small children themselves, can often be helpful, too. Simple acts of kindness or generosity such as bringing round a meal, doing your washing up, or looking after the baby while you rest, can be a tremendous help and make you feel cherished and

If you are lucky enough to have them nearby, your relatives can be wonderfully supportive. They love you and your baby and their relationship with your child gives him a sense of belonging to a wider family.

cared for. Alternatively, if your finances can stretch to it, you might consider having a home help or a doula. The term, which derives from Greek for servant or slave, refers to someone who cares for the mother postnatally (and in some instances accompanies her in labour), allowing her to concentrate on caring for the baby and breastfeeding. Doulas are fairly common in the US and are becoming more widely available in the UK (see Organizations, page 186).

SUPPORTIVE RELATIONSHIPS

In the weeks and months following birth, many new parents find themselves becoming closer to their own parents. You may remember incidents from your childhood and thereby gain new insights into the feelings of your parents. When grandparents are able to have contact with their grandchildren a special relationship often develops that means a lot to all concerned. If grandparents do not live nearby, regular telephone calls will help to keep them up to date with what is happening in your family. Photos sent by post or via the internet are always greatly appreciated and help to maintain contact.

Without the responsibility of full time care, grandparents often have more time and energy to play, and your child can benefit from spending time with other people who love him.

In a society where most of us no longer have relatives living around the corner, friends are crucial. Most new parents soon build a network of other families with babies around the same age. This enables you to get some adult company with whom you can share the ups and downs of new parenthood. You might also like to explore whether there are any postnatal groups or classes, such as a baby massage class, where you can be with your baby in the company of other new mothers and fathers. Times spent at these events can help you feel supported and give you renewed energy and enthusiasm for parenting, Many enduring friendships are formed in this way.

WORK AND CHILDCARE

Many mothers need to combine parenting with work outside the home. When the time comes, you may welcome the break from intense full-time care of your baby or you may feel it a terrible wrench to return to work as early as your maternity leave requires. The truth is that most mothers have mixed feelings about juggling motherhood with work ouside the home. Some mothers surprise themselves by discovering that they want to stay at home and, if this applies to you and you can afford it, you may want to consider delaying your return to work, working part-

COMBINING BREASTFEEDING AND WORK

There are various ways in which you can do this, depending on the practicalities in your particular situation. These include:

✿ Continue to breastfeed when you are with your baby and express milk at work to be fed to him by bottle while you are away.

✿ Have your carer bring your baby to work for feeds and cuddles.

✿ Go home to feed your baby in the day.

✿ Have your baby fed with formula when you are working and breastfeed at other times.

time, or giving up work altogether for a while. Some mothers take a less demanding job – even if only temporarily – that allows them to spend more time with their baby. Some find ways to work at home and, if this is an option for you, it can be a good solution. Others feel confident that it is right for them to combine outside work with motherhood. You need to create the best solution for you and your family.

If you must go back to work, there are ways you can maintain the close connection you have with your baby. Carry on breastfeeding if you can as this will nourish and strengthen your attachment (see box). A breast-feeding counsellor and some planning with your employer will help. When you are at home, have lots of body contact with your baby – for example, by using a baby carrier and sleeping with your baby at night. Be prepared to spend time with your baby after work, perhaps encouraging a long afternoon nap. Fostering closeness will help you and your baby to cope with the separations.

CHILDCARE OPTIONS

Your baby needs to be held, carried, and communicated and played with. This can be successfully and harmoniously done by someone else who is sensitive and responsive to his needs. There are several childcare choic-es, including workplace crèche, nursery, childminder, or nanny – each with its pros and cons. Consistency of care from a loving carer is essential, so when con-

CHOOSING A CARER

The following tips may be helpful in making your choice:

✿ Seek a carer through personal recommendation or through a reputable agency.

✿ Look for someone who understands your style of parenting and will keep it going in your absence.

✿ Observe whether your baby feels physically comfortable with the potential carer.

✿ Interview several candidates before making your choice.

✿ Check qualifications. A basic qualification should include childcare and development, feeding, health and hygiene, and first aid.

✿ Check previous experience. Find out how long the person was in her previous job, what her responsibilities were, why she decided to leave.

✿ If you have older children as well, ask how she will cater for their needs.

✿ Follow up all references in writing and on the telephone.

✿ Do not employ anyone under 18.

✿ Be very specific about how you expect your baby to be cared for, including feeding, sleeping, and comforting.

✿ Be clear about pay and the use of household facilities, such as the telephone. Don't be embarrassed about putting key guidelines in writing.

✿ Make sure your carer knows where to contact you at all times and leave a full list of telephone numbers for yourselves, other relatives, doctor, emergency services.

✿ When meeting the person for the first time observe her closely and try to pick up on cues. Does she seem honest, reliable, genuinely fond of and interested in your baby. Does she know what to expect of a small baby or child? How does your baby react to her?

✿ Follow your gut feelings and refuse the job to anyone that you have instinctive reservations about, even if they have the right qualifications.

sidering your options, choose carefully and try to make arrangements that will remain stable for the forseeable future. Depending on your baby's personality, the familiarity of a home environment may be important. You'll need to take this into account when deciding which type of childcare to choose. What is important is that the person who cares for your baby while you are absent is in tune with your style of parenting. If you have the option, one good solution may be sharing care with family members – grandparents, aunts/uncles, older cousins. Provided they are capable and trustworthy, this is a wonderful way to foster your child's relationship with his extended family.

THE RIGHT PERSON OR PLACE

Before leaving your baby with anyone, spend time with them to see how they interact with him. Have a potential carer visit you and your baby while you are home or spend some time at the nursery or home of the childminder when other children are there. When choosing a carer for your baby, find someone who is motherly and fun, who will hold and comfort your baby when necessary, and interact with him in the right way when he is in the mood for play. Such relationships contribute to your baby's world and enhance his development without disturbing the primal bond with you as parents. There is a vast difference between choosing an occasional babysitter, who will spend only brief periods with your baby (often when he is asleep) and employing a long-term carer, who will spend long periods of time with your baby and have an enduring influence on his world and development. It may be sufficient for a babysitter to have experience with and like babies and small children, but it is crucial that any regular carer is fully trained and qualified as well as sensitive to your baby and in tune with your ideas.

If you are employing a full-time nanny to care for your baby at home, think carefully about asking her to help with housework. It is wise not to burden your nanny with chores so she can concentrate on the main job of nurturing your baby the way you would yourself if you were there. It is important for your nanny to make use of the same support groups that you yourself would use.

> **NURSERIES AND WORKPLACE DAYCARE**
>
> Make sure any nursery you are considering meets legal requirements for registration and insurance. When visiting, observe whether the nursery is clean and safe, look out for a garden or outdoor space, and check how it is supervised. Look at the toys and equipment – are there sufficient for the number of children and are they clean and undamaged? Are they appropriate for the stage of development of the children? Find out what kind of qualifications and experience the staff have and what is the ratio of staff to children (one carer to three babies or small children is a minimum). Ideally, each baby should be able to bond with one carer, who is there consistently. Above all observe the children – do they on the whole seem happy and contented? Once your baby is settled at the nursery, visit regularly – sometimes unannounced.

Your baby needs to be able to trust the person who cares for her while you are away. Choose someone who will hold your baby a lot and comfort her when she cries.

Natural healthcare for your baby

Babies are usually remarkably robust, but equally, falling ill from time to time is a natural part of childhood. No matter how attentive parents are, accidents can happen, or in rare cases a baby can become seriously ill. While it is always wise to consult your doctor when your baby seems unwell, babies generally have a natural tendency to self-healing.

A healthy baby will generally overcome minor illnesses and accidents spontaneously with plenty of loving care and often without any special treatment. Getting through illness naturally helps to establish the foundations for a strong immune system as the body learns to ward off and fight infection. In addition, many experts in complementary therapies believe that minor illnesses are a natural mechanism for clearing toxins from the body.

The most important way you can support healing is to devote your time and attention to your baby. A baby who feels unwell may need to be held and comforted much more than usual. In this section you will find home care suggestions and complementary remedies to help support the natural healing processes when your baby is unwell, as well as clear guidance as to when to seek medical help.

Health choices

IT IS ESSENTIAL TO KNOW AHEAD OF TIME who you will consult when your baby is unwell and how to get hold of them quickly. If you wish to include complementary therapies in your baby's healthcare, try to find a family doctor who is sympathetic to these approaches. Locate practitioners of natural therapies such as homeopathy, herbalism, or cranial osteopathy in your area, who have experience working with babies. It is especially important to have expert advice from a qualified practitioner when using homeopathic or herbal remedies, as the treatment needs to be tailored to the individual and progress needs to be monitored. The suggestions I have made below are intended only as guidelines. You will need specific advice on suitable remedies and dosages from your practitioner. Some complementary remedies, herbs, and essential oils may be unsuitable for your baby, so always seek expert advice before you use them.

When your baby is unwell she will let you know by being unusually fretful, wanting to be held and picked up more than usual. She may indicate a pain by rubbing or batting the area with her hand. Alternatively, she may be lethargic and unusually sleepy or lose her appetite.

It is also wise to explore your local medical emergency facilities ahead of time, and discuss with your doctor the best way to summon help urgently in the event of a crisis. Finally read through this chapter at least once before you have a specific problem, so you will know where to find information when you need it. In particular, make sure you are familiar with symptoms that require immediate medical attention (see page 157).

USE OF CONVENTIONAL MEDICINES

Medications such as antibiotics and steroids may be needed if a baby is seriously ill, or if a minor illness doesn't respond to complementary treatment, persists for a long time, or causes undue suffering. However, with most common or minor ailments it is usually possible to avoid unnecessary use of medications with complementary care. Always read the packet insert for any medicine carefully and ask your doctor what to expect from the treatment and whether there may be side effects. Tell your doctor immediately if your child develops an adverse reaction.

ANTIBIOTICS

There is no doubt that antibiotics, when used appropriately, can quash infections that might otherwise become serious or even life threatening. Some bacterial infections (including those affecting the middle ear, throat, or urinary tract) may need antibiotic treatment. However, antibiotics are also commonly prescribed when natural healing is possible and would be much more beneficial to long-term health. Some babies and small children end up taking frequent courses of antibiotics, simply because their parents and doctor may not be aware of any alternatives. Many parents, natural practitioners, and medical professionals are concerned about the unnecessary use of antibiotics because of the risk of side effects. These may include:

✿ Allergic reactions.

✿ Reduced resistance to infection and disease, because antibiotics kill beneficial organisms in the gut, as well as harmful ones, and this may affect digestion and elimination and weaken the immune system.

✿ Over-frequent use of antibiotics may also increase the risk of recurrent infections, post-viral syndrome, and other chronic problems.

✿ Thrush (candida), a yeast infection that can follow a course of antibiotics.

✿ Antibiotic resistance, when infective organisms become resistant to antibiotics.

IMMUNIZATION

Paediatricians generally recommend that all babies are immunized, and in some countries immunization is compulsory. While vaccines were first introduced to combat serious infectious diseases, they are now also given for most of the common childhood illnesses and are offered to babies much earlier than they used to be. The arguments for and against immunization go to the very heart of the question of what is health and how we can best help our children to build a strong immune system.

WHAT IS IMMUNIZATION?

Immunization works by stimulating the production of antibodies through the introduction of a weak "live" or "killed" form of a specific infection (or a weakened substance produced by that germ) into the baby's system. In most cases, this gives the baby immunity to the disease. Currently babies are routinely offered immunization against diphtheria, tetanus, polio, measles, mumps, rubella (German measles), pertussis (whooping cough), Haemophilus influenzae type B or Hib (a bacterium that can

MINIMIZING THE SIDE EFFECTS OF ANTIBIOTICS

If your baby is prescribed antibiotics it is essential to finish the prescribed course. Afterward you can replace the flora in the gut by giving your baby a Bifidobacterium supplement for infants, which can be mixed in a little water. It is also advisable to give special mineral and vitamin drops for babies. In addition, if you are breastfeeding, you can also take a Bifidobacterium or Lactobacillus acidophilus supplement yourself, as some will pass into the breast milk.

BREAST MILK: THE NATURAL MEDICINE

The colostrum babies consume in the first days of life contains huge amounts of protective antibodies. Later, breast milk changes to provide specific immune factors to combat infections that are prevalent in the environment (see page 39). Feeding frequently is often the first line of treatment if you are breastfeeding. Sometimes an unwell baby may not seem hungry and may prefer regular sips of water. While this is a normal reaction for an unwell baby, it can also be a sign that a baby is more seriously ill, so be sure to check with your doctor.

cause meningitis), and meningitis C. Immunization against hepatitis B may also be offered and is routine in some countries.

THE DEBATE

Most medical professionals argue that immunization gives children protection against potentially devastating childhood illnesses and prevents them spreading through the community – a phenomenon known as herd immunity. They point out that before the existence of vaccines, many thousands of children and babies developed serious complications or died in epidemics of childhood illnesses. While most babies will recover well from the less serious childhood illnesses, a few babies will always be at risk of becoming very ill. While immunologists acknowledge that vaccines can cause side effects, they maintain that, overall, the life-saving benefits of immunization greatly outweigh the risks. The anti-immunization lobby argue that improvements to lifestyle, diet, and healthcare are the primary factors that have led to reduced mortality, and that suppressing some illnesses leads to the emergence of others. They maintain that the occurrence of disease is cyclical and is the main reason why some illnesses are no longer prevalent. There are also concerns raised by research about the effectiveness of certain vaccines in preventing disease. There are still many questions and no easy answers.

The following concerns about routine immunization have been raised:

❀ While immunization may protect against acute illnesses (short-term illnesses that come on suddenly), the price of this may be an increased incidence of chronic (long-term) disease. Some research suggests that the rise in problems such as asthma, allergies, autism, cot (crib) death, and other conditions may be connected with the introduction of routine immunization.

❀ Although the majority of vaccines cause only minor side effects, a small number result in serious side effects such as encephalitis (brain inflammation), permanent brain damage, and in a few cases death.

❀ While recent reviews of the research claim that they are safe, there have been concerns about the administration of a combination of vaccines together – for example MMR (mumps, measles, rubella) and Hib/DTP (Hib meningitis/diphtheria, tetanus, polio). Some experts feel that there is still insufficient knowledge about how different vaccines given simultaneously react with each other.

❀ Links have been suggested between autoimmune diseases, such as diabetes, in which the body's defence mechanisms attack itself, and immunization.

❀ There is no conclusive research into the potential long-term side effects of vaccines. While we know that

HOMEOPATHIC "VACCINES"

The homeopathic remedies called nosodes are sometimes described as "natural vaccines". These are said to help support the immune system, if a baby has a particular susceptibility to a disease either because of her constitution or because she has been exposed to that illness. Because, like all homeopathic remedies, nosodes contain so little of the active ingredient, they cannot be considered to be vaccines in the true sense of the word. Nosodes are thought to increase resistance to the disease rather than guarantee immunity.

natural disease provides lifelong immunity, we do not know if immunized babies could contract these diseases as adults, resulting in a worse outbreak.

YOUR CHOICES

Even in countries such as the United Kingdom, where immunization is not compulsory, you may be strongly advised by your doctor, friends, or relatives to have your baby immunized. If you decide to go ahead, you can choose to delay or stagger some immunizations until your child is older and more at risk of contracting these diseases. A newborn baby, for instance, is unlikely to sustain a deep puncture wound that could lead to tetanus infection and you could therefore opt to delay tetanus until she is walking and actively exploring the outside world, if she is in an area where tetanus is a threat. Interestingly, Japan has the lowest infant mortality rate in the world, yet vaccinations are not given to babies until after the first year. You may also choose for your baby to have some vaccinations but not others, based on individual circumstances. In some countries vaccines can be given separately rather than in combination. In reaching a decision:

❀ Consider your lifestyle and the risks to which your child is likely to be exposed. For example, a fully breastfed baby, who consumed a large quantity of colostrum and is likely to be breastfed throughout infancy, is less vulnerable to infection than a partially breastfed or formula-fed baby. There is no guarantee that a fully breastfed baby won't catch diseases, but they are likely to manifest more mildly.

❀ Consider the implications of your child contracting a childhood illness or a serious disease or suffering the side effects of a vaccination. Write them down. This may help you to weigh up your priorities.

❀ Gather as much evidence-based information as you can about the pros and cons of immunization and the different vaccines. (See Resources).

❀ Discuss all the issues with your partner or support person and with an informed, sympathetic professional such as your family doctor and/or an alternative or complementary practitioner.

MINIMIZING PROBLEMS

❀ An unwell baby is considered to be at increased risk of damage by vaccination, so make sure that she is completely well on the day of immunization. It is also important for your physician to assess the health of your child before vaccinating.

❀ Vitamin A and C supplements given in the weeks before a baby is immunized may help reduce the risk of complications and may also strengthen your baby's immune system.

❀ Ask a homeopathic practitioner about remedies that may help counter side effects before your baby is immunized and give them to your baby as advised.

NATURAL RESILIENCE

While not guaranteeing immunity to infectious illnesses, you can optimize your family's resilience to disease with a healthy, natural way of living. Promote vitality and good health through the following healthy lifestyle choices:

❀ Eat organically produced food with a high proportion of fresh fruit and vegetables in your diet.
❀ Ensure regular exposure to fresh air and sunshine.
❀ Get regular exercise and practise good posture.
❀ Allow time for plenty of rest and sound sleep.
❀ Maintain healthy relationships and a happy heart.
❀ Foster a positive mental attitude and peaceful mind.
❀ Provide a healthy home environment.
❀ Avoid toxins and chemical pollutants.

The basic tenets of attachment parenting – loving relationships, ongoing affectionate physical contact, and breastfeeding – plus all of the above, will help your baby to develop optimal resilience and positive health.

Complementary therapies

NATURAL THERAPIES SUCH AS HOMEOPATHY, herbalism, aromatherapy, cranial osteopathy, and flower essences are especially suitable for babies because of their safety and gentle action. These therapies work on the principle that the body has the ability to heal itself. They are designed to support the body as it recovers, to correct any imbalances of energy, and strengthen natural defences. Used correctly, they should have no dangerous or unwelcome side effects.

Homeopathic remedies are very easy to administer and can be very effective as a first line of treatment for minor ailments. After an initial consultation, the homeopath may prescribe remedies you can give your baby at home and may then follow up progress over the telephone.

With a little knowledge and experience, you can use natural remedies just as you would over-the-counter medicines to help minor complaints and common illnesses. The information in this chapter will help to point you in the right direction. It is also advisable to seek the advice of an appropriate practitioner who has experience in treating babies. Do not use natural therapies to treat serious or more complex medical conditions except under the supervision of a qualified practitioner. Natural remedies are not intended to be a substitute for conventional treatment in such conditions, but can often be used alongside conventional treatment to support the healing process. Always inform your doctor if you are using natural remedies in case of possible interactions.

HOMEOPATHY

In homeopathy, the symptoms of illness are seen as the body's attempt to heal itself and are therefore encouraged rather than suppressed. For this reason, remedies are prescribed that in a well person would cause the symptoms of the particular illness, in order to stimulate the body's self-healing powers. So, for example, for a cold that causes streaming nose and eyes, Allium cepa, a remedy derived from red onion, might be indicated. Homeopathic remedies are made from plants, minerals, and other natural materials, which are repeatedly diluted and shaken (succussed) until no trace of the original ingredient can be detected. However, the "energy" of the ingredient remains and this triggers the body's vital force. According to homeopathic thinking, our overall health depends on our constitution – that is, our inherent physical, mental, and emotional characteristics. The periodic use of a remedy that matches your baby's constitution – a constitutional remedy – will improve her general health and enhance her natural ability to fight disease and regain health.

AROMATHERAPY

Essential oils derived from natural plant sources, such as the bark, root, leaves, and flowers of trees, fruits, and herbs, are used in aromatherapy to stimulate healing. The oils may be added to a carrier oil such as grapeseed for massage, mixed in a little milk and dropped into the bath, applied as a compress, or dispersed into the air in a vaporizer or burner.

When inhaled, essential oils stimulate the part of the brain that helps to regulate emotions. When they are absorbed through the skin they travel in the bloodstream to the internal organs. Many essential oils possess specific soothing or healing qualities and can be used very effectively for their calming, antiseptic, antibacterial, or decongestant properties. Essential oils are very powerful and concentrated. They should never be taken internally or used without the guidance of an expert.

HERBALISM

Herbs have been used throughout the ages to heal and cure. Herbal remedies are available in the form of tinctures, ointments, creams, and herbal teas (infusions and decoctions) or can be used in compresses or in the bath. Because the whole plant is used rather than an isolated active ingredient as in orthodox medicine, herbs tend to be remarkably free of side effects. Herbs are most easily given to babies and small children in the form of an infusion or tea. Always seek the advice of a qualified herbalist on suitable herbs and appropriate dosages.

DILUTION OF ESSENTIAL OILS FOR BABIES

Never apply undiluted or neat essential oils to your baby's skin, and don't use essential oils before three months of age.

✿ For application to the skin, add one drop of essential oil to 30ml carrier oil.

✿ For bathing, add one or two drops to a little fresh milk and then add to the bath water.

✿ For inhalation, add one or two drops to water in a vaporizer.

Ensure good quality by purchasing aromatherapy products from a reputable supplier.

Cranial osteopathy involves gentle manipulation of the bones of the skull and lower spine. It is safe for babies and is without side effects.

CRANIAL OSTEOPATHY

The physiological effects of birth may lead to fretful behaviour or other health problems. This therapy is said to balance the flow of cerebro-spinal fluid that bathes the brain and spinal cord. This has been shown to be of benefit in easing the effects of a traumatic birth, reducing colic, incessant crying, reflux, and sleeping or feeding problems. Many paediatricians are impressed by the results. Recent studies confirm the value of this safe treatment for babies.

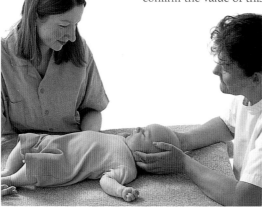

BACH FLOWER ESSENCES

Dr Edward Bach identified 38 plant remedies that he used to counteract the negative emotions that can affect psychological and physical health thereby helping the body to heal itself. A useful remedy is Rescue Remedy, a mixture of Cherry Plum, Clematis, Impatiens, Rock Rose, and Star of Bethlehem, used to counter emotional upset and panic. Flower essences contain alcohol, but can safely be given to a baby as only one or two drops are dropped into the mouth.

YOUR NATURAL HOME REMEDY KIT

This is a simple kit of basic remedies to keep in your home. For the appropriate use of each remedy, read the advice on the relevant ailment or condition later in this chapter and check with a qualified practitioner.

Homeopathic remedies

Soft tablets of 6c or 30c potency are usually best for babies.
Aconite: for the sudden onset of any illness.
Arnica: for falls, knocks, bruises, grazes, and shock.
Belladonna: a remedy for fever and inflammation.
Chamomilla: for teething, earache, and generally calming an upset child.
Arnica cream: for bruises.
Hypercal or calendula tincture: antiseptic and healing for cuts or wounds, or for cleaning the cord stump.
Urtica urens ointment: for minor burns and allergic rashes.
Bryonia alba: for dry coughs.
Rescue Remedy tablets: for shock or upset.

Herbal preparations

Aloe vera gel: for minor burns, cuts, and sunburn.
Calendula cream: for minor burns, scalds, sunburn, nappy (diaper) rash, and other skin problems.
Chamomile cream: for soothing inflamed skin.

Chamomile teabags or loose chamomile flowers: prepared as a tea for stimulating the immune system and calming emotions.
Echinacea tincture: for boosting the immune system at the onset of any infection.
Witch hazel (distilled): for application to bruises.

Bach flower essences

Rescue Remedy tincture: for all kinds of physical and emotional shocks.
Rescue Remedy cream: for cuts, grazes, stings, minor burns, and rashes.

Essential oils

Chamomile: for colic, teething, and calming.
Eucalyptus: for easing breathing in colds, flu, croup, and respiratory infections.
Lavender: for minor burns, inflammation, headaches, teething, and soothing upsets.
Tea tree: antiseptic, for grazes and cuts.

Caring for a sick baby

Your loving attention is the best medicine you can give any baby who is unwell, especially holding and physical contact. Cancel all other arrangements and focus all your attention on your baby. This will help you intuit what she needs to recover most easily. Keep her calm, quiet, and warm – although not too warm if she has a fever (see below). There is generally no need to stay indoors, unless the weather is foul or if she is really ill and cannot be moved. In fact dry, stuffy air can sometimes exacerbate the symptoms. A change of scenery and a dose of fresh air or some mild sunshine could do you both good.

A sick baby may lose her appetite. This is usually nothing to be worried about and in most cases is only temporary. Most sick babies will accept breast milk, so breastfeed little and often. If your baby doesn't

TAKING YOUR BABY'S TEMPERATURE

The most accurate way to take your baby's temperature is via the rectum. However, this is not advisable unless you have been trained how to do it properly. You can also take your baby's temperature with a thermometer under her armpit (as shown), though bear in mind that the reading will be 0.5°C (1°F) lower if you do it this way. Devices that measure temperature inside the ear are more accurate. Forehead strips measure temperature conveniently, although less accurately.

WHEN TO SEEK MEDICAL HELP

It is vital for every parent and carer to be familiar with danger signs that require emergency medical help and also to know the symptoms that require a medical opinion, albeit less urgent, because they may sometimes indicate a serious condition.

Seek emergency medical help if:

✿ Your baby appears limp, apathetic, or is difficult to rouse.
✿ Breathing is difficult, rapid, noisy, or laboured, or she becomes bluish around the lips.
✿ Your baby lost consciousness, for example, after a fall.
✿ Your baby has a fever of 39°C (102°F) or above, or a fever with chills or cold and clammy hands and feet.
✿ Your baby has a dark red rash that does not fade when pressed.
✿ Your baby has a fit for the first time.

Call the doctor promptly if:

✿ Your unwell baby is less than three months old.
✿ Your baby appears to be in severe pain. High-pitched crying can be a sign of pain in a baby.

✿ The soft spot (fontanelle) on your baby's head is bulging.
✿ Diarrhoea (watery bowel movements) or vomiting last longer than a day.
✿ Your baby's bowel movements contain blood and mucus.
✿ Your baby's vomit contains blood, is greenish, or your baby has several episodes of projectile vomiting in which the vomit is ejected forcefully.
✿ There are signs of dehydration such as dry, inelastic skin, more than eight hours without urination, sunken eyes, or sunken fontanelle.
✿ Your baby refuses feeds for longer than six hours.
✿ Your baby's abdomen is distended and tender.
✿ Your baby's cry is unusual – for example, prolonged, weak, or high pitched.
✿ You are concerned about your baby's health for any other reason.

FEBRILE CONVULSIONS

Febrile convulsions (fits) are caused by a rapid increase in body temperature. They affect three to four per cent of children aged six months to five years. In the vast majority of cases they are not harmful. Seek medical help for a first febrile convulsion, if your baby turns blue, if convulsions continue for longer than five minutes, or recur soon after.

want to feed, don't worry about your milk supply – it will soon come back when her appetite increases. If your baby is bottle-fed or being weaned, give small frequent sips of water, fresh juice, clear soup, or herbal teas such as chamomile.

FEVER

A feverish baby feels hotter than usual. Other signs include red cheeks, rapid breathing, sweating, listlessness, and irritability. Normal body temperature (taken by mouth or rectum) in a baby is 36–37°C (97–99°F). A temperature higher than this indicates a fever. A fever is usually a response to a viral infection such as a cold (see page 163). Some babies develop a high fever even with a mild illness, others, even when seriously ill, show only a slightly raised temperature. A fever in itself, unless exceptionally high, is not harmful. It occurs when microorganisms, such as bacteria or viruses, enter the body and provoke a reaction from the immune system. When feverish, the body cools itself by sweating, increased heart rate, and rapid breathing, helping the body to rid itself of toxins. Fever is one of the body's ways of fighting infection.

WHAT YOU CAN DO

The conventional approach is to try to reduce a fever. The natural approach is to keep your baby cool, without being over-concerned to bring about a rapid drop in temperature. Dress her in lightweight, loose-fitting cotton clothes that allow sweat to evaporate (a nappy/diaper and vest is fine for a baby). Keep the room at a comfortable temperature – neither too hot nor too cold – and aired, but free from draughts. The most important indication of when to seek medical help is your baby's general condition, not the figure on the thermometer. See panel on page 157 for symptoms that require urgent medical attention and keep a careful watch for any change in your baby's condition.

A feverish baby needs plenty of fluids to prevent dehydration. Continue breast- or bottle-feeding your baby on demand. You can offer dilute juice, water, or herbal teas as well. As your older baby's appetite revives, you can offer small quantities of fresh raw fruit juices such as carrot juice and vegetables. Offer light meals as soon as she seems interested.

Tepid sponging or a lukewarm compress will help to lower a fever. Avoid cold water as shivering closes down the blood vessels and increases body temperature.

NATURAL REMEDIES

FEVER

With expert guidance, select from the following:

Homeopathy
❀ **Belladonna**: for flushed cheeks and dilated pupils.
❀ **Pulsatilla**: for fever with runny nose, and clinginess.

Herbal remedies
❀ Elderflower, yarrow, lime (linden) flowers, or chamomile help to stimulate sweating. Make an infusion of any one of these and add to a tepid bath.

Aromatherapy
❀ For babies over three months, put a drop or two of lavender oil in the bath or vaporizer, or onto a cold compress to mop her forehead.

Newborn health

THIS SECTION DEALS WITH CONDITIONS that particularly affect babies in the first few weeks following the birth. At this time you will almost certainly be in regular contact with your midwife, family doctor, paediatrician, or other health professional, and can share any concerns you may have about your baby's health. If you think your newborn baby is unwell, seek medical advice without delay.

PREMATURITY AND SPECIAL CARE

Premature babies need to be born in a hospital where intensive care facilities are available. You baby's medical care will be expertly handled by the paediatric team. The type of care needed, whether just a few days of observation, some form of treatment, or life support, will depend on the baby's size and condition. Although the medical team will recommend and carry out any treatment your baby needs, your role is paramount. Bonding with a premature or sick baby is greatly helped by skin-to-skin contact and caring for her whenever you can.

It will make a huge difference to your premature baby to hear your voice, feel your touch, or even just to sense that you are right there. Contact may begin with stroking your baby through the portholes of the incubator and holding her hands and feet. Cuddle her in your arms as soon as this is possible.

WHAT YOU CAN DO

Research has shown that early and frequent contact with the parents, makes the baby absorb oxygen better, and gain weight more quickly. Touch given to pre-term infants through massage reduces stress, enhances development, and improves weight gain, leading to earlier discharge from hospital and later long-term advantages in growth and mental and motor development.

NEONATAL JAUNDICE

It is not uncommon for a newborn to show mild symptoms of jaundice (yellowish skin). This is caused by a high level of bilirubin, a

KANGAROO CARE

In a hospital in Bogotá, where they don't have sophisticated equipment, premature babies are carried snugly inside the mother's clothing. It was noted that these premature babies grow and thrive remarkably quickly. This method known as "kangaroo care" can be adopted in a modern hospital. As soon as you are able to hold your baby, you can try putting her inside your nightdress, against your skin, or use a baby carrier.

normal by-product of the breakdown of red blood cells. Unrestricted frequent feeding will encourage urine production to excrete the bilirubin. The baby may also need extra fluids during this time. Sometimes jaundiced babies can be very sleepy and may need to be woken up for feeds to ensure that they are getting enough fluids. Exposure to mild sunlight is also helpful. An extremely high bilirubin level in the blood increases the risk of deafness or cerebral palsy. This can be prevented by a course of phototherapy (exposure to ultraviolet light).

VITAMIN K DEFICIENCY

Vitamin K is produced by flora in the intestines. It enables blood to coagulate, which stops bleeding from an internal or external wound. All babies are born with low levels of vitamin K. This is because a newborn baby's gut does not yet contain the necessary microorganisms to produce the vitamin and only small quantities are passed through the placenta from the mother's blood. Production of vitamin K normalizes five to ten days after birth. While newborns are unlikely to be injured and bleed, very rarely a baby may develop excessive bruising or bleeding, called vitamin K deficiency bleeding (VKDB), and it can also occur between one and six months of age. Late VKDB is more likely in breastfed than bottle-fed babies because formula milks contain added vitamin K. Although only likely to happen to a tiny minority of babies, VKDB carries the risk of brain damage or death. Therefore giving all babies vitamin K soon after birth is routinely recommended. Research done in the 1990s raised concerns about a link between vitamin K and childhood leukaemia. Several follow up studies have investigated this link without a conclusive result.

Some hospitals offer oral drops instead of the injection. Although considered possibly less effective, these were not associated with cancer risk, and can be given in place of the injection. The drops are usually given after birth, at the end of the first week, and four to six weeks later. For maximum benefit, the entire course must be given at the prescribed times.

WHAT YOU CAN DO

Colostrum (the first milk) and hind milk (the richest milk at the end of the feed) contain more vitamin K. Thus if you begin to feed your baby as soon as he shows an interest after the birth, and you do not limit how long he is at the breast, you will ensure that he gets as much natural vitamin K as possible (see also Why breastfeeding is best, page 38). You can also enhance your diet with foods that contain vitamin K, such as greens and leafy green vegetables, cauliflower, tomatoes, carrots, potatoes, egg yolk, cow's milk, beef, liver, blackstrap molasses, yogurt, wholegrain and oat products, rice bran, and soya beans. You can also increase your intake of vitamin E, which enhances absorption of vitamin K, and avoid too much vitamin A, which inhibits vitamin K absorption. Alfalfa tablets are high in natural vitamin K.

HYPOGLYCAEMIA IN THE NEWBORN

In a full-term baby, blood sugar level normally drops in the first hour after birth and begins to rise again as the baby adapts to life outside the womb. Even babies who don't breastfeed immediately after the birth have a mechanism to gain energy from their own fat stores. One in ten babies risk developing hypoglycaemia, sustained low levels of blood sugar. These include premature or very small babies, unwell babies, and babies of diabetic mothers. If there are no symptoms, low blood sugar levels are rarely a problem. Formula feeds are sometimes recommended to raise blood sugar levels. However, this disrupts establishment of breastfeeding and frequent feeds of colostrum are generally equally effective. If there are initial problems with breastfeeding, spoon, cup, or syringe feed expressed colostrum or breast milk.

DEVELOPMENTAL DYSPLASIA OF THE HIP

About one in 400 babies is born with hip instability when the head of the thigh bone, the femur, slips out of the pelvic socket. Doctors routinely examine newborns and young babies for this problem. Minor hip problems usually stabilize naturally without any treatment during the first month. In some cases the baby may need to wear a harness or splint for six to ten weeks. Let your baby kick freely and carry him in a sling when you can to encourage good development of the hips. Some parents have reported good results from cranial osteopathy.

SUDDEN INFANT DEATH SYNDROME (SIDS)

SIDS, or cot (crib) death, is a very rare but tragic occurrence. The causes are still not fully understood, but a lot of research has been carried out in recent years, which has helped greatly to reduce the incidence of SIDS. The most vulnerable age is around 13 weeks. The latest recommendations to reduce the possibility of SIDS are:

✿ Have your baby sleep with you in your room for at least the first six months.

✿ If you sleep with your baby in your bed, never let her head be covered by a duvet or pillow. Use layers of lightweight cellular blankets instead.

✿ Never sleep with your baby in your bed if you or your partner smoke, have been drinking alcohol, taking drugs, or are extremely tired.

✿ Always put your baby to sleep on her back. Ensure that the feet are close to the foot of the cot (crib) to prevent her moving down (the feet to foot position).

✿ If a five- or six-month-old baby rolls over by herself, put her back on her back. However, there is no need to check repeatedly through the night.

✿ Use a firm, clean, dry mattress that is easy to clean. Don't leave your sleeping baby on a pillow, cushion, bean bag, or waterbed.

✿ Never use a pillow, duvet, or quilt (comforter) for a baby under a year.

✿ Avoid falling asleep with your baby on a sofa. If you feel drowsy put your baby in her usual sleeping place.

✿ Don't swaddle your baby at night, or use a sheepskin, electric blanket, or hot-water bottle.

✿ Avoid overheating the room. Maintain a comfortable temperature between 16–20°C (60–68°F).

✿ Don't let your baby sleep near a radiator or in direct sunlight.

✿ Prevent your baby from becoming overheated. Take off her hat and outdoor clothes when you come indoors, or in a heated car, bus, train, or shop.

✿ Never let anyone smoke in the same room as your baby.

Allergies

ALLERGIES OCCUR WHEN THE IMMUNE SYSTEM over-reacts to a normally harmless substance, known as an allergen, such as pollen, house-dust mites, or particular foods. The body produces antibodies, which are substances that are specially tailored to attack specific allergens. The action of the antibodies produces a variety of symptoms depending on the body system affected. The main allergies that affect babies in their first year are eczema, an allergic reaction affecting the skin (see page 176), asthma, breathing difficulty caused by narrowing of the air passages in the lungs (see page 164), and allergic digestive upsets, leading to diarrhoea or vomiting (see page 168 and Food allergy, intolerance, and sensitivity, below). Susceptibility to allergies is inherited, so if you or your partner have an allergy, your baby is at increased risk.

FOOD ALLERGY, INTOLERANCE, AND SENSITIVITY

True food allergy in which there is an immediate immune response, such as a rash or breathing difficulty, to a particular food is uncommon. It is estimated that a far greater number of children suffer from food intolerance (sometimes called delayed food sensitivity), in which the body is unable to cope with a particular food or foods. The onset of symptoms tends to be delayed, which can make it difficult to diagnose. The most common food allergens are nuts, shellfish, eggs, cow's milk, soya products, and wheat.

Respiratory problems

VIRAL RESPIRATORY INFECTIONS SUCH AS COLDS are the most common minor childhood ailments and are usually easily and simply treated at home. They are the most frequent cause of a raised temperature in babies under one year.

COLDS AND FLU

The common cold is caused by viruses that infect the upper respiratory tract (nose and throat). The familiar symptoms of a cold – runny nose, slight cough, and perhaps fever, help to eliminate the virus from your baby's body. Influenza (flu) is also a viral infection – in fact there are many different flu viruses. The symptoms in a baby are similar to those of a cold, although fever is likely to be higher and your baby may seem more unwell. If you suspect your baby has flu, consult your doctor. There is no specific treatment for either infection; antibiotics are ineffective against viruses and are not usually prescribed unless there is a risk of a secondary bacterial infection.

WHAT YOU CAN DO

If you are breastfeeding, offer the breast more frequently. It is difficult and frustrating for a baby to feed with a blocked nose. A simple tip is to squirt a little breast milk directly up

---

NATURAL REMEDIES

RESPIRATORY INFECTIONS

With expert guidance, select from the following:

Homeopathy

✿ **Aconitum napellus**: for colds or coughs that come on suddenly especially after exposure to cold, a dry, noisy hacking cough that is worse at night.

✿ **Allium cepa**: for a cold with watery discharge from the nose and eyes.

✿ **Belladonna**: for the sudden onset of fever, with a flushed red face.

✿ **Bromium**: for difficult breathing, cramp in chest, croup.

✿ **Bryonia alba**: for a dry, painful cough.

✿ **Pulsatilla**: for a stuffy nose, thick yellowish catarrh.

Herbal remedies

✿ Add a few drops of echinacea tincture to fruit juice for a weaning baby to boost the immune system. Give every two hours during acute infections. If you are breastfeeding, take echinacea yourself.

✿ Give a few teaspoons of chamomile tea to calm a baby who is wakeful because of cold symptoms.

Aromatherapy

For babies over three months:

✿ Add a few drops of eucalyptus or pine essential oils to a vaporizer to ease a blocked nose.

✿ Put one drop each of lavender, eucalyptus, and chamomile in a little warm carrier oil to massage the chest and upper back or add a few drops of each to the bath water.

✿ Put one drop of lavender essential oil on a paper handkerchief or on the bedclothes near to your baby's face when sleeping.

BRONCHIOLITIS

Caused by viral infection of the bronchioles (small airways in the lungs), bronchiolitis may follow a minor infection such as a cold. The main symptoms are a persistent cough or wheezing in addition to the usual cold symptoms. This condition requires urgent medical attention, but with treatment most babies make a full recovery, although a cough may persist for up to six weeks.

the baby's nostrils. This seems to dissolve and dry up the mucus. Stick to a light diet and avoid dairy produce, meat, and wheat, which are mucus-forming. Increase fluid intake by offering an older baby water, juices, soups, and herbal teas. You can keep the air humid with a humidifier, or make the bathroom steamy to open air passages and ease breathing. Your baby may cough to expel mucus that drains to the back of the throat. A warm humid atmosphere and extra fluids, especially warm ones, help open up the passages and loosen catarrh.

CROUP

Croup is caused by infection of the larynx, trachea, and bronchi (large airways). It starts with a cold and the child develops a harsh barking cough with a whistling sound when breathing in, a hoarse voice or cry, and may have difficulty breathing. It is most common at night or in the early morning. If your baby seems otherwise bright and alert, keep the environment humid and treat as for a cold (see above) though it is wise to inform your doctor and to seek immediate medical attention if symptoms worsen. In the meantime take your child into the bathroom and run the hot tap to humidify the air while holding her upright to ease breathing.

ASTHMA

Asthma is an allergic response to inhaled allergens (see Allergies, page 162). The symptoms are a persistent cough, wheezing, laboured breathing, and, in a severe attack, a blueish tinge to the lips. It does not usually occur before the age of six months and, like other allergic conditions, is more common in babies who have not been breastfed. Because a severe asthma attack can in rare cases be life threatening, always consult your doctor if you suspect this condition. Get help urgently for an acute attack of breathing difficulty. Orthodox treatment involves bronchodilator drugs to open the airways and inhaled steroid drugs.

NATURAL REMEDIES

ASTHMA

With expert guidance, select from the following:

Homeopathy

✿ **Arsenicum album**: for a baby with symptoms that are worse in the night or when lying down.
✿ **Chamomilla**: when symptoms are triggered by or accompanied by anger and irritability.
✿ **Pulsatilla**: for a baby with symptoms that are triggered by cold.

Herbal remedies

✿ Give a few teaspoons of chamomile tea to help to relax your baby and alleviate stress.
✿ A few teaspoons of tea made from one of the following herbs may help to relax the bronchi: coltsfoot, hyssop, licorice, mullein, thyme.

WHAT YOU CAN DO

Identify and avoid exposure to allergens. Make sure your baby has plenty of fluids to prevent mucus from becoming dry and thick. If you are breastfeeding, cut down on your own consumption of dairy, sugary, and fried foods. Daily massage may reduce the frequency of asthma attacks. Fresh air and regular exercise, such as baby massage and movement, help to improve lung function. For an acute asthma attack, try Bach Rock Rose or Rescue Remedy while waiting for medical help.

Ear and eye problems

COMMON EAR PROBLEMS IN BABIES INCLUDE middle-ear infection, a boil or a foreign body in the outer-ear canal, inflammation or blockage of the eustachian tube, and teething pain. Ear problems are less common in breastfed babies. Always seek medical advice if you think your baby has reduced hearing. Most eye infections are easily treated. However, always see your doctor about any eye problem.

MIDDLE-EAR INFECTION

This is usually caused by a viral infection, such as a cold, causing blockage of the eustachian tube. This may lead to a secondary bacterial infection. Occasionally the eardrum ruptures to release fluid and pus. Possible symptoms are pain, caused by fluid accumulating in the middle ear and pressing on the eardrum, and a raised temperature, and your baby may seem miserable and unwell with a loss of appetite. Conventional treatment consists of paracetamol (acetaminophen) syrup for pain and, in some cases, antibiotics.

WHAT YOU CAN DO

Gently wipe away any discharge from the external ear. Never poke a cotton bud or anything else down the ear canal. A warm compress or well-wrapped hot-water bottle can be soothing. Keep the air humidified to help keep the eustachian tube open and free from mucus. See also Colds and flu, page 163.

NATURAL REMEDIES

EAR PROBLEMS

With expert guidance, select from the following:

Homeopathy

Constitutional remedies are often very successful if a baby is prone to recurrent ear problems.

❀ **Aconitum napellus**: sudden onset of hot painful ear, fever, with thirst and maybe a dry cough.

❀ **Belladonna**: earache with fever, red face, hot moist skin, swollen glands

❀ **Chamomilla**: earache with teething, pain made worse by cold, one red cheek, especially in clingy babies.

❀ **Pulsatilla**: earache of gradual onset, often accompanying or following a cold, in a weepy, clingy baby with pale cheeks, and thick yellow-green mucus.

Aromatherapy

For babies over three months, dilute one drop of one of the following essential oils into 10ml of warm carrier oil and apply around the external ear.

❀ Chamomile
❀ Eucalyptus
❀ Lavender
❀ Tea tree

Cranial osteopathy

This can be useful for recurrent middle-ear infections.

PREVENTING EAR PROBLEMS

❁ Breastfeed for as long as possible.
❁ Identify and treat any allergies (see page 162).
❁ Treat colds promptly (see page 163).
❁ Make sure your baby gets plenty of fresh air and keep him away from smoky environments.

OUTER-EAR INFECTION

This may be caused by bacterial infection or by a foriegn body in the ear. Symptoms include inflammation, discharge, pain, and scaly skin. Conventional treatment is with anti-inflammatory eardrops and perhaps antibiotics. Paracetamol (acetaminophen) syrup helps to relieve pain.

BLOCKED TEAR DUCT

Watery eyes in a newborn baby may be caused by a blocked tear duct. If the discharge is thick or sticky, there may be an infection (see below). Blocked tear ducts usually unblock naturally after a few months. You can hasten this by massaging the duct (the tiny swelling at the corner of each eye close to the nose) with a clean finger six to eight times a day.

CONJUNCTIVITIS AND BLEPHARITIS

Conjunctivitis is inflammation of the transparent membrane that covers the white of the eye. It may be the result of infection, injury, allergy, or exposure to irritants. Symptoms include itchy, bloodshot eyes, watery or sticky yellow discharge, and/or sensitivity to light. Blepharitis is an inflammation of the eyelids most often caused by infection or allergy. The eyelids may be red and itchy with scaly skin.

WHAT YOU CAN DO

Bathe your baby's eyes with cooled, boiled water, a herbal infusion (see below), or breast milk, which is antibacterial. Use a separate piece of cotton wool for each eye, wiping gently from the inner to outer corner. Wash your hands before and afterward.

NATURAL REMEDIES

EYE INFLAMMATION

With expert guidance, select from the following:

Homeopathy

❁ **Aconitum napellus**: for red, inflamed eyes.
❁ **Euphrasia officinalis**: for swollen, inflamed eyelids, itching, tears with a thick discharge.
❁ **Mercurius**: for swollen, red lids with thin discharge.
❁ **Pulsatilla**: for thick, yellowish discharge.

Herbal remedies

❁ Bathe the eyes using a cooled infusion of one of the following herbs: chamomile, calendula, elderflower, marshmallow, rose petals.
❁ Use a few drops of euphrasia (eyebright) tincture diluted in a teaspoon of rosewater to bathe eyes.

Nutrition and digestion

YOUR BABY RECEIVES THE NUTRIENTS she needs to grow and develop initially from breast milk or formula and later from a mixed diet. If your baby doesn't receive sufficient nutrients, either because of inadequate feeding or because digestion or absorption of food is disrupted by illness, she will not thrive. Occasional digestive upsets (including vomiting, diarrhoea, and colic) are common in babies. Some babies have more sensitive digestive systems and take a while to get used to digesting and eliminating waste for themselves. Vomiting and diarrhoea are a means by which the body rids itself of toxins and are best not suppressed. Rarely, such symptoms indicate a more serious problem, so it is important to consult your doctor if symptoms persist. When babies are held a lot and have plenty of slow, calm body contact with their mothers, digestive problems are far less likely.

SLOW WEIGHT GAIN

Some babies are naturally slow to gain weight. All babies go through periodic growth spurts when they need to feed more often to increase the milk supply. If your baby has four to six wet nappies (diapers) daily, bright yellow, mustard-like stools, is gaining weight regularly, and has smooth, plump, elastic skin she is almost certainly getting enough milk. If your baby has poor weight gain, appears scrawny with loose wrinkled skin, and feeds frequently but appears unsatisfied, she may be

---

NATURAL REMEDIES

BUILDING UP YOUR MILK SUPPLY

Have plenty of fluids and pay attention to your diet. Include pulses, oats, nuts, and seeds (especially sesame seeds), raw fruit and vegetables, and green herbs such as coriander, borage, cress, and alfalfa. Rest and relax as much as possible.

Homeopathy
✿ **Pulsatilla**: for scanty milk supply and pain during feeding.

Herbal remedies
Drink teas made from one or more of the following herbs throughout the day:
✿ Borage
✿ Caraway seeds
✿ Dill
✿ Fennel seeds
✿ Fenugreek

✿ Milk thistle
✿ Raspberry leaf
✿ Agnus vitex castus, available as a tincture, works on the pituitary gland to help stimulate production of prolactin, the milk-producing hormone.

Other therapies
Acupuncture can help increase the milk supply by stimulating the endocrine system and balancing hormones. Cranial osteopathy for the mother can help to stimulate the let-down reflex.

Sleepy newborns need to be wakened and fed at least every three hours. Spending a quiet day together, resting, waking, and feeding may help your baby to get into a rhythm of regular feeds.

failing to thrive. If she is breastfeeding, this could be a sign that she is not getting enough of the higher-fat, high-calorie hind milk at the end of each feed. It is essential to seek the guidance of a breastfeeding counsellor or midwife. If your formula-fed baby is failing to gain weight satisfactorily, it could be the result of intolerance to the particular formula, or it may simply be that your baby needs feeding more frequently. In all cases, you should consult your doctor or paediatrician to rule out the possibility of an underlying condition.

WHAT YOU CAN DO

If you are breastfeeding, dedicate yourself to feeding as often as possible to increase the milk supply (see page 167). Ask your midwife or breastfeeding counsellor to observe your baby feeding to make sure that she is latching on and sucking properly. After your baby has fed from one breast, wind and change her to wake her up and give her the other breast. Repeat this several times to encourage the hind milk to be released. See also Solving problems, pages 54–7. If your baby is formula fed, make sure that you feed her as much as she wants whenever she seems hungry – night and day. If you think that the formula might be the cause of the problem, discuss alternatives with your doctor or other health professional.

VOMITING AND DIARRHOEA

Small babies often regurgitate part of their feed, and this is not true vomiting but possetting. As long as your baby is having regular wet and dirty nappies (diapers) and gaining weight, there is no reason to be worried. Possetting stops as the baby gets older. Winding the baby regularly and handling her carefully after feeds may help to ease the problem (see also page 55).

True vomiting, when the stomach contents are ejected, is a natural reflex and the occasional vomit is nothing to worry about. You should report persistent vomiting to your doctor without delay. In most cases vomiting has a minor cause such as wind or taking too much milk. More serious causes may include infection in the digestive tract (gastroenteritis), a childhood infectious illness, allergy, food intolerance, a hernia, or travel sickness. In a young baby forceful (projectile) vomiting after each feed may be a sign of pyloric stenosis, a condition caused by thickening of the pyloric muscle at the lower end of the stomach. This can usually be successfully corrected by surgery.

An unweaned baby with diarrhoea produces bowel movements that are greenish and more watery or mucousy than usual. This may accompany a cold, teething, or (in a breastfed baby) be a reaction to something the mother has eaten. In such cases diarrhoea usually subsides quickly and does not upset the baby. See your doctor if there are other symptoms of illness, such as fever, vomiting, loss of appetite, or dehydration (see below). In bottle-fed or weaning babies, diarrhoea may be a sign of intolerance to an ingredient in the diet or the formula or too much sugar in the diet. Underfeeding, which can occur when trying to follow a feeding schedule or sleep-training method, can result in loose, frequent, dark, mucousy, semi-transparent stools. The main danger of diarrhoea and/or vomiting, especially in a young baby, is that of dehydration. The main early signs of dehydration are reduced urine production (fewer wet nappies/diapers), dry, inelastic skin, sunken eyes, and/or sunken fontanelle. Call your doctor at once if you notice these symptoms

NATURAL REMEDIES

DIARRHOEA AND VOMITING

With expert guidance, select from the following:

Homeopathy
✿ Arsenicum album
✿ Nux vomica
✿ Ipecacuanha
✿ Sepia

Herbal remedies
Teas made from one of the following:
✿ Chamomile
✿ Dill
✿ Elderflower
✿ Fennel
✿ Spearmint

WHAT YOU CAN DO

If you are breastfeeding, give frequent, short feeds. Give a bottle-fed baby frequent sips of plain, previously boiled water to prevent dehydration. Do not offer large drinks of water, which can worsen symptoms. An older baby who is weaning will usually have little appetite, so breastfeed primarily if you can. Alternatively, give clear fluids such as water, broth, dilute apple juice, and herbal teas. Once symptoms have eased, introduce easily digested foods such as rice, bananas, dry cereal, dry toast, mashed potatoes, and well-cooked vegetables.

CONSTIPATION

Constipation refers more to the consistency of bowel movements than their frequency. It is normal for a breastfed baby to go several days without a bowel movement. If your baby seems to experience pain or unusual difficulty with defecation, or if the stools are hard and dry, she is constipated. Constipation is unusual in a breastfed baby, because the fluid content of breast milk is perfectly balanced; it is more common in bottle-fed or weaning babies.

WHAT YOU CAN DO

Make sure you make up formula feeds correctly and offer extra fluids. In a weaned baby, constipation is often a result of too little fluid and not enough fibre. Increasing these elements in the diet will usually correct the problem. Most fresh fruits and vegetables contain plenty of fibre. Wholegrain cereals and oatmeal porridge also help to stimulate the intestinal tract. Consult your doctor if constipation is accompanied by other symptoms such as painful, swollen abdomen, fever, vomiting, refusal to feed, or lethargy and listlessness.

COLIC

Recurrent episodes of abdominal pain in a baby are commonly called colic. This is very distressing for baby and parents and is all the more frustrating, because the specific cause is usually unknown. Possible explanations include air swallowing while crying or feeding, birth trauma, disruption of early bonding, allergy or food intolerance, over-stimulation or immature and fluctuating bio-rhythms. Studies have shown that colic is more likely if either parent smokes.

Colic may start when your baby is around two weeks old and usually ceases by about 12 weeks. Symptoms include prolonged, intense crying (often in the evening), a hard abdomen, and legs drawn up to the chest, flailing arms, and muscular tension throughout the body, redness and a clear expression of pain on the baby's face. If you think your baby has colic, check with your doctor in order to rule out any other possible explanation for her symptoms.

Massage your baby's tummy regularly when he is not distressed and has not recently fed. Place one hand on the belly and work gently with your palm and fingers in a clockwise direction.

WHAT YOU CAN DO

You can improve your baby's digestion by giving a few drops of liquid Lactobacillus acidophilus or Bifidobacterium supplement in powder form mixed in a little water. In

---

NATURAL REMEDIES

COLIC

With expert guidance, select from the following:

Homeopathy
✿ **Bryonia**: when symptoms improve if your baby lies still.
✿ **Cina**: for hard, bloated abdomen and better for rocking on shoulder.
✿ **Colocynthis**: for cramps in baby's stomach.

Herbal remedies
If you are breastfeeding, drink a cup of chamomile, dill, fennel, or licorice tea twice a day. If bottle-feeding, try giving your baby a few teaspoons of one of these teas before each feed.

Aromatherapy
Add one or two drops of one of the following oils diluted in milk or carrier oil to your baby's bath water: aniseed, chamomile, geranium, ginger, lavender.

Cranial osteopathy
This helps the baby to release tensions and improve general balance throughout the body and can be very effective for babies with colic. Sometimes just one session produces an improvement.

addition, follow the advice on comforting your baby (page 74) and try the following suggestions:

❀ Plan your day so you can slow down and devote yourself to your baby during the colicky time. Eat, drink, and rest yourself earlier in the day, or before you anticipate the onset of colic.

❀ Bathe and massage your baby just before the usual colicky time and enjoy calm, slow physical contact, reducing stimulation.

❀ Try getting your baby into a baby sling while still relaxed and going for a walk outside or keep it on around the house.

❀ Breastfeed without restriction to calm and soothe yourself and the baby. Check positioning and latch so that the baby doesn't swallow too much air, especially if the milk flow is very rapid.

❀ If breastfeeding, consider whether certain foods in your diet seem to make the problem worse and eliminate suspect foods if necessary.

❀ Burp your baby frequently.

❀ Hold your baby in the "tiger in a tree" position shown on page 56 with your hand on her tummy to move gas down the digestive tract.

You can give your baby herbal infusions with a dropper, on a teaspoon, or in a cup or bottle, depending on which he will take most easily.

URINARY INFECTIONS

Urinary infections are more common in girls than boys and are usually caused by germs from the anal passage entering the urethra from where they travel to the bladder. Symptoms include strong-smelling urine, crying, and apparent discomfort when passing urine. There may also be less specific symptoms such as fever, vomiting, and loss of appetite. If you suspect a urine infection in a baby you should always report it to your doctor. Conventional treatment is with antibiotics (see also page 151) and your doctor may recommend tests to discover if a structural abnormality is creating susceptibility to infection.

NATURAL REMEDIES

URINARY INFECTIONS

With expert guidance, select from the following:

Homeopathy

❀ **Cantharis**: for painful, stinging urination.

Other remedies

❀ Up to three times a day give a few teaspoons of tea made from one of the following: corn silk, chamomile, marshmallow, rose petals.

❀ Give sips of dilute cranberry juice (once a baby is having some fruit juices).

Mouth and teeth

Excessive dribbling is an indication that your baby is teething. This can happen even before there is any sign of a tooth appearing through the gums.

THE MOST COMMON PROBLEMS IN THE MOUTH are caused by teething or thrush. However, other problems, such as cold sores can occur, so be sure to get your doctor's opinion about any unusual sores or other problems in or around your baby's mouth.

TEETHING

Teething is the natural process whereby the baby's first (deciduous) teeth push their way up through the gums. Some babies show little sign of discomfort from teething and teeth suddenly appear, while others are quite upset by it. The first teeth usually erupt around five to six months, although early signs of teething under the gum surface may be present from around three or four months. These include red cheeks, dribbling, sore skin (from saliva), loose stools caused by swallowing excess saliva and possibly nappy (diaper rash), fever, irritability, sleep disturbances, biting/ sucking things, playing with the nipple to massage the gums, and refusal to feed. If you run your finger along your baby's gums you will be able to feel swollen ridges of emerging teeth. Once teething starts, the front eight teeth usually appear within six months. The full set of 20 milk teeth have usually appeared by about the age of two and a half years. If a teething baby develops a fever over 40°C (102°F), seems increasingly unwell, or develops other symptoms such as profuse diarrhoea or vomiting, you need to see your doctor.

NATURAL REMEDIES

TEETHING

With expert guidance, select from the following:

Homeopathy

❀ **Apis mellifica**: for swollen gums.
❀ **Calcarea carbonica**: for delay in teeth coming through and difficult teething.
❀ **Chamomilla**: especially for a baby whose gums are red, swollen and tender to the touch, who is irritable, worst at night, and comforted by being carried. You can get homeopathic chamomile teething drops or give cool chamomile tea well diluted.

❀ **Pulsatilla**: for teething babies who are clingy
❀ **Sulphur**: for swollen gums with throbbing pain.

Other remedies

❀ Essential oil of cloves has natural local anaesthetic properties: you can use one drop in one to two tablespoons of organic sunflower oil and use it to massage the gums
❀ Try giving your older baby a natural licorice stick to chew on.

WHAT YOU CAN DO

Give your teething baby something hard to chew – for example, raw carrot sticks, hard crusts of bread, or a teething ring. Proprietary teething gels help to numb the gums and alleviate soreness.

ORAL THRUSH (CANDIDA)

This is caused by overgrowth of *Candida albicans*, a yeast-like organism that is naturally present in the gut. Oral thrush appears as raised, creamy white patches on the tongue and inside the mouth that are not easily rubbed off. Underneath these patches may be sore and red, and may even bleed. An outbreak of thrush can be provoked by a course of antibiotics, which disturbs the natural balance of microorganisms in the body, or by immaturity of the immune system. It can be passed between mother and baby at birth, while breastfeeding, and it may also manifest as a type of nappy (diaper) rash (see page 174). Both mother and baby usually need treatment and sometimes the father does too. It can spread onto the mother's nipples and cause irritation and soreness. Sore pink nipples may be caused by thrush, even if you can't see any in your baby's mouth. Medical treatment consists of the application of an antifungal preparation.

Your teething baby may find it soothing if you rub his gums with a clean finger. Alternatively, you can use a small chip of ice.

WHAT YOU CAN DO

If you are breastfeeding, you need to tackle the infection in both your baby and yourself. To counter candida in your body, take Lactobacillus acidophilus and keep sugary foods to a minimum. Boost your immune system with supplements of vitamins A, C, and E. Garlic and the herbal remedies echinacea and goldenseal also strengthen the immune system. Ginger tea has antifungal properties. If your baby has been prescribed antibiotics, give her Lactobacillus acidophilus (see page 151). Don't try to remove patches of thrush from your baby's mouth as this will be painful and may cause bleeding. To treat your baby's symptoms, make a mouthwash with 1/8 teaspoon of Lactobacillus acidophilus powder in a 1/2 cup of water. Squirt this into your baby's mouth using a dropper. Items that your baby puts in the mouth should be cleaned with cool boiled water to which you have added five drops of tea tree oil and then boiled for about 20 minutes.

NATURAL REMEDIES

ORAL THRUSH

With expert guidance, select from the following:

Homeopathy

✿ **Arsenicum album**: for thrush with restlessness and fatigue.
✿ **Sulphur**: for thrush with overheating.
✿ **Thuja**: for thrush following immunization.

A homeopath may recommend constitutional treatment designed to boost your baby's immune system.

Herbal remedies

Teas made from the following herbs have antifungal properties and can be given as drops into your baby's mouth: fennel, marigold, rose petals, thyme.

Skin problems

TYPES OF NAPPY (DIAPER) RASH

If nappy (diaper) rash is severe, your doctor will determine which type it is and advise appropriate treatment.

✿ Thrush (candida) infection may occur after a course of antibiotics or if your baby has oral thrush (see page 173). The infection is more likely if the skin is already inflamed. A typical thrush rash is bright red with sharply defined borders.

✿ Seborrhoeic dermatitis, the same condition that causes cradle cap (facing page), may cause a widespread, scaly rash.

✿ Impetigo, a bacterial infection that causes blisters that gradually form honey-coloured crusts, may occur in rare cases when the skin is already inflamed and weakened.

BABIES HAVE DELICATE SKIN that is thinner than that of an adult. The sweat and sebaceous glands are comparatively immature and thus the skin is more prone to dryness and irritation. Little pimples with white heads, called milk spots, usually come up on the skin as a newborn adjusts to absorbing and digesting milk. There may also be small white spots over the bridge of the nose called milia. These are caused by blockage of the sebaceous glands, and should clear in a few weeks. Milaria, spots caused by blockage of the sweat glands, is more likely in hot weather and can be minimized by keeping your baby cool and her skin dry. Never try to squeeze spots on your baby's skin.

Rashes caused by the common childhood infectious illnesses are discussed on page 178. It is particularly important that you familiarize yourself with the the type of rash that sometimes accompanies meningitis. This is described on page 178.

NAPPY (DIAPER) RASH

Inflammation of the skin around the nappy (diaper) area can occur in a baby of any age. The usual cause is irritation from the ammonia produced as the baby's urine and stools break down. It may also be caused externally by friction on the skin or by heat and moisture in the creases around the groin. Nappy (diaper) rash can also be caused by an allergy to a specific food. In a breastfed baby, it may be a reaction to something the mother has eaten; in a bottle-fed baby, it may be the formula that is the problem, or in a

Help prevent nappy (diaper) rash by exposing the area to the air for a while at changing time.

NATURAL REMEDIES

NAPPY (DIAPER) RASH

With expert guidance, select from the following:

Homeopathy

✿ **Calcarea carbonica**: for a baby who sweats on the head and feet and whose sweat and faeces have sour smell.
✿ **Sulphur**: for a red, sore rash.
✿ **Thuja**: for a persistent rash.

Homeopathic calendula powder is excellent for helping to dry the skin thoroughly and alleviates a moist rash, especially in the creases.

Herbal remedies

✿ A warm bath to which you have added an infusion of calendula or chamomile flowers will be soothing for your baby and mildly antiseptic. Immerse your baby's lower half into it for about five minutes.
✿ Calendula cream applied regularly is soothing and healing.

Aromatherapy

For babies over three months:
✿ Make up a soothing massage oil using one or more of the following oils in a base of organic carrier oil: calendula, bergamot, chamomile, geranium, lavender, sandalwood, rose (for amounts, see page 155).
✿ Tea tree essential oil is antibacterial and antifungal. It is available as a gel for application to the skin.
✿ As a preventive measure, make a soothing and cleansing lotion to use at each nappy (diaper) change. Add five drops of essential oil of lavender to a spray bottle filled with distilled or spring water. Spray onto your baby's skin and wipe with cotton balls.

weaning baby a particular food. When treated naturally, nappy rash should improve in two or three days and then disappear completely within a few more days. As the treatment for each type of rash is different, it is important to get any persistent rash diagnosed by your doctor. Medical treatment may be needed and, depending on the rash, may involve applying an antibiotic or antifungal ointment, or a mild steroid preparation.

WHAT YOU CAN DO

If your baby has nappy (diaper) rash, change her as soon as possible after soiling or wetting. Cleanse the skin with cotton wool and warm water and dry thoroughly. Between changes expose the area to the air for as long as possible. Use a plant-based nappy (diaper) gel to protect the skin from moisture and irritants. Calendula cream is especially soothing. When laundering cloth nappies (diapers), add 10 drops of tea tree oil to the rinse water and dry thoroughly in the fresh air, if possible.

SEBORRHOEIC DERMATITIS AND CRADLE CAP

Seborrhoeic dermatitis is a type of skin inflammation with no certain cause, although it may be linked to a yeast or fungal infection. It is common in the first few months of life and can spread to the forehead, eyebrows, behind the ears, neck, armpits, and the nappy (diaper) area. The symptoms are a red, scaly rash or,

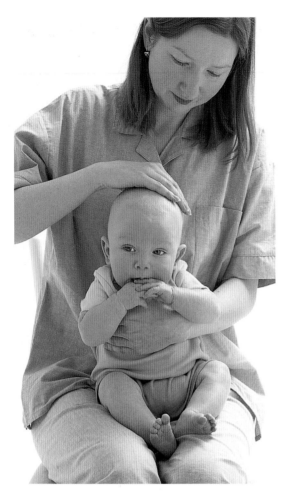

Use one of the gentle methods (described right) to loosen and remove cradle cap. Never try to pick off the scales. You can massage the scalp with oil when your baby is seated on your lap or while feeding.

when it affects the scalp, greasy, white or yellowish-brown raised patches known as cradle cap. No treatment is needed for mild seborrhoeic dermatitis, but seek a medical opinion if the condition is widespread.

WHAT YOU CAN DO

If you are breastfeeding try taking a daily spoonful of flaxseed oil which is rich in essential fatty acids needed for healthy skin, and drink burdock root tea to help control any yeast or fungal growth. Lactobacillus supplements will also help to balance gut flora and avoid fungal overgrowth. Unsightly cradle cap scales can be gently removed by washing with a mild baby shampoo. To loosen the scales, rub the baby's scalp with olive, wheatgerm, or sesame oil with perhaps a couple of drops of lavender, rosemary, or sandalwood essential oil and leave overnight. Wash away the scales with a mild shampoo. Herbal treatments include washing the scalp with an infusion of burdock, chamomile, or meadowsweet. Leave the infusion to dry and then apply olive oil to soften the scales. Homeopathic remedies include Graphites for a scaling scalp and Sepia for moist dandruff.

ECZEMA

There are many different types of eczema but the most common is atopic eczema (atopy means a tendency to have allergic reaction). In a baby eczema may appear as inflamed patches on the face, body, forearms, and legs. Seven out of ten children with atopic eczema have a family history of allergy. The most common eczema-causing allergens are house-dust mites, animal dander (skin debris), pollen, and certain foods and medications. Irritant substances, such as soap, detergents, household chemicals, wool, synthetic fabrics, dust or sand, and cigarette smoke, can also trigger an outbreak. Eczema may be made worse by hot baths, change of climate, central heating, tiredness, chemicals in swimming pools, stress, and illness. In some cases eczema disappears as the child gets older (see also Allergies, page 162). Conventional treatment is usually with steroid creams or antihistamines. These treatments are best reserved for minimal use when symptoms are severe because of the risk of side effects.

WHAT YOU CAN DO

Try to minimize your baby's exposure to suspected allergens. Dress her in cotton clothing and keep her nails trimmed to reduce harm from scratching. Moisturize the skin daily by applying generous amounts of emollient cream. Avoid using soap and ordinary bath

ECZEMA

With expert guidance, select from the following:

Homeopathy

✿ **Calendula ointment**: for weeping eczema.

✿ **Graphites**: by mouth or as an ointment for moist rash with yellowish discharge, dry cracked, rough skin.

✿ **Rhus toxicodendron**: for a blistery rash.

✿ **Sulphur**: for a rash that is worse for heat.

✿ **Urtica urens ointment or gel**: for dry, scaly eczema.

Constitutional treatments recommended by a homeopath may also be effective.

Herbal remedies

Chamomile or calendula ointments may reduce itching and inflammation.

Aromatherapy

For babies over three months, under the supervision of a qualified aromatherapist, you could use one of the following essential oils in the bath, in a lotion, or mixed in a carrier oil for massaging into the affected skin:

✿ Bergamot

✿ Cedarwood

✿ Roman chamomile

✿ Geranium

✿ Lavender

✿ Rose otto

✿ White sandalwood.

preparations. Instead use a proprietary liquid moisturizer and skin lubricant that you add to your baby's bath water. Alternatively, an oatmeal bath can be very soothing for dry eczema. Place a cupful of oatmeal in muslin and tie to make a bag. Put it under the running tap or in the bath and dab the wet bag over your baby's skin. Wet wrapping, in which bandages are applied over moisturizing ointment, is another possible treatment for severe eczema.

If your baby has eczema, be sure to keep the skin well moisturized by applying emollient cream several times a day.

URTICARIA (HIVES)

This is a common skin reaction with raised, red, itchy weals, with a paler centre. The main causes are a reaction to an allergen in food (commonly strawberries, shellfish, peanuts, eggs, or food additives) or drugs such as penicillin, or skin contact with irritating plants such as nettles or poison ivy, exposure to sunlight or extremes of heat or cold, and insect bites or stings. Prevention involves identifying and avoiding the triggers. Symptoms may fluctuate and usually disappear within 24 hours. Meanwhile, use calamine lotion or make a paste with bicarbonate of soda and apply to soothe the itching. A burdock and chickweed infusion in a warm bath is also soothing. An oral antihistamine medicine is the usual conventional treatment.

In rare cases, urticaria (hives) is accompanied by sudden and severe swelling of face, eyelids, tongue, and throat, known as anaphylactic shock. This is a life-threatening condition that requires emergency treatment.

Childhood infectious illnesses

THE MOST COMMON CHILDHOOD INFECTIOUS illnesses are caused by viruses, and infection normally gives lifelong immunity. If you suspect that your baby may have one of these infections, seek medical advice to get a definite diagnosis before you start home treatment. There is usually no need for undue concern if a healthy baby is affected, but in rare cases there is a risk of serious complications. Be alert for any of the emergency symptoms listed on page 157.

CHICKENPOX

Caused by infection with the varicella zoster virus, chickenpox has an incubation period of 14 to 21 days. The main symptoms are fever and crops of small, red spots that turn into itchy blisters, which later crust over. Conventional treatment, if any, may consist of paracetamol (acetaminophen) syrup to reduce fever and anti-histamine medication to relieve itching. Antibiotics may be prescribed if there is a secondary bacterial infection. If a woman contracts chickenpox in early pregnancy, there is a slight risk to the unborn baby. Seek medical advice if your baby develops the disease and you think you may be pregnant.

WHAT YOU CAN DO

Maintain your baby's fluid intake by breastfeeding frequently or, in a weaned or bottle-fed baby, offering extra drinks. Chamomile or elderflower tea may help to bring down a fever and soothe the rash. Keep your baby's fingernails short to minimize damage from scratching. Calamine lotion may relieve itching. A few drops of essential oil of lavender, chamomile, or tea tree in a tepid bath is also soothing.

MENINGITIS

In meningitis, the membranes that enclose the brain and spinal cord become inflamed as a result of infection. Symptoms in a baby may include:
✿ Fever.
✿ Lethargy and abnormal drowsiness.
✿ Vomiting.
✿ Neck stiffness.
✿ Dislike of bright light.
✿ Flat, red rash that does not disappear when pressure is applied.
✿ Blotchy or pale skin.
If you suspect that your baby may have this serious illness, seek immediate medical advice from your doctor or local hospital emergency department. When meningitis is suspected, hospital admission for observation is a wise precaution.

RUBELLA (GERMAN MEASLES)

This usually mild viral infection has an incubation period of 14 to 21 days. Symptoms may include a slight fever, swollen lymph nodes in the neck, a flat, light red rash that spreads from the face to cover the whole body. Maintain your baby's fluid intake by frequent breastfeeding and/or extra drinks, but no other special treatment is necessary. It is essential to keep a baby with rubella away from pregnant women.

MEASLES

This is a highly infectious viral infection with an incubation period of 10 to 14 days. First symptoms usually include a fever, cough, runny nose, and red, sore eyes. These are followed by the appearance of small white spots in the mouth and a flat, blotchy rash, which usually begins behind the ears and later extends to the whole body. Most children recover quickly, but because of the risk of serious complications, it is essential to seek medical attention. Follow the advice on treating feverish illnesses (page 158).

ROSEOLA INFANTUM

This viral infection has an incubation period of 5 to 15 days, and is common in babies over six months. The first symptom is usually a high fever that lasts for up to four days. As the fever subsides, a faint pink rash appears on the body and limbs, lasting a few days. Complications are rare in healthy babies and there is usually no medical treatment required. Follow the advice on treating a fever on page 158.

WHOOPING COUGH

Whooping cough is caused by the *Bortedella pertussis* bacterium. The symptoms may initially include runny nose, cough, and slightly raised temperature. Seven to 14 days later, the child develops bouts of coughing, followed by the characteristic "whoop" as air is inhaled through the narrowed windpipe. Vomiting may follow violent bouts of coughing. The cough may persist for up to three months. An otherwise healthy baby usually recovers well. Antibiotics given early in the illness may shorten its duration. Babies with severe symptoms may be admitted to hospital.

WHAT YOU CAN DO

The use of a humidifier may help relieve congestion. Lavender, thyme, or eucalyptus essential oils added to the bath water or a vaporizer may also assist breathing. A few teaspoons of thyme, elecampane, or hyssop tea every two hours may also relieve symptoms. Massage can help to clear the chest. Bach flower Rock Rose or Rescue Remedy may help to calm and ease panic for both mother and baby during bouts of coughing. Call your doctor if your baby becomes exhausted or breathing becomes laboured.

MUMPS

This is a viral infection that affects the saliva-producing parotid glands in front of the ear. The illness is relatively uncommon in the first year of life. The incubation period is two to three and half weeks. The symptoms usually include a fever, followed by the characteristic swelling of the face. Complications are unlikely in a baby, but you should nevertheless consult your doctor.

WHAT YOU CAN DO

Rest at home with your baby and feed frequently. Give a weaned baby plenty of extra fluids, but avoid juices, which stimulate saliva production and therefore may increase discomfort. Warm or cool compresses applied to the swollen glands may help to relieve pain or tenderness. Conventional treatment includes liquid paracetamol (acetaminophen).

Accidents and first aid

Immerse a minor burn in cold water for several minutes.

IN THIS SECTION YOU WILL FIND GUIDANCE for common injuries and household emergencies. To learn how to deal with more serious emergencies such as concussion, if a baby is not breathing or is unconscious, it is advisable to attend a first aid and baby resuscitation course. Those who may share the care of your baby, even occasionally, should attend too. Invest in a good first aid book. Even though some of the serious incidents described are very unlikely, knowing what to do before emergency help arrives can save a life. The information here is intended to help you provide appropriate care in less serious situations.

GENERAL ADVICE

If you are in any doubt about whether or not your baby needs emergency treatment, don't hesitate to contact your nearest hospital emergency department or call an ambulance. If your baby has sustained a blow or fall and seems drowsy or loses consciousness, however briefly, you should call the emergency services. If you think she may have broken a bone or may have an internal injury, don't move her unless it is absolutely necessary, to avoid further injury. In an emergency, do your best to stay calm, breathe evenly, and think carefully about what to do. Keep your baby warm, and comfort her by holding her, if safe to do so, and by reassuring her through the familiar sound of your voice.

BURNS AND SCALDS

Burns are caused by dry heat. Scalds are caused by damp or wet heat. The symptoms and treatment are the same for both. Mild burns and scalds damage only the outer layer of skin, while more serious burns cause more serious damage to the underlying tissues. Serious burns may cause clinical shock (dangerous fall in blood pressure). All but the most minor burns should be seen by a doctor.

Immediate action
Immerse the affected area in cold, running water immediately and continue for 10–15 minutes. This is the only action you should take for large burns while waiting for medical help.

Natural care
For minor burns, pat dry gently and apply a generous amount of homeopathic burn ointment with a light touch and don't rub in. Give your baby Rescue Remedy. The following homeopathic remedies also can be used:
✿ **Arnica**: for shock and blistering.
✿ **Cantharis**: for stinging burns.
✿ **Urtica urens ointment**: for stinging burns causing redness and weals.
✿ **Essential oil of lavender, calendula cream, and pure aloe vera gel**: can also be used to soothe minor burns.

CUTS AND GRAZES

Once a baby is crawling, she is at risk from minor injuries. Severe cuts are not common in babies and need immediate medical attention and may need to have the skin edges held together with special adhesive strips or stitches.

Immediate action

Clean thoroughly with water. If necessary, hold the area above the level of the heart, if possible, to slow bleeding. Exposure to the air aids healing; however, the area may need to be covered with a loose dressing to keep it clean.

Natural care

✿ Give your baby a drop or two of Rescue Remedy.
✿ Homeopathic Hypercal solution is an excellent antiseptic cleanser. Put 10–20 drops in warm previously boiled water and cleanse with cotton wool. Then apply a few drops of neat Hypercal to a fresh piece of soaked cotton wool and hold over the wound. A solution of tea tree oil is also an effective antiseptic.
✿ Calendula or Hypercal cream can then be used daily to hasten healing.

BRUISES

Bruises are caused by blood leaking from broken capillaries and pooling under the skin. Bruising is rare in a young baby, but may occur more frequently once your baby is on the move and starts to bump her head and other body parts frequently.

Immediate action

✿ Immediately after a bump give your baby a drop or two or a tablet of Rescue Remedy. Hold a cold compress over the affected area and apply moderate pressure. Then dry and gently rub some homeopathic Arnica cream into the skin, repeating often until the bruise fades.

✿ The homeopathic remedy Arnica taken orally is also excellent for bruising. You can give your baby Arnica 6 three times a day, starting as soon as possible, while the bruise is tender. This remedy can safely be given to newborns or, if you are breastfeeding, take Arnica yourself.
✿ A pad of cotton wool soaked in distilled witch hazel and applied to the affected area is another soothing treatment for bruises.

BITES AND STINGS

The most common stings that affect babies are from bees, wasps, horseflies, ants, spiders, jellyfish, and plants such as stinging nettles. Usually, they cause local swelling, redness, or infection.

If the child is allergic to the sting, in rare cases there may be a serious allergic reaction known as anaphylactic shock (see page 177). If there is swelling of the eyes, lips, or mouth, seek emergency medical attention; your child may need an injection of adrenaline or antihistamine. An animal bite that breaks the skin should always be seen by a doctor. A tetanus inoculation may be necessary.

Natural care

✿ Give your baby a drop or two of Rescue Remedy. For animal bites wash with previously boiled warm water with 20 drops of homeopathic Hypercal tincture. Cover with a sterile dressing and seek medical advice.
✿ If an insect sting is visible remove it with tweezers.
✿ Neutralize a bee sting with bicarbonate of soda, and a wasp sting with lemon juice or vinegar.
✿ Aconite is a homeopathic remedy for shock. Give Apis if the skin is hot, red. and swollen.

CHOKING AND SWALLOWED OBJECTS

Babies will put any object that they pick up into their mouths, so it is essential to ensure that nothing they could potentially choke on, is within their grasp. But however vigilant you are, there is a risk that your baby may choke on something. Suspect this if there is sudden difficulty breathing in a previously well baby. Her face may turn blue, may try to cry, may make strange noises, or may not make a sound.

Immediate action

DO NOT shake the baby or turn her upside down.
✿ Lay her face down along one of your forearms with her head at the hand end, supporting her chest and chin with your hands.
✿ Lower your arm to bring the head lower than the rest of the body.
✿ Give five sharp slaps on the back.

If this does not clear the obstruction:

✿ Turn your baby over face up, keeping the head lower than the body.
✿ Place two fingers in the centre of the chest just under the breastbone and give five sharp downward thrusts. This simulates coughing and may bring up the object.
✿ Look in the mouth to see if you can clear the object with your finger but don't put your finger down the baby's throat unless you can clearly see the object to hook it out.

If there is still no result, call an ambulance and keep repeating the procedure back and front until help arrives.

SHOCK

Shock can be caused by a serious injury or allergic reaction (see also Uritcaria (hives), page 177). This causes a sudden drop in blood pressure that deprives the vital organs of their oxygen supply. Symptoms may include clammy, cold skin, pallor, shallow rapid breathing, fainting, and dizziness. Severe shock can cause unconsciousness and may be life threatening. Emergency medical attention is needed.

Immediate action

Cover your baby with a blanket to keep her warm. Raise the legs above the level of the heart to encourage circulation to the heart. Give plenty of emotional comfort and calm reassurance.

ELECTRIC SHOCK

Although a rare occurrence, there is a risk that the tiny fingers of a curious, crawling baby could come into contact with an electric current. This is a preventable accident so ensure that all electrical appliances and supply points are baby proof (see Safety in the home, facing page).

Immediate action

Disconnect the power by standing on a dry surface and use a wooden broom handle, chair, or other nonconductive material to move your baby away from the source. Treat as for shock (above). Get emergency help.

SAFETY IN THE HOME

Before your baby gets to the crawling stage, look through your home with safety in mind. As soon as she can move around, she will be exploring the environment. She will be into every low-level cupboard, so remove anything toxic or harmful and fit special safety catches on all drawers, cupboards, or appliances that may be dangerous.

✿ Be sure to keep everything that you don't want your baby to touch out of reach, so you are not constantly saying "no" and "don't", which will dampen her enthusiasm and confidence.

✿ All sharp corners that will be at the level of your baby's head when standing need to be covered once your baby is on the move.

✿ Safety gates at the top and bottom of stairs are essential. Your baby will need to learn to negotiate stairs when you are there to supervise but at all other times gates should be in place.

✿ Electrical wires and flexes need to be tacked safely to the walls and sockets covered so that curious little fingers can't get at them. Keep the television, video, and music system out of your baby's reach.

✿ Make sure that rugs have non-slip underlays.

✿ Cover potentially hot radiators, and have secure fireguards in place if you have an open fire.

✿ In the kitchen, ensure that nothing can be pulled off counters or the hob, and that your baby cannot reach hot food or appliances.

✿ In the bathroom, the medicine cabinet needs to be out of reach and locked. A safety latch on the toilet is useful. Place insulated covers on the hot tap to prevent burning and it is wise to set the hot water temperature to a maximum of 65°C (150°F). Non-slip surfaces are essential in the bath and on the floor in the bathroom, especially if you are stepping in and out of the bath holding your baby (see page 83).

SAFETY IN THE GARDEN

Fresh air is essential for you and your baby and you may want to make your garden a safe place to play before your baby starts to explore. Here are some guidelines for a childproof garden.

✿ Avoid using chemical pesticides or fertilizers.

✿ Make sure that fences and gates are secure with locks out of reach of a child.

✿ Keep your shed or garage locked and wherever possible store tools and dangerous items on high shelves.

✿ If you have a greenhouse, try to locate it away from the play area and ensure that it is made of safety (shatterproof) glass.

✿ Cover drains and water butts with childproof lids.

✿ Washing lines need to be high up and secure.

✿ Babies can drown in just a few inches of water, so if you have a pond, make sure that there is a securely locked barrier around it or you may consider filling it with stones for a few years or turning it into a sand pit. This needs a cover that will prevent animals from using it as a litter box.

✿ Extract all poisonous plants from your garden. Seek advice from a garden store or from a horticultural society.

✿ Ensure that sharp or scratchy plants such as roses or holly are away from the play area.

✿ Teach your baby from the start not to eat plants, flowers, berries, or dirt and remove any seeds or berries that are inedible.

✿ If you install play equipment such as a baby swing, make sure it meets national safety standards and is positioned over a soft surface such as grass or bark rather than concrete or stone.

✿ Never leave your baby unattended in the garden.

Resources

FURTHER READING

General

Susan Allport, *A Natural History of Parenting*, Souvenir Press 1998.

Janet Balaskas, *New Natural Pregnancy*, Gaia Books 1998.

Jay Belsky and John Kelly, *The Transition to Parenthood: How a First Child Changes a Marriage*, Delacorte Press 1994.

Nicky Bradford, *Your Premature Baby*, Frances Lincoln 2000.

Cassandra Eason, *A Mother's Instinct*, Aquarian Press 1992.

Alison Gopnik, Andrew Meltzoff, and Patricia Kuhl, *How Babies Think*, Weidenfeld & Nicolson, London 1999.

Anne Hubbell and Edie Farwell, *The Tibetan Art of Parenting*, Wisdom Publications 1997.

Deborah Jackson, *Mother and Child*, Duncan Baird Publishers 1999.

Deborah Jackson, *Three in a Bed*, Bloomsbury 1999.

Sheila Kitzinger, *The Year After Childbirth*, Oxford University Press 1994.

Marshall Klaus and John Kennel, *Bonding*, Penguin Plume 1983.

Jean Liedloff, *The Continuum Concept*, Penguin Arkana 1989.

Vimala McClure, *The Path of Parenting: 12 Principles to Guide your Journey*, New World Library 1999.

Lynne Murray and Liz Andrews, *Social Baby*, PC Publishing 2000.

Michel Odent, *The Scientification of Love*, Free Association Books 1999

Peggy O'Mara, *Natural Family Living*, Pocket Books, Simon and Schuster 2000.

Joseph Chiltern Pearce, *Magical Child*, Paladin 1979

Martha Sears with William Sears M.D., *25 Things Every New Mother Should Know*, Harvard Common Press 1995.

William Sears M.D., Becoming a Father – *How to Nurture and Enjoy your Family*, La Leche League International 1998

William Sears M.D., *The Fussy Baby: How to Bring out the Best in Your High-Need Child*, Penguin Group 1985, also La Leche League International/Signet 1995.

William Sears M.D., and Martha Sears, *The Baby Book: Everything You Need to Know about Your Baby from Birth to Age Two*, Little, Brown and Co. 1993.

William Sears M.D., *Nighttime Parenting - How to get your Baby and Child to Sleep*, La Leche League International 1996.

Tine Thevenin, *The Family Bed: An Age Old Concept in Child Rearing*, Avery Publishing Group 1992.

Thomas Verny and John Kelly; *The Secret Life of the Unborn Child*, Warner Books 1993.

Health

The American Red Cross First Aid and Safety Handbook, Little, Brown and Co 1992.

Edward Bach and F.J. Wheeler, *The Bach Flower Remedies*, Keats Publishing 1979.

Dr. Sarah Brewer, *Super Baby*, Thorsons 1998.

Miranda Castro, *Homeopathy for Pregnancy, Birth and Your Baby's First Year*, St. Martin's Press 1993.

First Aid for Children Fast, Dorling Kindersley 1999.

Sue Frederick, *A Mother's Guide to Raising Healthy Children ~ Naturally*, Keats Publishing, Contemporary Publishing Group 1999.

Anne McIntyre, *The Herbal for Mother and Child*, Element 1996.

Randall Neustaedter, *The Vaccine Guide: Making an Informed Choice*, North Atlantic Books 1996.

Michel Odent, *Primal Health*, Century 1986.

Paul Offit M.D. and Louis Bell M.D., *What Every Parent Should know About Vaccines*, Macmillan 1998.

Shirley Price and Penny Price Parr, *Aromatherapy for Babies and Children*, Thorsons 1996.

Aviva Romm, *Natural Healing for Babies and Children*, The Crossing Press 1996.

Julian Scott, *Natural Medicine for Children*, Gaia Books 1996.

Dr Andrew Stanway, New Natural Family Doctor, Gaia Books 1996.

Robert Ullman and Judyth Reichenberg-Ullman, *Homeopathic Self-Care: The Quick and Easy Guide for the Whole Family*, Prima Publishing 1997.

Janet Zand, Rachel Walton, Bob Rountree, *Smart Medicine for Healthy Child*, Avery Publishing Group 1994.

Healthy home and environment

Lynn Marie Bower, *The Healthy Household*, The Healthy House Institute 1995.

Tanyia Maxted-Frost, *The Organic Baby Book*, Green Books 1999.

Beverley Pagram, *Natural Housekeeping*, Gaia Books 1998.

David Pearson, *The Gaia Natural House Book*, Gaia Books 2000.

Melody Potter and Erin Milam, *Healthy Baby – Toxic World*, New Harbinger Publications.

Feeding and nutrition

Diane Bengson, *How Weaning Happens*, La Leche League International 1999.

Ina May Gaskin, Babies, *Breastfeeding and Bonding*, Bergin and Garvey 1987.

Gwen Gotsch, *Breastfeeding Pure and Simple*, La Leche League International 1994.

Karen Kerkhoff Gromada, *Mothering Multiples*, La Leche League International 1999.

Patrick Holford, *The Optimim Nutrition Bible*, Piatkus 1999.

Kathleen Huggins, *The Nursing Mother's Companion*, Harvard Common Press 1995.

Dr. Jack Newman's *Guide to Breastfeeding*, HarperCollins 2000.

Michel Odent, *The Nature of Birth and Breastfeeding*, Bergin and Garvey 1992.

Mary Renfrew, Chloe Fisher and Suzanne Arms, *Bestfeeding – Getting Breastfeeding Right for You*, Celestial Arts 2000.

Chemical Tresspass: A Toxic Legacy; Reducing Your Risk, World Wildlife Fund.

Breastfeeding Guide for the Working Woman, La Leche League International.

The Womanly Art of Breastfeeding, La Leche League International, also Plume, New American Library 1997.

Baby massage and other activities

Allison England, *Aromatherapy and Massage for Mother and Baby*, Vermillion 1999.

Françoise Freedman, *Water Babies*, Lorenz Books 2001

Lauren Heston, *Water Baby*, Element 1999.

Ashley Montague, *Touching. The Human Significance of the Skin*, Harper & Row 1986.

Peter Walker *The Practical Art of Baby Massage*, Carroll and Brown 2000.

Peter Walker, *Baby Massage – A Practical Guide to Massage and Movement for Babies and Infants*, Piatkus 1995.

Peter Walker, *Practical Art of Baby Massage* (Video), Active Birth Centre.

ORGANIZATIONS

UK

Active Birth Centre
25 Bickerton Road
London N19 5JT
Tel: 020 7482 5554
e-mail: info@activebirthcentre.com
www.activebirthcentre.com
Postnatal groups, baby massage and
baby gym classes; mail order own-brand
mother and baby products.

Association of Breastfeeding Mothers
PO Box 207
Bridgwater
Somerset TA6 7YT
Tel: 020 7813 1481
e-mail: abm@clara.net
www.home.clara.net/abm

British Allergy Foundation
Deepdene House
30 Bellegrove Road
Welling
Kent DA1 3PU
Tel: 020 7388 4097

Cot Death Helpline
Tel: 020 7235 1721

CRY-SYS
27 Old Gloucster Street
London WC1N 3XX
Tel 020 7404 5011
Support for parents of babies who cry
excessively or have difficulty sleeping

Doula Association of Great Britain
PO Box 33817
London N8 9AW
e-mail: info@doulas.org.uk
www.doulas.orq.uk

Foundation for the Study of Infant
Deaths (FSID)
Artillery House
11-19 Artillery Row
London SW1P 1RT
Tel 020 7222 8001

Institute for Complementary Medicine
PO Box194
London SE16 1QZ
Tel: 020 7237 5165

International Cranial Association
478 Baker St
Enfield EN1 3QS
Tel: 020 8367 5561
Fax: 020 8202 6686
e-mail: kbs07@dial.pipex.com
Cranial ostepathy association

La Leche League Great Britain
PO Box 29
West Bridgeford
Nottingham NG2 7NP
Tel: 020 7242 1278
www.laleche.org.uk
Support for breastfeeding mothers

National Childbirth Trust (NCT)
Alexandra House
Oldham Terrace
London W3 6NH
Tel: 020 8992 8637
Breastfeeding counsellors and postnatal
groups

National Infrmation for Parents of
Prematures - Education, Resources and
Support (NIPPERS)
17-21 Emerald Street
London WC1N 3QL
Tel: 020 7820 9471

National Institute of Medical Herbalists
56 Longbrook Street
Exeter
Devon EX4 6AH
Tel: 01392 426022

Parentline Plus
Tel 0808 800 222
www.parentline.co.uk/
Helpline for parents and carers

Primal Health Research Centre
59 Roderick Road
London NW3 2NP
Fax: 020 7267 5123
e-mail: modent@aol.com
www.birthworks.org/primal health
Research on vaccination and health

Relate
Herbert Gray College
Little Church Street
Rugby
Warks CV21 3AP
Tel: 01788 573241
Relationship counselling

Society of Homoeopaths
2 Artizan Road
Northampton NN1 4HU
Tel: 01604 621400
Fax: 01604 622622
e-mail:
societyofhomoeopaths@btinternet.com

Twins and Multiple Births Association
(TAMBA)
Harnott House
309 Chester Road
Little Sutton
Ellesmere Port CH66 1QQ
Tel: 0870 121 4000/0151 348 0020
Fax: 0870 121 4001/0151 348 0765
e-mail: enquiries@tambahq.org.uk
www.tamba.org.uk

Suppliers
For information on ecological nappies:
www.nappyfacts.co.uk

For nutritional supplements:
Lifestyles Healthcare
Tel: 0870 532 9244

USA

American Herbalists Guild
PO Box 70
Roosevelt, UT 84066
Tel: 435-722-8434
Fax: 435-722-8452
e-mail: ahgoffice@earthlink.net

American Association of Naturopathic
Physicians
8201 Greensboro Drive, Suite 300
McLean, VA 22102
Tel: 703-610-9037
Fax: 703-610-9005

Attachment Parenting International
1508 Clairmont Place
Nashville, TN 37215
Tel/fax: 615-298-4334
www.attachmentparenting.org

Depression After Delivery (DAD)
PO Box 1282
Morrisville, Pennsylvania 19067
Tel: 800-944-4773

Doulas of North America (DONA)
1100 23rd Avenue East
Seattle, WA 98112-3521
Tel: 206-324-5440
e-mail: AskDONA@aol.com
www.DONA.com

La Leche League International
1400 N. Meacham Road
Schaumburg, IL 60173-4840
Tel: 847-519-7730
e-mail: lllhq@llli.org
www.lalecheleague.org/

Lamaze International
2025 M Street, NW
Suite 800
Washington, DC 20036
Tel: 202-367-1128/800-368-4404
Fax: 202-367-2128

National Association of Postpartum Care
Services
PO Box 1012
Edmonds, WA 98020
Tel: 800-453-6852
e-mail: mthrcre@gte.net

National Center for Complementary and
Alternative Medicine
PO Box 8218
Silver Spring, MD 20907-8218
Tel: 888-644-6226
Fax: 301-495-4957
www.altmed.od.nih.gov

National Vaccine Information Centre
(NVIC)
512 West Maple Avenue, Suite 206
Vienna, VA 22180
Tel: 800-909-SHOT/703-938-0342
www.909shot.com

North American Society of Homeopaths
1122 East Pike Street, Suite 1122
Seattle, WA 98122
Tel: 206-720-7000
Fax: 208-248-1942
e-mail: nashinfo@aol.com
www.healthy.net/nch

Australia and New Zealand

Australian Childbirth Education and
Parenting Association (ACEPA)
Tel: (07) 266 4030

Australian Early Childhood Association
Woomerah Avenue
Darlinghurst NSW 2010
Tel: (02) 331 7773

Australian Natural Therapists
Association
PO Box 308
Melrose Park
South Australia 5039
Tel: (8) 371 3222

La Leche League (NZ)
20 Douglas Avenue
Mount Albert
Aukland 3

Lone Parent Family Support Service –
Birthright
Goyden Street
Narrabundah ACT 2503

Nursing Mothers Association of
Australia
PO Box 231
Nunawading Vic 3131
Tel: (3) 877 5011

Index

Main entries are in **bold**.

A

accidents **180–2**
allergic reactions
    to cow's milk 38, 61
allergies 152, **162**
Allport, Susan 25
anaphylactic shock **177**, 181
antibiotics 151
areolae 27, **46**
aromatherapy **155**
asthma 152, **164**
attachment, maternal **24–5**,
    42
autism 152

B

baby bath 84–5
baby blues 31
baby carriers **72–3**
    front 73
    side sling 73
baby cup 63, 64
baby-led feeding **52–3**
    bottle-feeding 60
baby massage 88–9
    step-by-step 90–1
baby sleeping bag 126
baby wearing **72–3**, 159
babymoon **30–5**
Bach flower essences **156**
    home remedy kit 156
    Rescue Remedy 77, 164,
    180
bathing **83–5**
    diluting essential oils 155
    topping and tailing 83
bedclothes/mattress 126,
    127
bed-sharing **121–5**
    and sex life 125
    benefits of 122–3
    guidelines 124
bedtime 128
Bifidobacterium supplement
    151, 170

bilirubin 159, 160
birth 12–13, 21
    after pains 31, 44
    days following **24–7**, 30–1
birthmarks 29
bites **181**
blepharitis **166**
body contact 24, **33–4**, 159
bonding, mother/baby 20,
    21, **25**
books, picture 109, 113
bottle-feeding **58–61**
    equipment 60
    guidelines 60
bowel movements **78–9**,
    157, 168
brain, development of 38, 39
breast/bottle milk
    combination 57, 58–9
breast milk 38, 40
    antibodies in 38, 39, 151,
    162
    building up supply 167
    changes in composition
    39, 40, 41
    colostrum see colostrum
    composition of **38**
    contamination/toxins 41
    digestion of 52
    hind milk 40–1, 48
    mature 38
    transitional 38, 51
    when comes in 51
    see also expressed milk
breast pad 74
breast pump 57
breastfeeding 25, 31,
    37–57, 65
    and working 57
    at night 122
    baby-led feeding 52–3
    benefits for mother 39
    correct positioning 46
    feelings about 42–3
    guidance 44–6
    painful 135, 167
    problems 54–7, 167
    see also working mothers

breastfeeding counsellor 54
breastfeeding positions
    44–6
    cradle hold 45
    criss cross (V) hold 49
    reclining/lying down 47,
    48
    underarm position 45, 49
breasts 25, 42–3
    care of 44
    leakage from 44
    problems 135
    size of 40
    see also engorgement
breathing 25, **35**
    difficulties 182
bronchiolitis **164**
bruises **181**
burns **180**
burping 56

C

caesarean section, and
    breastfeeding 46, 47–8
carer 146–7
    choosing 146
carrying your baby **72–3**
changing bag 97
changing table 82
chickenpox **178**
childcare options 146–7
childhood infectious
    diseases/illnesses 151,
    178–9
choking **182**
clingy 111
clothes
    newborn 86–7
colds **163–4**
colic **170**
colostrum 39, **50–1**,
    151
    expressed 48
comforting **74–7**
communication
    between parents 139
    with baby 70

communication
    development
    newborns 98
    3–4 months 101, 104
    5–9 months 104, 108
    10–16 months 111
complementary therapies
    154–6
conjunctivitis **166**
constipation **169**
contraception 141
conventional medicines 150
co-sleeping 35, **121**, 122
cot (crib) 121, 122, 127
cot (crib) death 123, 152,
    161
couples, relationship of
    140–1
    conflict 140
    time together 140
cow's milk 38, 52
    formula 61
cradle cap **175–6**
cranial osteopathy 75, **156**
crawling 105, **108–10**
crib see cot
croup **164**
crying **74–7**
    at night 130
    calming your baby 77
    immediate response to 74
    reasons for 75
cuts **181**

D

defecation **78–9**
dehydration 157, **169**
depression 136, 137
development, encouraging
    baby's
    newborn 97, 100
    3–4 months 103
    5–9 months 105, 107, 110
    10–16 months 112
developmental checks 97
diaper rash see nappy rash
diapers see nappies

diarrhoea **168–9**
digestion problems 167–71
diphtheria 151, 152
disposables 79, 80
dive reflex 29, 114
doulas 32, **145**
dribbling 172
drinking **63–4**, 112
dressing 86–7

E

ear problems 165–6
eating **64–7**
eczema **176–7**
electric shock **182**
elimination **78–81**
emergency medical help 157
emotional development
    in womb 13
    newborns 98
    3–4 months 101, 104
    5–9 months 104, 108
    10–16 months 111
endorphins 13, **20**
essential fatty acids (EFAs)
    39, 61
essential oils **155**, 162
    home remedy kit 156
expressed milk 55, **57**
eye contact 99
eyes
    focusing 99, 101, 102
    problems 165, **166**

F

falling in love with your
    baby 20, 23, 25
family life/dynamics 96, 142
family support 144, 147
fathers
    and bottle-feeding 59
    and breastfeeding 43
    and the birth 12, 15, 27,
    137
    relationship with mother
    32, 138–41
    sharing care of baby 71
febrile convulsions **158**
feeding 33, 105, 108
    at night 119, 129
    expressed milk 57

when out 97
    see also baby-led, bottle-,
    breastfeeding, working
    mothers
fever 157, **158**
finger foods 67
first aid **180–2**
flu **163–4**
focusing see eyes
follow-on formula 61
fontanelle 28, 157
food allergy, intolerance,
    and sensitivity **162**
foods, first **64–7**
    solids 62, 65
foot care 86
formula-feeding 58, **60–1**
    LCPs 61

G

games, interactive 95, 106,
    109
gape 46
German measles see rubella
goat's milk 61
grandparents 144, 145, 147
grasping 29, 103
grazes **181**
growth **53**, 131, 167

H

hair washing 84, 85
hand-eye coordination 103,
    106, 110
health **150–3**
    see also specific ailments
healthy lifestyle 153
hearing in the womb 12
herbalism **155**
    home remedy kit 156
Hib 151
Hib/DTP vaccine 152
high-need babies, 35, **77**
hip problems 161
HIV positive mothers 58
hives see urticaria
holding **72–3**
    upside down 106
home
    preparing/cleaning 16–17
    safety in 183

homeopathy 47, 75, **155**
home remedy kit 156
    nosodes 152
hormones 13, **20**
hunger
    and crying 33, 52, **75**
    at night 129
hypoglycaemia **161**

IJL

immune system 17, 50, 162
immunization **151–3**
impetigo 174
independence 111
jaundice **159–60**
labour 18, 20
Lactobacillus acidophilus
    supplements 151, 170, 173
latching on 40, **46**, 51, 55
laundering 80, 81, 86
let-down reflex **40**, 44, 57
lone parenting/sole carer 16,
    96
love hormones 20

M

massaging 75, 88–91
mastitis 135
measles 151, 152, **178–9**
meconium 51, 78
meningitis 152, **178**
mental development 94
milia and milaria 174
milk production 24, 27
milk spots 35, 174
MMR vaccine 152
mothers **134–7**
    and baby in womb 13
    diet/nutrition 54, 135–6,
    160
    emotions after birth 21,
    23, 31
postnatal depression 174
physical/emotional
    wellbeing 134, 136
mothering the mother 31–2
motor development
    newborns 99
    3–4 months 102
    5–9 months 105, 109
    10–16 months 113

mouth 172–3
multiples, breastfeeding 49,
    59
mumps 151, 152, **179**

N

nanny 147
nappies (diapers) 78, **81–2**
    see also disposables,
    washables
nappy (diaper) rash 81,
    174–5
    types of 174
natural remedies **154–6**
    home remedy kit 156
newborns 20, 21
    appearance of 28–9
    bed-sharing 123
    crawl position 100
    feeding 50–1, 55, **60**
    finding the breast 25
    health 159–61
    massaging 89
    nightclothes 125
    reflexes 29
    sensory awakening 98–100
    swaddling 86, 87
    see also sleep patterns
night feeds **47–8**, 121, 122,
    123, 130
night-waking 131
nightclothes 125
nipples 25, 44, 46
    size of 40
    sore or cracked 135
nursery 17
nurseries (daycare) 147
nutrition problems 167–71

O

Odent, Dr Michel 20, 25
oils 35, **85**, 88, 185
older children 143
    welcoming the baby 27
    regressive behaviour 142
oral thrush (candida) **173**
organic foods 67
oxytocin **20**, 39, 40

PQ

pain 75
parents
  relationship **138–41**
  sleeping arrangements
  120–1
pertussis *see* whooping
  cough
physical development 94,
  101
placenta 13, 20
play 94, 96, 97
  newborn 99
  3–4 months 102
    106, 109
  10–16 months 112
polio 151, 152
pollutants
  in breast milk 41
  in home 16
possetting 55–6, 168
postnatal depression (PND)
  31, **137**
premature babies
  breastfeeding 47, 48–9, 55
  special care 159
preparation for birth 14–17,
  18
prolactin **24**, 38, 40, 74
pyloric stenosis 57, **168**
quiet alert state 23

R

rashes 174–5, 178–9
recognition 23, 24, 104, 111
reflexive movements 13, 25,
  100
respiratory problems 163–4
rooting reflex 13, **25**, 29
roseola infantum 179
rubella 151, 152, **178**

S

safety
  in bath 83
  in garden 183
  in home 17, 102, 109, **183**
  swimming 115
salt 65
scalds 180

screaming 77
Sears, Dr William 35, 77, 118
seborrhoeic dermatitis 174,
  175–6
seclusion after birth 30
self-feeding 112
senses
  in womb 12
  newborns 99
  3–4 months 101
  5 months + 104, 108
sex 125, 140, **141**
shock **182**
sibling relationships **142–3**
  coping with rivalry 142
sick baby, caring for 157
signals, responding to baby's
  71, 74
sitting **104–5**
  supported 103
  tailor position 104, 106,
    107
skin
  care of baby's 35, 85
  problems 174–7
skin-to-skin contact 23, 24,
  26, 71, 159
sleep patterns
  mothers' 118, 122
  newborns' 33, **119**, 122
sleep training 130
sleeping 33, **118**
  daytime 130
  falling asleep 129
  in parents' bed **120–1**
  in parents' bedroom 17,
    121
  position (on back) 118
  problems 131
  settling baby 128–30
smiles, social 98
smoking 16
social development
  newborns 98
  3–9 months 101–3, 108
  10–16 months 111
sole carer/lone parenting 16,
  96
songs 95, 106
soothing *see* calming
sounds 95, 99, 102, 108, 112
  in womb 12–13
soya-based formulas 61

speech, development of 95
"spoiling" 71, 74
squatting 113
standing
  supported 103, 106
stings **181**
sucking first 26
sudden infant death
  syndrome (SIDS) 123, **161**
sun protection 85
support network
  after birth 144–7
  before birth 18, 32
swaddling 86, 87, 125
swallowed objects **182**
swimming **114–15**
Syntometrine 25

T

talking 111–13
teeth/teething 105, **172–3**
temperature 158
  of home 17, 25
  regulation of baby's 24,
    123
  nighttime environment
    126
  taking baby's 157
teats (nipples) 61
tetanus 151, 152, 153
thrush 172, **173**, 174
tiredness 31–2
toddler, and nighttime 119
toxins 16, 17, 79
toys 95, 113
  3–4 months 102
  5–9 months 106, 109
twins, breastfeeding 46, **49**,
  59

UV

umbilical cord 25, 35
unsettled babies 35
urination 78–9
urinary infections **171**
uticaria (hives) **177**
vaccines/vaccination 151,
  153
vitamin
  A and C 153
  D 38

K deficiency 160
K deficiency bleeding
  (VKDB) 160
vocalization
  newborns 99
  3–9 months 101, 104, 108
  10–16 months 112
vomiting 55–7, 157, **168–9**

W

Walker, Peter 88
walking 111–13
washables 80–1
water baby programmes 115
weaning 61, **62–7**
  foods to avoid 63
weight 52, 53
  slow gain 167
whooping cough 151, **179**
winding 55–6, 75
  positions 56
working mothers
  and childcare 145–7
  and feeding 57, 59, 146
workplace daycare 147

Acknowledgments

AUTHOR'S ACKNOWLEDGMENTS

I am very grateful to my husband Keith and my son Theo for enabling me to dedicate so much time to writing this book. I would like to thank Anthea Sieveking for the wonderfully sensitive photography and also the parents and babies who so generously allowed us to photograph them. Thanks to Cathy Meeus for her masterful editing, Hugh Schermuly and Nick Buzzard for the beautiful design and layout. To my agent Rosemary Scoular and to Sophie Laurimore many thanks for the invaluable support and encouragement. I am also very grateful to Pip Morgan for his help in the early stages. To Patsy Westcott, Jill Benjoya Miller and Diane McDonald, my thanks for your assistance with research. Thanks to Peter Walker for his generosity and help with baby massage and to Chandana Walker and her son Harley for the water baby photograph. To Naomi Stadlen, my thanks for her help with the breastfeeding chapter and to Paul Gorman for help with the cover. For help with the photography, thanks to Pat Scott, Kim Balaskas, Kira Balaskas and Mario Constantine, Caroline Gaskin, Diane Harvey Kumer and Diane McDonald. Also to colleagues and staff at the Active Birth Centre for their support, to Anne McIntyre for advice about herbs and aromatherapy and to Diane McDonald for advice on homeopathy. Last but not least, thanks to Alan Stuart for innumerable cups of tea and wonderful hospitality during the photo shoots.

PUBLISHER'S ACKNOWLEDGMENTS

Gaia Books would like to thank the following:

For kind permission to reproduce copyright material in this book Wisdom publications, 199 Elm Street, Somerville MA 02144, USA. www.wisdompubs.org (p.31); Butterworth Heinemann, a division of Reed International & Professional Publishing (p.41); Greenwood Publishing Group Inc (p.43 and p.50)

For the loan of equipment for photography: Green Baby, 436 Essex Road, London N1 3QP.

For expert advice on the text: Polly Carmichael; Dr Jacob Empson; Anne McIntyre; Dr Frances Williams.

For styling and props: Tanya Volhard.

For proofreading the text and compiling the index: Lynn Bresler.